DATE DUE

DEC 23 1988	
MAR 08 1989	
NOV 24 1991	
MAY 13 1992	
FEB 26 1993	
JUN 28 1993	
NOV 26 2007	

Applying Expert Systems in Business

Other McGraw-Hill Books by the Author

Local Area Networks (1984)

Interactive Message Services (1984)

Management Workstations for Greater Productivity (1986)

Fourth and Fifth Generation Programming Languages, Vols. 1 and 2 (1986)

Applying Expert Systems in Business

Dimitris N. Chorafas

McGraw-Hill Book Company
New York St. Louis San Francisco Auckland Bogotá
Hamburg London Madrid Milan
Mexico Montreal New Delhi Panama
Paris São Paulo Singapore
Sydney Tokyo Toronto

Library of Congress Cataloging-in-Publication Data

Chorafas, Dimitris N.
Applying expert systems in business.
Includes index.
1. Management--Data processing. 2. Business--
Data processing. 3. Expert systems (Computer science)
I. Title.
HD30.2.C475 1987 658'.05633 86-2794
ISBN 0-07-010880-3

234567890 DOC/DOC 893210987

ISBN 0-07-010880-3

The editors for this book were Martha Jewett and Galen H. Fleck, the designer was Naomi Auerbach, and the production supervisor was Thomas G. Kowalczyk. It was set in Baskerville by McGraw-Hill Computer Assisted Publishing.

Printed and bound by R. R. Donnelly & Sons Company

Contents

Preface ix

Chapter 1 Management Perspectives 1

Responsibilities of Top Management 1
Strategic Planning 2
Responsibilities of Middle Management 5
The Past Is Prolog 6
Information Systems Policies in Manufacturing and Distribution 9
Background for Implementing Online Technologies 13
The Intelligent Workstation 16
Definitions of Key Terms 20

Chapter 2 Decision Support and the Information Center 21

What Is Meant by "Information Center"? 21
Goals of an Information Center 23
Project Management for an Information Center 26
Organizing for Decision Support 29
Decision Support in an Office Automation Environment 30
An Expert Online: Models and Spreadsheets 34
PC-to-Mainframe Communications 37

Chapter 3 What Is Meant by Artificial Intelligence? 42

The Search for Machine-Based Knowledge 42
Three Decades of AI Effort 43
Goals for the 1980s 46
Implementing High Technology 50
From AI to Robotics 55
Artificial Intelligence Markets 58

Chapter 4 Expert Systems and the Industrialization of Knowledge 62

Knowhow and Virtue 62
A Crisis in Data Processing 63

Layers of Expert Systems Implementation 66
Why Decision Support Leads to Expert Systems 70
The Industrialization of Knowledge 72
Expert Systems in Weapons Development: A Case Study 74

Chapter 5 Knowledge Engineering 78

What Is Meant by Knowledge Engineering? 78
Architecture of the Expert System 80
Organizational Information as a Knowledge Network 82
Example with the Pentomic Organization 86
Frames and Languages 89
Tools for the Knowledge Engineer 92
Serving a Purpose 94

Chapter 6 Knowledge Management 97

What's the Sense of Knowledge Management? 97
The Knowledgebank 98
Knowledge Acquisition 102
The Computer-Based Interview 105
The Role of Misinterpretation 106
Structuring Expert Systems Research 108
Approaches to Knowledge Exchange 110

Chapter 7 The Human Window 114

Conversing with an Intelligent System 114
The Expert System Asks for *Your* Response 116
Using Fourth-Generation Languages 119
Two-Dimensional Programming 121
Introducing Management Graphics 124
Dataland Project at MIT 127
A Role for Interactive Videodisks 128

Chapter 8 The Inference Machine 132

Changing Meaning of the Word "Machine" 132
The New Empire of Logical Entities 133
Models and Modeling 136
The Sense of Logical Inference 140
Alternatives in Chaining Solutions 143
Search Strategies 144
Results with Different Search Procedures 146

Chapter 9 Induction, Deduction, and Fuzzy Logic 148

A Plan of Action 148
Inductive and Deductive Approaches 150
Semantic Networks 152
Fuzzy Sets 154
Risk-Adjusted Solutions 157
Machine Learning 160

Chapter 10 Languages and Shells for Expert Systems 163

The Concept behind the Use of Shells 163
Lisp, Prolog, and the Others 165
Expert Systems Shells 168
Commodity Shells and Toolkits 170
Prototyping 172

Reveal and Exsys 176
Other Currently Available Shells 179

Chapter 11 Expert Systems Projects 184

Planning an Expert Systems Project 184
Directing and Controlling Esystems Projects 186
Starting the Expert Systems Project 189
Expert Systems Building 191
Learning What to Do and Applying what We Learn 194
Testing the Expert System 197
A Test for Dependability 199

Chapter 12 Applications of Expert Systems 203

A Bird's-Eye View of Current Applications 203
Proprietary Applications 206
Commodity Applications 210
Using Expert Systems within the DP Organization 212
Addressing Software Issues 214
Expert Systems in Manufacturing 215
Expert Systems in Banking 219

Acronyms and Abbreviations 224
Index 227

Preface

After years of gestation, expert systems are emerging from the R&D laboratories and working their way into commercial, industrial, and financial applications. This business use of machine intelligence has generated considerable excitement not only among potential users but also in the press.

There are many reasons for this positive reaction, some of which have to do with the capabilities of the expert systems already applied. But also a good deal of interest invariably centers on the future impact of expert systems on management. The inevitable changes can be of a magnitude which is actually difficult to perceive, yet it has to be estimated.

The goal of this book is to explore the questions of change and impact in a comprehensive manner and present information that will be useful during the transition period. It is addressed to senior management—the strategic decision makers—but also to the leaders of the data processing organization.

Practical examples and case studies are given in most chapters. Emphasis is placed on the human dimension of artificial intelligence. This is important for several reasons. First, by assisting the human mind, this new technology impacts our life on both its professional and its personal sides. Second, an integral part of the growing interest on practical applications of expert systems has to do with *downsizing*. Third, while intelligent machines need powerful processors, we all know the projected increase in personal computer processing power.

We have gone a long way from theory to implementation, and so the need for comprehensive coverage is increasingly felt. Yet today managers must buy several special reports and attend a number of seminars to learn expert systems definitions and discover that the systems do indeed have practical applications.

An *expert system* is a *practical resource* able to handle complex problems, tackle issues requiring a high level of human judgment and expertise, and communicate with its user through an effective dialog. Expert systems ask questions, give advice, and justify the advice.

The building of expert systems is the business of *knowledge engineering*. This is the process of capturing and representing knowledge in a computer-oriented sense. The output must be simple, effective, and comprehensible to the human user. Compared to those practical concepts, *artificial intelligence* has a more theoretical background. It is concerned with symbolic reasoning, problem solving, augmentation of human intelligence, and the eventual creation of machine-based processes of imagination.

Intelligence augmented by computers will most likely be the main trend of the 1990s, but from the mid-1980s to the early 1990s machine intelligence will be embedded in a number of applications which will become parts of our lives. Implementations are materializing within a specific organizational context. That is what this book is all about.

There are reasons for pushing the use of expert systems forward in manufacturing, marketing, finance, engineering, medicine, data processing proper, and other professional fields. Increased competition is a business reason; new solutions exemplified by robotics present a technical one. But the most fundamental reason is the size of a growing population. As of late 1985:

- 40 million computers inhabit the planet.
- Over 20 million computers were shipped in 1984 and 1985.
- The value of the worldwide installed computer base exceeds $300 billion.
- Programming investments in U.S. corporate data centers (1965 to 1985) approach $1 trillion.

Transaction processing may have been the booming applications area 10 years ago, but now message services and decision support have stolen the show. Millions of computers and billions of dollars are increasingly oriented to those tasks.

The users are becoming the motive for the new applications, and they demand able solutions *now*, not tomorrow. Through friendly fourth-generation languages, proficient users have been programming their own computers and finding the experience rewarding. As their numbers increase, we can expect more emphasis to be placed on intelligent business systems. This will happen rapidly, even though computer literacy has been a desirable goal for only a few years.

Today, in business, system analysts with the skills to coach end users into designing their own systems are being more appreciated than programmers. Typically, such analysts pay attention to interactive methods and efficient dialog, as well as machine intelligence. At the same time, the more classical thinkers in the data processing departments are awakening—and for good reason. Many companies expect to find themselves in trouble by the end of the century when millions of programs become obsolete.

Given the business orientation of this book, Chapter 1 first considers the responsibilities of top management, including strategic planning. It then reviews some of the best results obtained so far with information systems. They are typically on the middle-management level, and they provide a good point of departure. Chapter 2 focuses on two subjects: how to establish and operate an information center and how to put decision support systems to profitable use. Expert systems require a global database. The information center will provide the needed infrastructure, which is a prerequisite. Another critical side of such an effort is organizing beyond decision support.

All this is written, in a management-oriented form, to explain why it is not enough to develop components. We must also be aware of system integration. We should be able to justify the investment to the board of directors and win top-management approval. Only when those issues are well understood is it time to talk of artificial intelligence: We will be so much more effective if we have done the proper preparatory work. That is why the subject is introduced in Chapter 3.

Artificial intelligence has gone through epochs. In the 1950s, research focused on *neutral nets*. An outcome of that work was *Perceptron*. The 1960s placed emphasis on *heuristics*. *Knowledge representation* was the high point of the 1970s. *Mycin* is a monument to that effort. The focal point of the 1980s is *computer learning*, and the results are nicely represented by *Eurisko*.

As the research phases succeeded one another, the subject approached maturity. This is reflected in the organization of the text: Chapter 4 is addressed to expert systems and the industrialization of knowledge they make feasible. Given the importance of this topic, the reader may be tempted to skip the first two chapters and start with artificial intelligence and expert systems. That would be a great mistake. This book is not about pure expert systems; it is about *expert systems in business*, and that is a different matter.

Applying expert systems in business requires the proper infrastructure, and that includes the issues which are the subject of the introductory chapters. Only after that foundation has been laid do expert systems constructs make business sense.

Chapter 5 is devoted to knowledge engineering. It starts with the architecture of the expert systems, looks at organizational information as a knowledge network, and presents examples with the pentomic organization. It then discusses frames, languages, and tools for the knowledge engineer.

The subject of Chapter 6 is knowledge management; the topics range from knowledgebanks to the very important process of knowledge acquisition and the orientation of expert systems research. Chapter 7 discusses the human window. It emphasizes interactivity, gives examples of questions asked by the expert system, and introduces fourth-generation languages—and also management graphics and the use of videodisks.

With that background established, the time is ripe for talking of the part of the system which is mathematics. The inference engine is the subject of Chapter 8. Chapter 9 stresses induction, deduction, and fuzzy logic. Fuzzy sets are explained with examples. The pure management reader may wish to leave out Chapters 8 and 9, though they are important to an understanding of what goes into the implementation of the inference engine.

The following two chapters talk of languages, shells, and project management. Chapter 10 introduces Lisp, Prolog, the notion of shells and toolkits, and some of the better commodity shells are described. It also places emphasis on prototyping. Chapter 11 explains why many projects fail and what should be done to make them successful. It then advises on how to start an expert systems project and what to do to test the resulting structure properly.

The subject of Chapter 12 is applications of expert systems. Some of the most successful ones are reviewed; the applications domains range from manufacturing and banking to the data processing organization's own operations. As several of these examples help demonstrate, the use of expert systems in business improves *dependability of the decision-making process*. Humans can forget relevant factors, especially if under stress or in situations where time is critical. Intelligent machines do not forget them.

Expert systems increase the consistency with which importance is assigned to different decision factors and probabilities are dealt with. They present greater accessibility as well. Human experts can be on holiday, on call, or otherwise unavailable. The industrialization of knowhow sees to it that the intelligent machine is always at your service.

* * *

Finally, I express my thanks to everybody who contributed to this book: my colleagues, for their advice and the insight which they provided; the people who took part in my seminars, for the puzzling and most interesting questions; Galen H. Fleck, for his care and interest in editing the text; and Eva-Maria Binder, for assistance in preparing the drawings and doing the typing.

Dimitris N. Chorafas

Applying Expert Systems in Business

Chapter 1

Management Perspectives

"Who has nothing to do with the computer has nothing to do in life." ROBERTO VACCA

Responsibilities of Top Management

Management, Webster's dictionary tells us, is the act, art, or manner of managing. It is careful treatment, executive ability, and skill in managing. Managing involves six fundamental functions—forecasting, planning, organizing, staffing, directing, and controlling—which are executed by managers.

Managers hold dominant positions on the business stage. Their thoughts, plans, theories, statements, decisions, and actions are the stuff of which business, administrative, and financial news are made. They are collectively regarded as a distinct social group with views and knowhow to run the resources under their command.

Too often, the spotlight that gives industrial and financial leaders prominence is the income they are reported to receive from the enterprises with which they are connected. Success in a management career is measured by personal financial gain. Yet only a few persons in each profession realize high incomes for their work, and still fewer receive princely amounts.

Opportunities for successful careers are open to all, but whether they are to be industrial tycoons, financiers, engineers, lawyers, medical doctors, priests, army officers, entertainers, or politicians, few of those who take the opportunities will be acknowledged as renowned leaders. They will be distinguished for their intelligence, knowhow, authority, and skill with decisions, and also for their appeal, adaptability, staying power, determination, and persistence.

Einstein aptly remarked, for these people any sphere of activity will do. Whether they become officers, tradesmen, or scientists depends on circumstances. Conspicuous leadership is not a matter of chance. "Luck" is what happens when preparation meets opportunity. The opportunity is offered by the environment, but steady, lifelong preparation must be carried out by the person who wants to succeed and is willing to invest in his or her own brains.

Business, whether industrial, financial, or in professional specializations, has been both fueled and limited by its environment—and by the objectives of the men and women working in it. Any field of activity involves both internal and external relations. In these last years of the twentieth century, such relations can be enhanced or handicapped through the use of computers and communications. They are enhanced if we promote personal productivity and organizational innovation; they are handicapped if we simply throw money at the problems which we are facing and thus add to the layers of resistance.

Having the best information equipment at our disposal, and paying dearly for it, is no guarantee of success. And although we invite failure by relying on an obsolete workplace, modernity itself is no guarantee of unquestionably good results. Thornton, the former chairman of Litton Industries, once said that the true task of leadership is *the management of change.* That is quite true, but managers should be aware of this: Every time they try innovation, they risk being bruised by the organization's prevailing culture. Hence there is the need for determination and for the uncanny will to prevail.

Strategic Planning

Adjustment and innovation are conditions that should exist both in the internal affairs of a business and in the environment in which the business lives and operates. Both processes, however, require direction, which is given by *strategic planning.*

Strategy is a master plan against the corporate opponents. Within the master plan, and subordinate to it, are other more detailed plans for finance, personnel, product development, marketing, and information systems. Survival calls for paying attention to a pentomic organization shown in Figure 1.

Top management addresses itself to strategic planning, policy decisions, the administration of change, and top-level contacts with the external world. It is difficult to draw an exact dividing line between policy and strategy, because established policies have a strategic effect on the course the organization follows.

Policies are typically established as guidelines for specific actions. They help us avoid making repetitive decisions on the same or similar

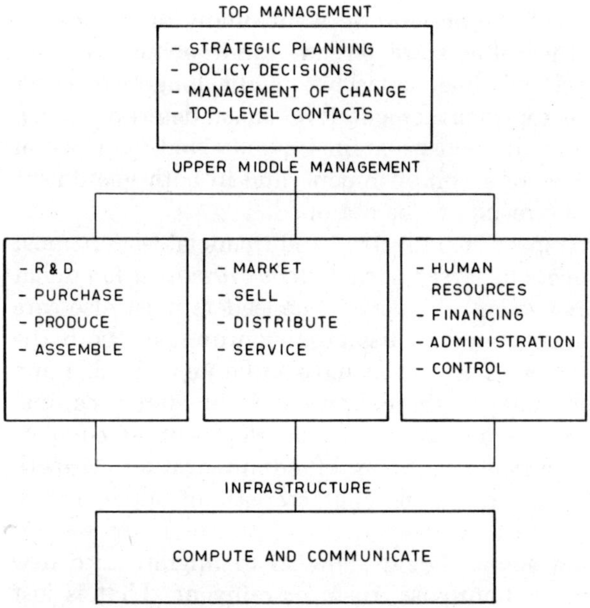

Figure 1 The pentomic organization: structure and infrastructure for the 1990s.

issues. They are employed to interpret or shade the emphasis and meaning of strategies. Strategic planning helps senior management to concentrate on essentials. It makes feasible a general harmony of effort; it sees to it that everything fits together and every contributor plays a full part. The following are the functions of strategy formulation:

1. Establish and then explain objectives in concrete terms.
2. Define long-term policies.
3. Develop milestone plans for the implementation of policies.
4. Establish product line developments.
5. Set (or check) costs and benefits for products and services.
6. Place emphasis on human capital and its steady training.
7. Decide on the timing of the moves necessary to reach goals.
8. Establish policy on technology transfer and avoid obsolescence.
9. Conduct reviews and acid tests to ascertain how the organization stands against competition.

Strategies have a great influence on operating decisions; therefore, their possible aftermaths must be examined in advance. Lightly studied strategies would have few of the actions we want, many of the effects we do not want, and other effects we do not know about. We can do things in short periods of time, but what is the long-term cost? Strategic planning at the top-management level must determine such factors as the funding of plans and programs, quality and quantity of human resources, timetables of accomplishment, and in both qualitative and quantitative terms, the results to be obtained.

Within this strategic perspective, industrial and financial leaders must *manage, consult, and educate against the entrenched organization.* That is the bottom line of management of change. The leaders must also care about the infrastructure. In a modern business environment, both the *strategic plan* and the *information system* have to be kept flexible and dynamic. They must contribute to the enhancement of human capital, the amplification of market perspective, the development of competitive procedures, and an efficient process of administration. Growth and survival rests on all three functions characteristic of upper middle management.

The solutions which we adopt should allow us to migrate into new structures without having to improvise, rush, or reinvent. That is just as true of the strategic plans we develop as of our computers and communications plans. As a matter of fact, the former should cover the latter. Information systems projects should not be undertaken in a haphazard manner or because "that's the trend." In this as in any other implementation domain, a good project is one that has us doing, for $1, a job that once cost us $5.

The good news is that senior management started to recognize that a profitable future depends on innovative automation. Modern information systems applications should have the dual objective of:

1. Improving management productivity and cutting clerical costs.

Management productivity depends both on better decision making and on our ability to eliminate delays and lost time while concentrating on the essential management tasks.

2. Enhancing the organization's ability to meet customer needs in an able manner.

By gaining access to a new and fast-growing customer population for existing services, we also enable new services (or even new businesses) to be built on the foundation of our existing customer base. The capable use of information systems also lets us approach markets in which our presence was insignificant or nonexistent.

These are new approaches to the use of electronics in management. They reflect the increasing appreciation of the fact that computers and

communications have become a strategic-level tool, w
banking, commerce, manufacturing, or public admini

But if strategic information systems open new per impose new prerequisites. They need to be long-terr must address issues on a broad scale. Our plans must human, financial, and technological resources while placing particu emphasis on low-cost techniques.

Being a low-cost producer will be an overriding requirement into the mid-1990s, but that does not mean strategic information systems will be cheap. Efficiency makes the difference. *If we have the funding, we will get the technology. If we have the brains and the technology, we will control the future.*

Responsibilities of Middle Management

When we build a strategic information system, we must address the needs of sophisticated customers in the market we are after. Logically this requires an improved system for communications and management—to be provided by communications technology—enhanced with advanced systems for decision support.

We must also think of brain intake. To find enough qualified people, we must create and sustain their motivation. Managers and professionals work under pressure. They will better accept such an environment if they see a growth in their intellectual capabilities. The responsibilities of middle management are indivisible from those of the professionals working for the organization. A *professional* is the person serving the customer with advice and assistance. New technology makes it mandatory to redesign that job.

The new perspective should be not of more routine work, but of tools to provide better advice and more evaluation of profits by account. Administrative chores and trivial duties should be weeded out of professional jobs. But changeover from current practices to a new system will not be easy. As Max Hopper, executive vice president of technology at Bank of America, commented, "This job is like trying to change the tires on a moving car."

To have a lasting effect, we should not focus on the technology per se. Our attention must be concentrated on current and future needs and on choosing the best technology to meet those needs. That is the best way to be of service to end users. Information system projects that get results are those that not only are end-user-oriented but also obtain user acceptance and support.

Winners do not automate what they do today, whether with paper or classical data processing (DP). Losers do so, and they end up making the same mistakes faster. Winners are keen on taking the proverbial ȝ, hard look. They also see the need to find solutions which will ıake system sense over a 10- to 15-year life cycle.

The Past Is Prolog

In terms of what can be achieved with the current information systems technology, the past is prolog. Technology, economics, marketability, serviceability, and product factors press for continuing development of new, more powerful information systems.

Organizations able to read the direction of future developments are keen to sharpen their tools: They are effectively using computers and communications to exchange business data, electronic memos, and still images among their own plants. Automated transactions are growing in number and sophistication. Office automation is slowly coming of age, and it is leading to increased productivity and to reductions in the use of paper and travel.

Private and public networks interconnect machines and their users. Public databases offer a variety of legal, financial, technical, medical, educational, recreational, and governmental information services for a fee. Many traditional ways of doing business are changing. An informational labor force supplies a new wave of services.

Every four years or so there is a new cycle of information system offerings, as Figure 2 shows. After the relatively slow growth of the batch years (1953 to 1964), we had timesharing, realtime, and distributed data processing. Then the pace accelerated. As experience with computers and communications accumulated, the mid- to late 1970s saw increasing interest in decision support systems, which before

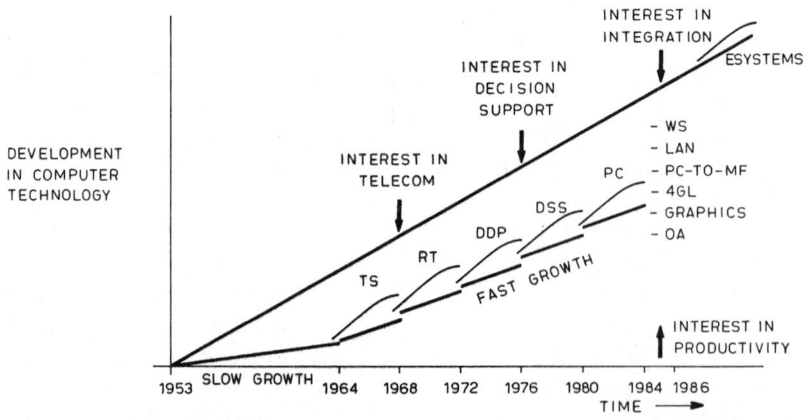

Figure 2 Development in computer technology; every 4 years there is a new cycle.

long were carried out on personal computers. We now have intelligent workstations (WSs), local area networks (LANs), PC-to-mainframe connections, fourth-generation languages (4GLs), and graphics presentation—all blending into the broader scope of office automation (OA).

Electronic mail, computer conferencing, teleconferencing, business transactions, access to very large databases, management planning, personal calendaring, graphics presentation, color enrichment, and voice mail are themes of this new program. They are also fundamental components of the system that high technology offers management. Text, data, graphics, and voice are exchanged through an information center organization that is distinct from but associated with classical data processing.

Those are the components of the *knowledge revolution* in manufacturing, and General Motors is a first-class example of their application. At General Motors, Roger Smith, the CEO, and H. Ross Perot have set out to achieve a *thorough redesign of systems used to manufacture durable goods.* Said the chairman: "We decided we were going to build our future, not stumble into it backwards."

Here are the highlights: GM is the single largest user of computers, next to the U.S. government, but in the past computer applications were developed haphazardly. Many functions were duplicates of others, and there were also serious gaps. The new design makes computers and communications the central nervous system of GM. It will link managers, project leaders, manufacturing engineers, robots, and salesmen with computers. The new mottos are:

- Sensitivity to the market
- Willingness to adapt to changing conditions
- Implementation of high technology
- Steady competitive drive

The goal is to make GM *the premier technology power in the world.* "We are going to build our company for the twenty-first century," said Roger Smith. That is a show of determination, and it also exemplifies what should be the *necessary commitment* from top management.

Today, much of the reluctance of senior management to a total commitment is based on the early stages of the information technology. Another prominent concern is that the use of computers and communications may determine the organizational strategy rather than being an instrument of the strategy. Ill-informed middle managers emerge from that smoke screen only to put forward the *difficulty of predicting* cost/benefit relations in many potential applications. Yet, their real fear is what may happen to their careers as a result of *changes in organizational structure.*

At long last, computers and communications are affecting organizational structure and reporting relationships. None of those changes are viewed with alarm by clear-eyed managers who comprehend the new look that information systems bring to the internal organization, the resulting opportunities, and the professional challenges.

The General Motors example is at the top-management level, and it is also the first of its kind. In the following sections we will outline some of the cases most characteristic of the past decade in which middle management was both the prime mover behind and also the primary beneficiary of adoption of the new technology.

An accumulating wealth of knowledge based on computer implementation and two decades of communications experience provide the documentation that *information technology should be seen as a key resource.* There is significant value for any organization in an electronic link between headquarters, factories, sales offices, and customers.

Computers and communications links make it simple to distribute product information and to collect and process orders. They also *tie in* the customer to the supplier. However, organizations have to decide if they wish to be technology leaders or technology followers, and they must plan accordingly:

- Technology leaders are innovators; they exploit their position of being first in the marketplace with a new system.
- Technology followers respond to the activities of the leaders, from whose experience and mistakes they hope to profit.

Such "hopes" are not necessarily justified. Technology leaders are first in selecting the right sales prospects through the use of computer-based information. They minimize unnecessary travel time for their own management, improve effectiveness, and speed up communications.

Managers and professionals should look at technology as being a partner in decision support, as helping to reduce wasted time, as improving the effectiveness of group meetings, and as providing new and powerful tools such as expert systems. Organizations that ignore those changes are likely to suffer as their present competitors move ahead and new competitors break into their markets. But technology for technology's sake is not the "business of business." Investment decisions should fit within a properly established strategic plan, and they should be rich in innovation. Routine is good, but new ideas are even better.

We must understand market movements as they impact our business whether we are producers or consumers. Figure 3 dramatizes the fact that there is an irreversible process of merging classical DP and the widespread text processing with formerly pure communications. This is forming a new aggregate and also a host of products.

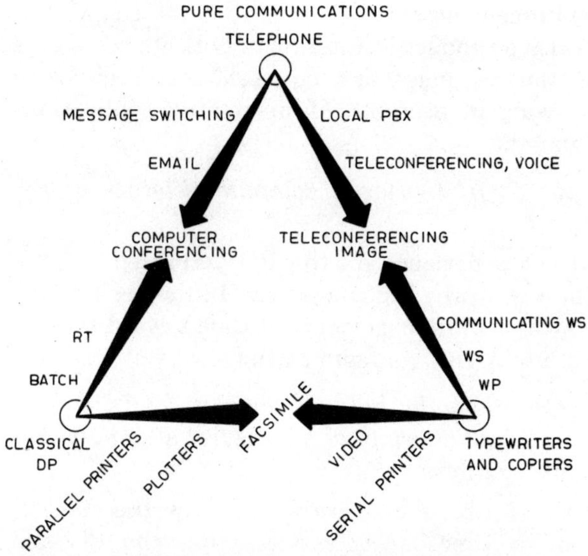

Figure 3 Understanding market movements: the merging of different technologies into one system

If we are not able to bring forward new ideas, our competitors may do so. The *obsolescence of systems projects* is rarely appreciated, but it is there. At Bankers Trust, a critical evaluation found that *the usefulness of 80 percent of ongoing DP projects no longer existed*:

- Competitors had leaped ahead.
- The market needs had changed.
- Delays had made certain computer projects nearly unnecessary.

A fast-moving environment calls for a strategic look at information systems projects while critically evaluating the projects against the new policies established by top management, the market drives, and the professional needs. Such an examination will reveal that *business strategy* and *computers and communications* are not independent of each other. *They are very closely related.*

Information Systems Policies in Manufacturing and Distribution

No matter in which industry computers and communications are applied, implementation examples are often surprisingly similar. The common goals are smothering internal costs and enhancing customer service.

Expanding horizons of implementation see to it that the supplier of information services provides a product of interest to both its customers and other suppliers. Also, the customers may be reselling the service to their client bases. The following are examples of imaginative applications of information technology.

- *United Technology put as first priority computer literacy at the senior management level.*

An intensive 3-day hands-on experience on the PC permitted the top 1100 executives to learn how to work with computers. In the background of that policy is a major switch in management attitude toward the use of computers as personal, intelligent, communicating workstations.

- *At Bangor Punta Corporation, the holding company of Lone Star Cement and Piper Aircraft, personal computers and local area networks have been installed at the board level.*

The 35 companies of the group have long been served by the General Electric Information Systems timesharing service. Now the PC and LAN application is primarily addressed to the chairman of the board, the president, the senior VP/finance, and other authorized executives. It includes a decision support system with graphics capability, financial analysis models, and access to public databases.

- *At Gould Industries an interactive management information system has been designed and has been in operation since 1976. It is used at board meetings and committee sessions.*

Every night, all operating divisions of Gould, domestic and international, update the management database run on two superminis at headquarters, which are near O'Hare Airport in Chicago. Although the information systems of acquired divisions differ among themselves, all of them use the same matrix for management reporting. Information is interactively available to top and middle management through a videotex-type implementation.

- *The Sylvania Commercial Lighting Division of GTE supplies sales personnel with portable computer terminals.*

The sales representatives access a system to analyze prospective customers' lighting requirements. They can prepare sales proposals on-site and thereby obtain better sales orders and get them faster.

- *Owens Corning Fiberglass uses data on energy efficiency to help builders evaluate the insulation requirements for new building designs.*

Such evaluations are provided free of charge to builders who meet minimum standards of energy efficiency if they agree to purchase insulation from the vendor.

- *Some suppliers of aircraft parts have developed an inventory locator service. It allows air carriers to specify the parts they require for repairing airplanes undergoing maintenance.*

When asked, the service automatically generates *request for quotation* messages to the supplier. The service also provides a parts number cross-reference database to assist users in identifying interchangeable parts.

- *Whitbread, a leading British brewery, keeps in its database the inventory records of wholesalers and retailers (pubs). Consumption is simulated by a seasonally adjusted model.*

Informed by the model on stocks that are running out, the salesperson contacts the client online and suggests types and quantities needed—and asks for confirmation.

Whitbread has also realized a first-class application on videotex, in fact, the first in the world in terms of timing. It is addressed to top executives and to middle management. It covers everything from timely snapshots on financial data to inventory and production status and from alarm signals to a testbed corrective action.

- *A Swedish dairy cooperative provides retailers with estimated requirements in the form of pro forma orders. The retailer then has the option of either using or changing the prespecified orders.*

The pro forma orders assist the retailer in the specification as well as requirements stage of the life cycle, and applications cover as many as six life cycle stages. As in the Whitbread example, the system can nicely be implemented online with PCs installed at the dairies. The PC can also provide other local services such as billing and accounting.

- *Westvaco, a supplier of paper products to printers, has developed WestTrak. When a customer order is about to be shipped, WestTrak informs the customer's computer that the order is in transit and provides essential identifying information about the shipment.*

When the order arrives, a receiving clerk transmits an identifying bar code to the printer's computer, which then immediately records the availability of the resources placed in inventory.

- *General Electric Supply Company provides a computer-based tool to assist customers in inventory management.*

For a specified time, GESCO commits a prearranged quantity of items that are purchased repetitively. As in the case of Whitbread, the distributor keeps inventories for customers and, in effect, upgrades the wholesaler's or retailer's inventory on the basis of observed and/or simulated market demand.

- *At USAA Insurance, personal computers and local area networks are used for the handling of property, auto, casualty, and life insurance policies.*

The network of workstations spreads to all regional and branch offices. Each WS is able to communicate with others and with shared mainframe resources. The new "claims processing system" was developed on PCs and LANs over a 10-month period versus the 3-year delay that mainframe applications usually face.

- *The Metropolitan Insurance Company found that dedicating a PC to each person radically changes the way of doing business.*

Data entry done at the local level is significantly simplified; sales agents use the PC to do prospecting; the PC has been advanced to the agents; and new managerial functions that have been implemented have significantly improved executive productivity.

- *England's South East Electricity improved its service and increased its sales by installing a private videotex system with 100 terminals, each equipped with a printer.*

The sales staff in each of the board's 77 electrical retail shops has immediate access to up-to-date versions of the product catalog, together with all the information on any product including dimensions, features, and illustrations of costs for individual customers. Staff savings alone are expected to pay for the system, and net benefits were expected in the first year of operation. The major benefit, however, is projected to be an increase in sales through greater certainty about stock levels and delivery dates.

- *Arthur Andersen has developed an integrated middle-management-oriented package addressed to billing, inventory control, replenishment and purchasing, accounts receivable, and sales analysis.*

Its billing module, to take one example, permits three types of action: open-order billing, prebilling, and postbilling. Open-order billing has two steps: original order entry and billing at a later date. If goods are shipped as ordered, minimal operator input for billing is required. Otherwise, the system leads the operator through the order and requests the quantity shipped and the quantity back-ordered. As soon as the operator enters the billing information, the open accounts receivable records are updated. This interactive process through computer guidance is one of the key characteristics we will stress when we talk of expert systems.

In the examples which we have considered, the knowledge of how to do the job is largely provided by the responsible managers and professionals; the computer provides the online communications, processing, and presentation support. The latter knowledge is encoded in the work process, but little attention has been paid to how to make the knowledge explicit.

Requirements are changing, however. Companies have increasingly found that growth of demand brings with it the need for greater functionality. To manage an expanding process, we require low-cost uniformity, and that is another door for the entry of expert systems.

Background for Implementing Online Technologies

Although top management will give (or approve) the main direction, implementation of online technologies is up to middle management and the professionals. The implementation cannot be in one step. Basic choices are necessary, and so are concrete timetables which can bring tangible results in quick succession.

Variety in project orientation should be welcome. Some projects may be oriented toward decision support; others will feature communications-intensive activities as their high points. Some firms will choose to streamline their internal operations first; others will address the skills of their system designers toward the marketplace.

- *Brook Bond Oxo installed a voice response system to speed up and increase the accuracy of its ordering process.*

Until 1982, the company's 250-strong sales force recorded orders on customer cards, transcribed the details onto printed forms, and used an answerphone service to dictate orders to the computer center. That created a bottleneck which had a pervasive effect on the organization. The answer was a Comdial voice response system in which each salesperson was equipped with a special touch-tone telephone adapter. The recorded voice messages repeat the information so the salesperson is certain the order has been transmitted correctly.

Sales information is processed within 24 hours, which gives distribution managers more time to plan loads and routes for end-of-week deliveries. Postal charges, telephone charges, and telephone answering machine charges have all been reduced, and the accuracy and immediacy of management information have been improved.

- *England's Mothercare, a retail chain specializing in everything for mothers and babies, installed videodisk systems in tests at 4 of its 210 branches.*

The installation consisted of a color television, a standard videodisk player, a numeric keypad, and numbered photographs of the products being promoted. Potential customers pressed appropriate buttons on the keypad to select short presentations showing the products being used and highlighting the safety features. After 24 weeks, sales in the branches fitted with video systems were 20 percent higher than in control branches. Now the videodisk player solution is generalized.

- *Distriphar is a Paris-based subsidiary of Roussel-Uclaf responsible for storing, marketing, and distributing pharmaceutical products to wholesalers, pharmacies, hospitals, doctors, and laboratories. It installed a value-added network service to improve communication between its main distribution depots and its customers.*

The network is based on the French videotex service and gives its customers access to a range of information including warnings, safety information, product data, and useful contact names and telephone numbers. The system, which is used by 850 pharmacies through Minitel terminals, allows Distriphar's customers to order products directly. It automatically takes account of any discount arrangements. Distriphar believes the service has increased its sales volume while reducing the paperwork and costs associated with the order process. It expects that eventually 3000 clients will use the service.

- *Betriebswirtschaftliches Institut der Kreditgenossenschaften, the development organization of the German Popular Banks and Agricultural Banks, uses videodisk together with hard-disk equipped PC and videotex linkage to promote client services at the branch office.*

This goes well beyond a banking application and into general-merchandising implementation. To help the competitive position, applications cover real estate sales and vacation plan sales, including reservations. Training is also a strong feature.

- *Bergen-Brunswig, a pharmaceutical supply distributor, monitors product sales data for druggists and then uses the data to support its* space management *product.*

For a monthly fee, customers are advised on shelf arrangement and potential upgrades related to product choice. Bergen-Brunswig also leases hand-held computers to its customers. Orders can be entered via the devices to one of several warehouses and are shipped the following day.

- *Many retail drug stores, as a service to their customers, provide a detailed accounting of their customers' drug purchases, social security numbers, income tax deductions, drug compatibilities, and other information.*

Even a small local druggist, with the aid of a personal computer, can offer very attractive services.

- *Medicare-Glaser's therapeutic interaction detector tests a prescription against other therapeutics that customers may be taking and flags potential problems.*

- *Distributors such as American Hospital Supply, McKesson Pharmaceuticals, General Electric Supply Company, and Arrow Electronics have established sophisticated round-the-clock order entry systems that accept customer-entered orders without human intervention.*

- *Chevron retail dealers are now using personal computers to notify customers that they are due for service visits and to support the mechanics who maintain the customers' cars.*

A running record of previous maintenance also is provided. This service encourages customers to consistently rely on Chevron dealers for maintenance needs.

- *The PC has been successfully used as a marketing tool by large, medium-size, and very small firms.*

A PC that was originally installed in a 50-people firm of a dental prosthetics laboratory for accounting purposes was soon employed to improve the productivity of the salespersons. It cut down wasted time by 65 percent and improved acquisition from 1 per 40 salesperson calls to 1 per 8.

- *Avis uses ATM-like machines to shorten the car-return process.*

Customers enter a few pieces of data, and the machine concludes the rental transaction and returns an itemized receipt.

- *The Washington Hotel in Tokyo is using an automated registration robot to check guests in with no manual assistance.*

On the way out, the robot accepts the customer key and presents a bill for refreshments, telephone calls, and the like.

- *Several taxi firms have installed in-cab terminals that display the number of empty cabs cruising in various cab zones.*

Drivers use this information to calculate where requirements are greatest.

- *New magazines, such as the* I.B. Magazette *and* Mentor, *published on computer disks let the reader interact in novel ways with articles and advertisements.*

The common ground in all these references is that strategic information systems provide firms with competitive advantages. They can help companies become *both innovators and low-cost producers* for given products or services. They also assist in defining a service within a market niche and in differentiating that product offering from the offerings of competitors.

Advanced microelectronics, software technology, computer-aided design, online sales, dispatching and inventory management, office automation, computer-integrated manufacture, and information exchange capabilities are examples on the fast-expanding horizons of the information-processing technologies. Decision support and expert systems are other examples. Each needs an intelligent interface to the end user, and that is the *workstation*.

The Intelligent Workstation

The intelligent workstation (WS) is a personal computer dedicated to the end user: One machine, one person is the principle. The hardware features one or more microprocessors, central (high-speed) memory, hard disk, and line discipline for communications, modem, and output and input units (video, printer, graphic tablet, mouse, and keyboard).

The software endowment includes an operating system (OS), database management system (DBMS), communications protocols, integrated software (spreadsheet, graphics, word processing), calendaring services, and logical decision support gear—from modeling to expert systems. Such a software endowment reflects market demand and with it market opportunity. Figure 4 puts this fact into perspective. The demand for productivity tools is on the increase, and so is the demand for software programs for communications. They are becoming the items most in demand during the next couple of years.

Historically, computers have been centralized resources. Because of their high cost and relative scarcity in their paleolithic age, computers were shared either through different programs on a batch basis or (later on) on a time-sharing basis. Even if those approaches still form 90 percent or more of today's computer systems, microcomputer-based personal computing has made time-sharing obsolete in supermicro, mini, and mainframe systems.

Instead of sharing a large but monolithic computer and fighting for a time slot through a wire of 3-kilohertz (Hz, thousands of cycles per second) bandwidth, we can now use personal computers placed under our desks over a 15-megahertz (MHz, millions of cycles per second) channel. The able manager does not need to know the meaning of "cycles per second" to understand that the difference is greater than three orders of magnitude.

Whenever the power at our disposal changes by an order of magnitude, all of management thinking must change. The influence of more than three orders of magnitude is overwhelming. *After 30 years of our working for the computer, the computer now works for us.* Engineering workstations for computer-aided design (CAD) offer one example. The greatly expanded power of new-generation microcomputers has opened

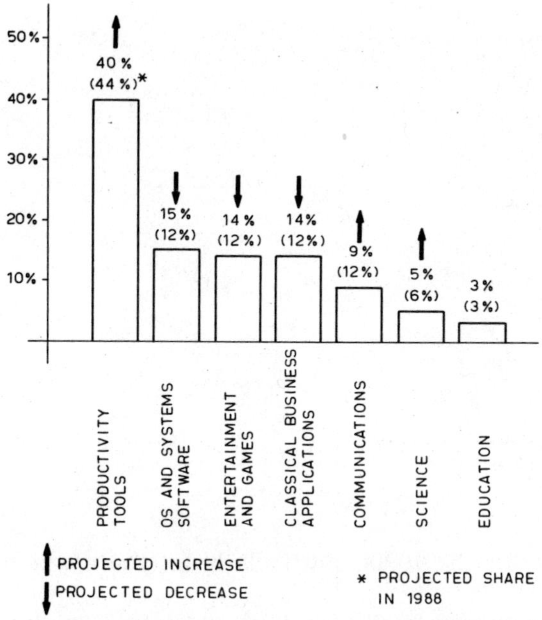

Figure 4 Software business opportunity—the sharing of a multibillion market by different product offerings.

the possibility to firms of all sizes to capitalize on the benefits of CAD. Engineers, architects, designers, and industrial artists are among the professionals who can now take advantage of this technology.

Programs have become abundantly available in two-dimensional (2-D) and three-dimensional (3-D) design, solid modeling, drafting, kinematics, finite-element analysis, structural studies, printed-circuit design, circuit simulation, and so on. Desktop access, short training periods, ease of use, and dedicated computing resources bring this technology within everyone's reach.

Most likely to benefit from the computing and communicating power embedded in workstations will be the larger firms that have the human and financial resources necessary to capitalize on technology. The projected market share for PCs by the end of this decade divides into two unequal parts: 80 percent for the larger firms, including their managers and professionals, and 20 percent for the smaller firms (Figure 5).

The forecast is for an explosion in workstations of all types, and this will mean that the staffs we employ from now on will be increasingly familiar with computers. One of the aspects of this increased literacy is that people generally will become more expert on software. This

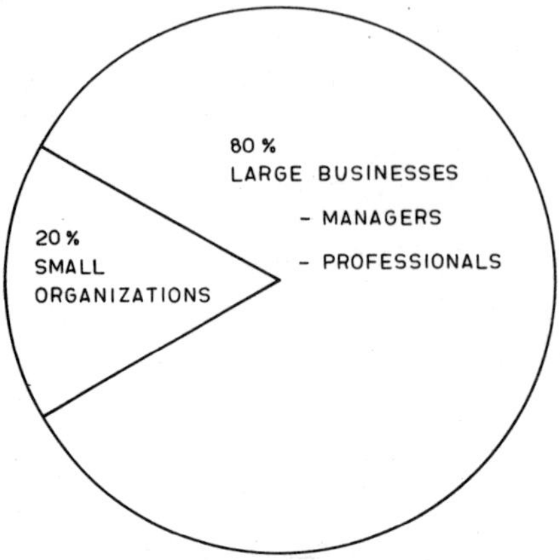

Figure 5 Projected PC market share in the 1985 to 1989 timeframe.

will create a major problem for the 1990s, particularly for the banking industry: that of security.

To face the challenge of greater security, we need at least authorization and authentication techniques and in some cases cryptographic protection. Depending on the application we must choose between:

- Low-level protocols (specifying from, to, and error checks)
- Higher-level protocols (affecting speed and format conversion and encryption and featuring file transfer characteristics)

We must provide network software and uninterrupted services, and we must do so with full understanding of market movements.

Telecommuting is another feature to be brought into the spotlight. Increased quantity and improved quality of work are reported for working at home through PCs, while turnover and absenteeism problems appear to be reduced. Through access to electronic mail and message systems, routine work tasks are handled more efficiently, and it is possible to direct an uninterrupted effort to some of the more complex work.

Just because so much power is in the balance, one of the criteria should be the demonstrated ability of new information systems projects to benefit from technological innovation by using it to the profit of the sponsoring organizations. New-generation PCs now under development are believed to have all the power and functionality of full mainframes. According to some estimates, the potential cost reduction from today's processors could be as much as 80 to 90 percent.

Facts and forecasts of greater computer power at the workplace, and lower costs, must be among the key points of projects in computers and communications. Organizations that ignore these changes are likely to suffer as their competitors move ahead and new competitors break into their markets.

But technology for technology's sake is not the horizon of business. Investment decisions should fit within properly established strategic plans. Technology will continue to change. Hardware will become less expensive and more powerful. Software and programming languages will evolve—and in any case software has generally outstripped our capability to exploit it effectively.

Integration must be a cornerstone of our efforts—from system-wide to workplace level. With the increasing levels of automation in a firm, it has become rather commonplace to see two or more display terminals on the same desk. They are there to satisfy a need to access different systems at the same time. Companies often fail to realize that this redundancy is costly not only in terms of the hardware itself and the inherent communications capabilities that support it but also, and most particularly, in terms of the human usability of such a solution. A key ingredient of the preparatory work is to assure *generality in the capabilities of workstations* and to fully streamline the system.

As an increasing number of terminals require access to more and more database-data communications facilities, the importance of system solutions increases. The number and types of users operating online should definitely influence the design of the entire information system rather than just the communications end of the system. Access to external (public) databases should be cross-country to make feasible reception of data at the executive desk instantaneous rather than delayed by days or weeks. Management applications demand timely and documented answers to the questions posed, and without the intermediation of assistants.

Software is necessary to handle typical end user operations such as formatting, visualization, and copying. The software supports generic commands or primitives which the end user can easily learn. There is a small set of native commands that can be used throughout the system. Examples are the commands *rename, format, move, copy,* and *delete.* Each performs in the same way regardless of the type of object selected.

But, in the last analysis, an efficient information system depends on more than hardware and software. If a system is to work, we have to consider the most important variable: *people.* How do we direct our managers and professionals for highest productivity? How do we establish workable, cost-effective solutions? How do we select the supports suited to our requirements?

Definitions of Key Terms

Artificial intelligence is a scientific field concerned with creating computer systems which can achieve a human level of sensory activities and reasoning.

Expert systems are software constructs that experts in specific fields enrich with their knowledge. They give advice and justify the opinion which they offer.

These definitions are intended to identify, in this introductory chapter, a terminology new to management. Each term will be fully explained in a later chapter.

Chapter

2

Decision Support and the Information Center

"Knowledge wears out if we don't use it."
A PRINCIPLE OF SCIENCE

What Is Meant by "Information Center"?

Information center technology, intelligent personal workstations, PC-to-mainframe interconnections, communicating databases, and fourth-generation languages are today the most exciting areas of information processing. They put us within reach of the automated society which, until now, has largely been in the realm of science fiction writers.

Our postindustrial social environment operates effectively only by having information open to everybody and getting each individual to respond. Our future depends on shared information. This is particularly true of all factors affecting business decisions (Figure 6).

Knowledge is power, but knowledge and information have two special characteristics that contrast them to physical assets.

1. The more we share them, the more of them we have.
2. If we stop sharing them, they decay and eventually become negative assets.

In a broader sense, the *information center* (Icenter) is a mainframe-*and* PC-based system designed primarily for managers and professionals. It helps in establishing easy access and effective communication links, but it also extracts, filters, and compresses information from internal and external sources.

Information centers typically reside on hosts and any number of personal computers. Users communicate with the software through a keyboard, keypad, graphic tablet, mouse, or touch-sensitive screen.

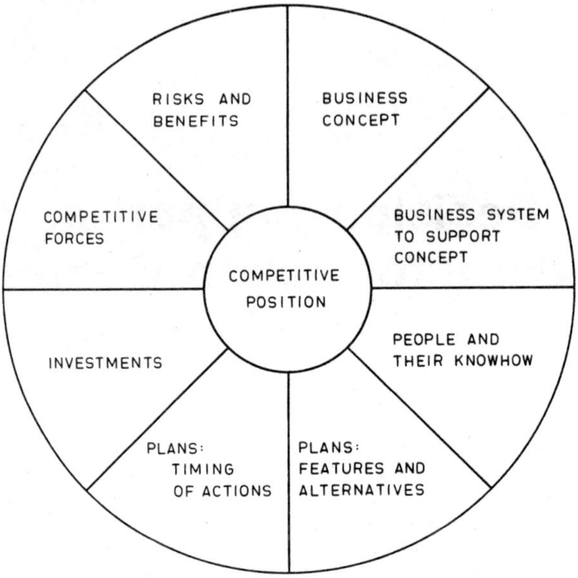

Figure 6 Factors affecting business decisions.

In an easy, assisted, and forgiving manner, the information center is intended to help business people with limited or no computer experience do their jobs better and faster. End users can:

- Create formal reports
- Apply what-if experimentation
- Convert the results of experimentation into graphics
- Access databases
- Manage data
- Retrieve and analyze information
- Develop business plans
- Control projects
- Perform financial and statistical analyses
- Convert data into color displays

Software supporting the information center permits interactive file creation without professional assistance, but with data security at the library level or through passwords for specific files. Also available are built-in fourth-generation programming languages to help the user expand the applications.

Goals of an Information Center

Like programming environments, information centers are areas of rising competition. They are not so gaudily marketed as classical DP installations; but if we are right about the underlying technical nature of the information systems task, they should have more staying power.

In an Icenter orientation, we no longer talk about where to mechanize a program life cycle or about the programmer's own symbol-processing capabilities. Our goal is much broader; *it is to look at classical DP as a subset of office automation. The information center is an integral part of OA.*

The purpose of establishing and operating an information center fits into notions which have just been outlined. The center is built to serve three basic goals:

1. *Provide the necessary background for sharing information among top management, middle management, and professionals in the organization.*

These are the people who were the least served during the first 30 years of the information revolution. Yet, because of the acceleration of technology, product life cycles have been dramatically shortened, perhaps to less than their depreciable lives.

The new automated office system brings together persons, processes, and media in the form of computers and communications. The Icenter allows them to interface (Figure 7). Survival in a fiercely competitive environment greatly depends on management ability to have the infor-

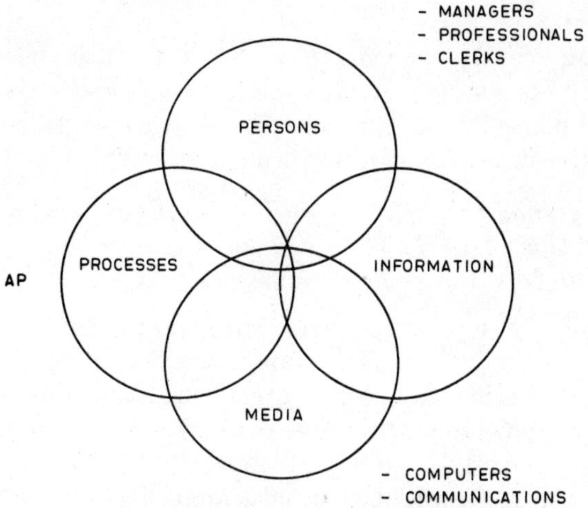

Figure 7 An office system involves persons, processes, information, and media.

mation it needs when it needs it—and in a form it can comprehend. This information is decision-oriented, and it must be possible to manipulate it with the appropriate tools.

The information center is not addressed to transactional activities. The latter are more or less well supported by the classical realtime operations. The goal of the Icenter is management service. The systems approach should cover Icenter design, connection to the transactional database, user access capabilities, and—most important—information delivery.

Such a goal is consistent with the fact that, to gain competitive advantages, an organization must have steady and easy access to timely and accurate information. Therefore, information center design must be based on understanding of management-level information technology to deliver it to users properly.

2. *Dissociate the management information system activities from the transactional chores and thus avoid a confusion in the operations of classical DP through an unwanted transformation of current day-to-day activities into a simultaneously accessed two-tier system.*

Not only have classical DP center operations been basically oriented toward transactions (money in and money out) but they also have had a twisted history of development. Files are rarely integrated into a coherent, comprehensive database.

Just the same, transactional procedures do not necessarily use DBMSs—some of them do and others don't. Furthermore, with 2 to 10 million Cobol statements in the library it is unwise to move too much in the foggy bottom of classical DP activities. There is the risk of destabilizing the old system.

Hence, the information center approach is to link the new management-oriented database—which is typically relational—to the old one (which is usually hierarchical) through data extract routines. This provides significant freedom in design and leads to the third goal:

3. *Use the expertise we gained through 30 years of computer practice and 20 years of communications experience to develop a comprehensive information system for managers and professionals.*

Such a system will typically be supported by mainframes at the level of the *text and data warehouse* and by PCs under the users' desks. For decades, information processing has been centered around a rather unproductive structure: the traditional DP department. Now a wave of new policies has come into view.

Old policies saw to it that managers and professionals had to wait in line a year or two for help from classical DP. Even when their turn came, it seems they never got just what they wanted. Only recently has a competitor emerged in the form of the information center and its end user orientation. This is creating an opportunity to make widespread applications of management principles to corporate computing.

What we are essentially developing within the Icenter framework is a rich and actual internal database, an able complement to the long list of external databases the manager and professional user of the information system is free to access. This brings into focus the first prerequisite: a good deal of *planning* activity, that is, *defining the information center and identifying who will be involved and how.*

The second basic prerequisite is *designing*. It includes selecting system architecture, OS, DBMS, equipment, and staff and defining the policies and overall strategy. The third key issue is *developing* the stage at which products and services are chosen. This, too, is instrumental in putting the Icenter into practice. Fourth, there is need for properly managing and evaluating the time at which plans are put into action and Icenter activities are evaluated for their effectiveness.

Planning and designing must be given predominant places because, this time around, we have the experience necessary to do the work in the right manner. Indeed, an estimated two-thirds of an information center's troubles can be traced to mistakes made during the start-up phase. The right planning must cover technical issues:

- Initial information (product) selection
- Possibilities of networking PC
- File-handling procedures
- The maintenance of information elements
- Fourth-generation language selection
- Quality control requirements

Better results are obtained when there is corporate management involvement and the concept is to make the Icenter a valid service organization. End users should definitely be involved in planning information center activities, promoting teamwork, and building long-term commitments to technological solutions. At the same time, information systems people and policies should be keen on improving senior management support.

An information center implementation will, then, be successful if company information is re-sorted and custom-designed for the executives. The Icenter should allow the executives to track key data and strategic statistics, through their PCs, in the center's database. This puts emphasis on the need for able solutions in PC-to-mainframe communications, beyond the level of traditional dumb terminal–to–mainframe linkage. It underscores connection methods and protocols.

Choices must be made. Will we use dedicated lines, polling and selecting, dial-up contention, or value-added network? The answer is part of a more general problem which includes:

- Cost
- Response time
- Dependency on mainframe-supported applications

PC-to-mainframe communications are an integral part of the query: How and why can intelligent terminals be of help? The answer is computer power under every desk, but the solution is multifunctional: It includes ways to simplify the programming job, accelerate timetables, and be punctual in meeting user demands.

Other goals, too, have to be addressed: offloading host MIPS (millions of instructions per second), allowing deferred file data transfer, and reducing response time. One of the goals is assuring greater applications versatility; another is highly improved systems availability and reliability.

Project Management for an Information Center

The implementation of an office automation environment with strong decision support system (DSS) features implies change. Such a change must be both procedural and in the habits of people; it must significantly influence the way the people are working. Change will be better accepted, and the system will become more successful, if we move swiftly.

The characteristics of modern information systems are short development cycles, low start-up costs, the use of small but expert teams, well-defined and well-contained projects, and concrete and fully observed timetables. This provides increased efficiency in implementation and greater ability to integrate systems and components, but it also calls for project management.

It is one thing to obtain senior management commitment; it is another to arrange for broad-based participation; and it is still another to identify objectives, alternatives, and constraints. There is a counterpart to those statements. If management wants something done, it should make somebody responsible for it. The person to be selected as project manager must:

- Be experienced in systems development
- Know the organization
- Be motivated toward improving productivity

The project manager's responsibilities must include maintaining awareness of development tools and productivity techniques, identifying potential systems development areas, and promoting the need for computers and communications in managerial and professional positions.

Management should also appreciate that the anticipated changes will affect many in the organization and not just the technicians. By having managers and professional users participate in the planning phase, advantages can be achieved. Their enthusiasm and support are stimulated. Since they participate in building the plan, they commit themselves to carrying it out. Also, a more accurate assessment of the environment is obtained. This is important in establishing a valid working basis.

Organizational prerequisites also should be properly appreciated. A project is an organizational unit dedicated to the attainment of a precise, short- to medium-term goal. The successful completion of a project in time, within budget and in conformance with specifications, can best be achieved on a project management basis.

The project manager's mission should be in writing. The manager's aim is to create a defined product, service, or process. The primary tool is the brainpower of the people under the manager's authority: professional specialists in their fields. The next most important tool is the authority the project manager is given by management to cut red tape. In principle:

1. Projects must never be permanently structured.
2. Projects must be dismantled upon completion.
3. The project staff should be a mix of different specialties, including end users.

Furthermore, *goals and criteria for success should be expressed both in qualitative and in quantitative terms.* It is very important to establish from the beginning the right sort of metrics which will enable the manager to thoroughly evaluate progress. The usefulness of the evaluation, in fact, lies as much in its compliance with timetables as in the specific quality of the results.

The budget is another issue which should be carefully outlined. It should be established per phase within a project and then be reviewed, revised, and consolidated as the project moves on.

Well-run projects will typically put forward a clear, comprehensive explanation of how each function is going to be implemented at each managerial, professional, and clerical level. Here is an example. In its recently announced Office Automation Strategy, AT&T has defined areas of activities to which it is addressing itself. AT&T calls them The Workstation-Type Centers, and they are three:

1. A voice-data terminal for the executive
2. A Unix PC for the professional
3. A word processing system for the secretary

Even this definition, though necessary, is not complete. There should be included realistic and characteristic profiles of executives, managers, and professionals whose jobs are to be automated; otherwise, the OA project rests on generalities.

This is what I mean by *establishing precise goals.* At the same time, it is necessary to properly elaborate on the text and data flow this project will be using. That evidently points to information center implementation. In the way we have been discussing it, the information center is not necessarily just a physical place. It is also, if not mainly, a conceptual area. It is, therefore, difficult to put walls around it, but it is necessary to give a comprehensive definition within the company's own environment.

Choices have to be made. Will the Icenter database share resources on the mainframe that is processing transactions (a bad practice) or use a dedicated machine? This option is outlined in Figure 8, which also points to the fact that information center databases should be relational.

Don't ever use ossified, hierarchical structures because of "investments of the past." The past is past. New concepts need new solutions. The Icenter database must certainly be dynamic and typically distributed,

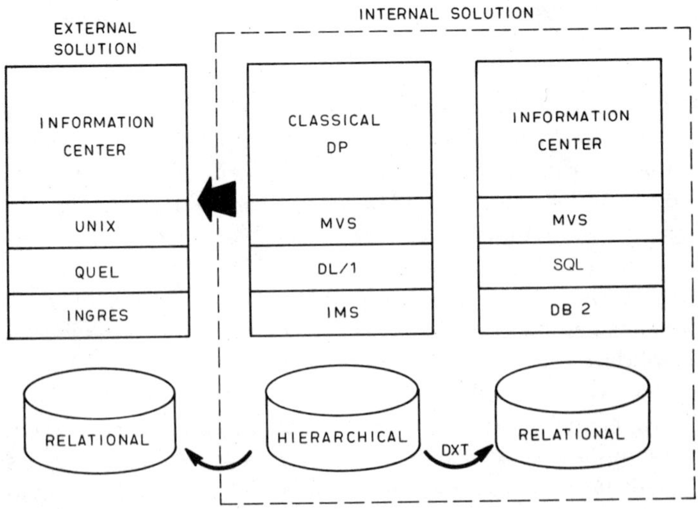

Figure 8 Information center solutions external and internal to the current computer resources.

and it is often unstable. Many organizations would be dismayed by such instability. Only the minority will use it as an opportunity for progress.

The management-oriented projects of which we are talking abide by different guidelines than plain old data processing. They aim at decision assistance, the provision of uninterrupted service, emphasis on security and protection, and the assurance of availability and reliability. One of their characteristics should be short timetables. As stated in another connection, long timetables see to it that, by the time a system is developed, demands have changed and the system no longer provides the needed solutions. Worse yet, long timetables discourage the user.

Those are reasons why formal approaches must be developed through project management. But lip service will work no miracles. *A project must be a well-defined activity set up to produce predetermined results.* It involves resources:

1. Knowhow and therefore personnel
2. Money and therefore budgets
3. Time, projected in timetables
4. Other resources such as computers and communications

A project should be closed down if it fails to reach its milestones, overruns its estimated costs, misuses its human resources by periodically diverting them to secondary issues, and goes out of control. Projects should not drift aimlessly. They should be subjected to rigorous design reviews and management control.

Organizing for Decision Support

The subject of this book is expert systems, but the book is written for management. It would be wrong to include in it mathematical equations and, by doing so, shoot over the heads of its intended readers. It would be just as wrong to not bring all relevant organizational issues into the picture. This is the reason why the first chapter is addressed to the responsibilities of top management and the second chapter to decision support.

As a December 6, 1985 article in the *Christian Science Monitor* aptly suggested: "One of management's best friends this year has not been a fancier personal computer, but rather a human being—the information management consultant—who can tell a company how to use its number crunchers." The information management consultant focuses his attention on two issues:

1. The infrastructure
2. Developments beyond the now classical data processing chores

Such higher-up developments are decision support and expert systems. They represent the culmination of experience in making computers useful. But let's not keep a fact of life in the shade. Though many think that decision support and expert systems are mainly mathematical, algorithms represent only 20 percent of the task. The balance is information.

To collect, sort, organize, store, and access this information, we must *know how to use our experience effectively*. What did we learn from 33 years of DP practice?

1. Information systems are a matter of culture, not of machines.
2. We get little from our investment unless we have clear goals.
3. Without the proper knowhow, results will be minimal.

This puts emphasis on the need for *computer literacy* and also on the prerequisites: strategies, policies, and procedures. Any successful effort will start at the top-management level and move all the way down the organization. The senior executives must set the example.

In any organization there are three basic entities in information-handling perspectives: a system of record, the users, and management. The entities are dynamic and interact. The information elements included in a distributed system of record feed the end users. The latter make decisions based on the results of processing. In turn, these decisions cause management to change both the day-to-day and the longer-term operations of the company.

Those three sentences help explain why organizations can use decision support systems to competitive advantage. In firms that use DSS, competitive information systems become a regular feature of management practice. This is another reason for more emphasis on direct, interactive computer assistance.

As was said earlier, a discussion of the mathematical aspects of decision support, though scientifically exciting, is of less immediate concern to management practice. What is important, however, is to emphasize that *competitive information systems require a level of discipline that is rarely seen in older management approaches*. Yet this discipline is the key to success.

Decision Support in an Office Automation Environment

Many users of computers and communications, from corporate treasurers to wealthy individuals, need three distinct financial applications: cash-flow planning, analysis of alternatives, and status tracking. A sound status-tracking program should also include a budgeting system useful in controlling income and expenses (cash flow).

In cash-flow planning, a budget can be helpful, but it is also necessary to have a financial program that will help project an ideal budget for a year. This can offer a valid annual picture of income and expenses, which can be developed by using a spreadsheet. A spreadsheet presents considerable flexibility in structuring income and expenses.

For the evaluation of alternatives a financial analysis program is needed. It can be useful in testing purchase or investment decisions. First standardizing and then automating the calculations would simplify amortization, depreciation, and return-on-investment studies.

Finally, for status tracking it is possible to use the records created for entering check transactions. The result will be of help in presenting a picture of assets versus liabilities. The difference between the latter and the former yields net worth.

Another significant area for decision support systems is cost analysis. There are two cost references when we commit large amounts: up front and ongoing. Knowing our liquid assets is important when we handle up-front costs. Understanding our cash flow helps us determine whether we can pay the continuing costs. Cash flow planning presents an annual view of income and expenses. By doing so, it helps improve finances and associated managerial decisions.

Quite helpful in this same sense is a checkbook-balancing program:

1. Allowing description and updated inventory of assets and liabilities
2. Maintaining all financial transactions
3. Tracking the budget in a plan versus actual form
4. Automatically generating tax reports and other documents required by authorities and equity holders

Just as important are parametric aids for analyzing financial information. Such aids typically permit the user to study insurance plans, estimate risk, relate current investment to goals, keep track of net worth, evaluate alternative tax strategies, and hedge different investment types including multiple currencies.

In this section we have described most of what can be said about decision support systems in financial planning and control. *Sounds wonderful? It is not.* Although what has been stated is valid, what has not been stated can make that insignificant. The difference lies in the wealth of information elements in the database (DB)—from our personal microfiles (stored on the hard disks of our WSs) to the distributed corporate text and data warehouses and the public databases we can access.

As many people fail to appreciate, the database is the real wealth:

- Give an executive the most wonderful DSS model and little or no data, and there will be no use for the model.
- Guarantee the same executive a steady stream of pertinent, updated data handled through a simple model and you have laid the cornerstone to success.

President Eisenhower is reputed to have said: "The plan is nothing. Planning is everything." It is the *process* which is important, and it must be established in a sound, steady, but also dynamic manner. Its form must be transparent to the user. This can be achieved in an office automation environment if we establish the right perspective from the start. Figure 9 makes this point. The whole information system in a firm can be divided into three layers:

1. Top management
2. Middle management and professionals
3. Transactions and word processing (secretaries and clerks)

Strategic planning is the domain of top management, most particularly the policy makers. Top management also looks into operations planning, but that is specifically the area in which middle management and professionals act. Decision support and expert systems are addressed both to top management and to the upper layer of middle management.

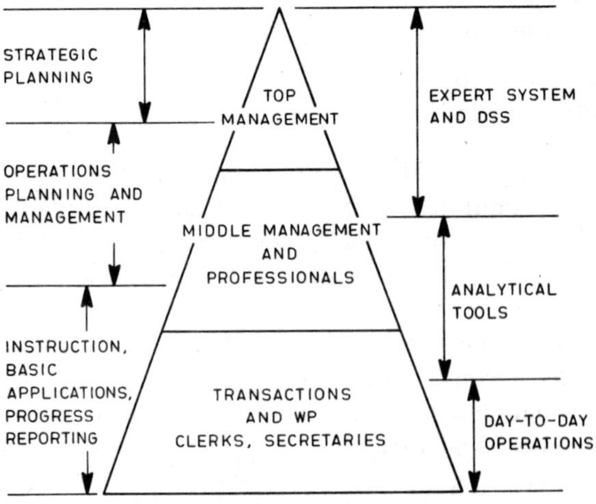

Figure 9 Information systems should be looked at as composed of three layers each with specific objectives.

A large variety of analytical tools, of lesser sophistication, appeal both to professionals and to the people more directly connected to transactions. Word (text) processing, which for all practical purposes has merged with data processing, is at the bottom of the pyramid.

From 1975 to 1984, office automation was easily confused with word processing. That is no longer true. What is a valid, forward-looking definition of OA on which we can all agree? The definition which I propose consists of four key components.

1. *The new frontier in the battle for productivity*

Like every new frontier, it calls for fundamental studies, particularly studies oriented toward doing things in a different way: less paper, more machine intelligence, and greater integration.

In terms of analysis, development, and implementation, office automation is *a state of mind.* The key issue is *the management of change.* This requires a transition plan for adaptation and continuity.

2. *The means to support and enhance the mental productivity of managers and professionals*

A wave of change is now hitting managerial, professional, and clerical jobs in financial institutions. Throughout the years, few highly qualified executives had the *uncanny ability to see major trends before anyone else—and to capitalize on those trends.*

The highly competitive environment within which we now live makes it mandatory to *assist all managers and professionals to see the future more clearly.* That is what we aim to do with decision support, what-if evaluation, and *expert systems.* The primary goal of office automation in any company should be the *mental productivity of the company's managers and professionals.* Otherwise, the automation will not be worth its cost.

3. *A powerful tool for the preservation of company resources*

The foremost resources of any bank or industrial concern are clients, its own personnel, money, strategic products, and equipment. An office automation effort should definitely support those resources.

The goals should be stated by top management: "What is our organization going to be in 1999?" Office automation should then help management focus on strategic planning. In that sense, OA is a strategic information system.

4. *The implementation of high technology*

Precisely because of the cutting edge of science and technology, implementation is a never-ending process involving system studies, personal computers, new software offerings, spreadsheets, database management facilities, and artificial intelligence. *Those references have in common the emphasis on information*, which is now not only a commodity but also a valuable resource.

An Expert Online: Models and Spreadsheets

We have been speaking of project management and end user participation as two of the pillars on which a valid decision support system rests. Uninterrupted data flow provided by the information center is the third pillar, and the fourth is the establishment of precise goals.

The goal of DSS is to assist in *analysis* related to decision-making tasks: forecasting, planning, directing, controlling, and reporting. Only when the area of applications has been properly focused on can we talk of *modeling*. Modeling is necessary when a combination of human judgment and automation can be more effective than the person alone.

A *model* is the idealization of a real situation* which permits us to experiment on a scale while obtaining reasonably valid results. This is the essence of:

- What-if
- Simulation
- Ad hoc analysis
- Monitoring of business operations
- Information access and query

Unlike the plain old vanilla ice cream of DP performance, modeling, and therefore decision support, is usually nonprocedural. Increasingly, the technical vehicle has included approaches which do not follow a precise computational procedure as the batch routines do.

Computer simulation maps the real world into computer memory and subjects it to rigorous treatment defined parametrically by the user. For example, a *financial model* simulates money flows that arise as the result of underwriting risks. These flows may include premium receipts, claims payments, investment of funds, investment income, expenses, taxes, and dividends. The net result of all money flows occurring in a given period of time is shown by changes in the balance sheet, which represents the state of the company.

A *descriptive model* is neutral with regard to the simulated decisions specified by the user. Such a model typically calculates the results of management decisions taken in conjunction with a specified economic

---

*We will return to this subject when we talk of inference.

scenario. The user can run the model many times and vary the numerical values of decision parameters as required. An *optimizing model* would generate a set of decisions guided by a set of goals and constraints established by the user.

What-if employs the speed and power of the computer to evaluate the effects of alternative management strategies and different economic environments. The user will typically ask a series of questions of this kind: "What if inflation rises to 10 percent over the next 2 years?" "What if interest stays at 8 percent?" Results can be used as an aid to planning at a strategic level or by researchers looking into more theoretical issues.

An *accounting model* is more limited: it investigates changes in balance sheet levels that result from money flows calculated according to fundamental accounting identities. This is in contrast to econometric models, which attempt to forecast the values of such items as gross national product and the impact of economic indicators.

In contrast, a *dynamic model* simulates the changes in the state of a company which result from changing economic environments or other factors. In addition, it can simulate changes which arise from sudden discontinuities, superimposed trends, or cycles.

Although less sophisticated than an expert system, decision support software is a partner of the end users in many offices. It will typically involve:

1. Database retrieval and a report-writing facility
2. A relational database

The functions have characteristics which include data expression on a video display using a table and simple commands (operation and instruction). They allow end users to operate easily on their own and make use of help features.

There is today a cornucopia of offerings in *DBMS and query* fourth-generation programming products. Just as easily, users can find simpler *query only* languages available as commodity software. They can be operated stand-alone or combined with the following:

3. Spreadsheet packages
4. Table-handling functions
5. Other data process activities (logical and arithmetic operations, conditional expressions)
6. Graphical and picture operations

A *spreadsheet* is a tabular structure whose cells are interconnected in a preprogrammed form transparent to the end user. This feature allows the user to employ the spreadsheet both as horizontal applications software and as a user-friendly fourth-generation language. The spreadsheet permits financial planning. It is the end user software for microcomputers par excellence.

Through spreadsheets, managers and executives can maintain a variety of information from which sales analysis reports can be developed. The system produces various types of standard profit and sales reports and handles data for custom-developed displays to meet unique reporting requirements in each firm.

As another application example, spreadsheets assist in the proper management of inventory: maintaining accurate inventory information, valuing inventory properly, and using forecasting and item performance analysis. They provide for online record keeping for inventory items and adjusting the inventory balances, as well as for multiple-location inventory processing, status inquiries, and inventory transfers between locations.

The spreadsheet is a decision support tool, but decision support is not just a spreadsheet. What is important to remember, however, is that spreadsheets (lots of them from different makers) are available as commodities. The project manager has a problem of choice but not the option of reinventing the software. That is a wasteful practice sometimes carried beyond all reason because of other, ill-conceived practices of years past. Management should be on the lookout for such irrationalities, and it should strictly forbid them.

The availability of commodity software at very reasonable prices has transformed the economics of computer use and the scope of computer applications. Through decision support systems (DSS) we have been developing a solid understanding of where and how to use computers to help managers improve their decision making.

Spreadsheets have greatly changed some of the aspects of the managerial effort and have made it feasible to project, analyze, control, and forecast interactively. Through commodity software, managers analyze, schedule, and plan the costs of business projects. They obtain summarized reports which stress exceptions, cash flow commitment, and schedule analysis.

These are elements of interest both to professionals and to strategic planners, the more so when the spreadsheets are enriched with graphics capabilities: bar, pie, and line charts that express detailed and consolidated reports by strategy, product, and cost center. The user can analyze data in tabular or graphical form, produce variance reports from actual, forecasted, and planned quantities, and create forecast reports by customer, product, district, territory, and region. These examples document the reference that spreadsheets are commodity products intended to be useful in refining, examining, analyzing, and presenting information.

Although the goal is to assist the decision maker through well-rounded, friendly, and off-the-shelf modular support packages which can be obtained at very reasonable prices, spreadsheets should not be confused with decision support. They are only a tool for that use. Furthermore, value-added spreadsheet offerings have developed into *integrated software* (Isoft) which integrates a DBMS, graphics capabilities, word processing features, and sometimes calendaring in the same package.

Other horizontal software offerings include free formatted data entry facilities, data verification, picture making and maintenance, file entry processing, management modeling, and the like. End users can execute a management model simulation, display results, and make reports by using computer-based management reporting functions.

With the current power of modeling, analysis, and graphics on personal computers, visual presentation of information is one of the highlights in decision support. In the coming years, the ideal operating environment for personal computer users will contain many characteristics developed within the artificial intelligence research area, with the emphasis shifting to expert-based systems.

Software will be providing access to a large database of knowledge by using natural-language commands to retrieve the desired information. Nonprocedural approaches will become the rule. The executive will pose on a WS the query: "What is the company policy regarding make or buy?" and the system will respond with examples.

We will return to these concepts in the following chapters after the notion of artificial intelligence has been introduced. But prior to that we must meet a prerequisite: The following section treats the all-important subject of PC-to-mainframe communications.

PC-to-Mainframe Communications

At Bankers Trust, the worldwide computers and communications network is designed around the premise that *the key element in banking is information exchange*. As a first condition, communications must be so advanced that any intelligent terminal (WS) can link to any data processing (DP) cluster or to any database (DB) in any location. The network must assure there is enough information transfer capacity (text, data, image, voice) and very little contention.

Such a policy assures an aggregate of information services at management's disposal. Although computer support is structured in a distributed environment, there is comprehensive integration into a three-layered structure: end user support, department system(s), and corporate mainframe(s) (Figure 10). This is fundamental in a decision support and expert system implementation, in which a wide range of users must be supported through:

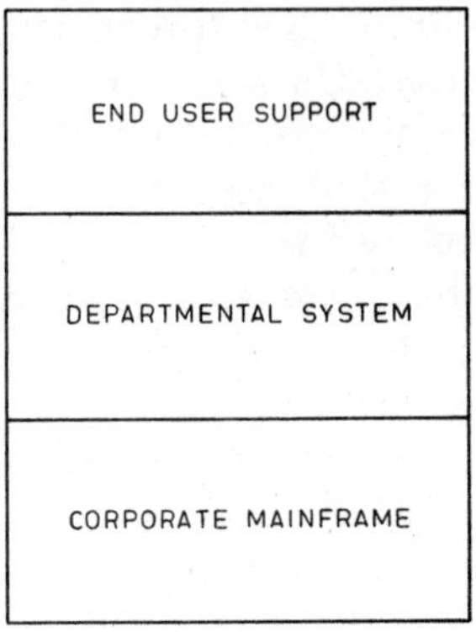

Figure 10 A three-layered structure: from central to distributed systems.

1. Interactive dialog
2. Easy database access and manipulation
3. Timely answers to management questions
4. Computer-enriched presentations
5. Menu approaches
6. Help pages
7. Full screen editing

The earlier reference to information transfer capacity is another way to say that a rational, long-lasting solution should go well beyond a discrete islands approach and assure a clear integration of two types of processes that are reflected in the information system:

1. *DP/WP orientation,* the structure of a system processing large text and data volumes (whether online or batch) in a predefined sequence
2. *Artificial intelligence* (AI) capabilities to forecast, analyze facts, evaluate alternative possibilities, plan, recommend solutions dynamically, and document the advice given

Both are in need of PC-to-mainframe communications as well as a formalization of the process of exchange. The last thing we want is to allow everybody in an organization to do what they please with their PCs, that is, to exercise no control over the process. At the same time, we want to introduce intelligent WSs as soon as possible.

Both goals can be reached if *the workstations are networked.* There is no place for individual, noncommunicating machines in a modern environment. Each device should be part of an aggregate, and the devices should have software in common.

End users should not be put in a position of seeing a machine with a split personality. We must provide:

- Consistency at current requirements
- Ability to integrate higher levels
- Interconnect facilities

all at costs which are reasonable.

As we will see in the following chapter, the operating system on mainframes and minis must include intelligence to communicate with the individual workstations, and vice versa. The better we can maintain a compatible, well-controlled environment the closer we are to a valid solution.

Basically, workstation-to-mainframe communication is structured around the concept of a conversation:

- *Connection* is the creation of the data path.
- *Transmission* is the sending of information over the logical link.
- During *reception*, information is received from a logical link.
- *Disconnection* is the destruction of a logical link. Any resources are returned to the system.
- *Interruption* has to do with the notification at the other end of the link of some unusual condition or event.

The mechanism must provide a range of facilities to programs and processes. The facilities include *link transparency*, in regard to the physical characteristics of the communications links, and *error-free transmission.*

Packet assembly and disassembly are used in the sense that applications may agree to exchange data in blocks of up to the number of Kbytes (K = 1024) supported by the line discipline. For *data transparency* reasons, programs should not be restricted to a certain set of valid characters; they may contain any values.

In any communications mechanism, *automatic data conversion* between ASCII and EBCDIC characters may be necessary. To lower communications volumes, and hence costs, *data compression* by removing repeated characters before data transmission may be advisable.

Communications machines use *protocols.* As we said in Chapter 1, a protocol is a formal set of conventions governing:

1. Format
2. Transmission
3. Control of text, data, graphics, voice, or other forms of information

Protocols constitute logical levels of connection to the physical elements: cables, modems, line, and switching nodes. Originally called line disciplines, simple, early protocols were of the start/stop type. Modern protocols have a layered nature. They include advanced communications and databasing concepts. They also handle error detection, correction, and recovery procedures.

Still, protocols primarily standardize known, *not* new, things. They are short formalisms reflecting an established practice such as the *separation of control from data signals* featured by nearly all data communications techniques.

There is also a communications software challenge: do it yourself versus buy it ready-made. The second is the better alternative provided it fits existing hardware, basic software, and applications software. Other communications requirements include data security, integrity, journaling, recovery, and restart.

Efficient, company-wide communications services are typically structured into an *open system,* and they are supported through network control. Open systems differ crucially from traditional electronic data processing (EDP) systems. Their users can be induced to accept new services (and facilities to reach new users), in a way not possible with closed systems.

Open systems reach beyond the confines of the operating organization. The customer can see the improved service directly. That was seldom true of the old EDP, which was kept close within the organization and petrified beyond possibility of change. Greater flexibility offers both the opportunities needed by end users and challenges to open system operator(s). The latter can add to the services and become more competitive and successful.

Yet, with open systems there are no benefits to be had without exposure to risk. Three major issues can be identified: possibly losing control over features, assuring that users are properly trained, and making the security mechanism effective.

Let's recapitulate. Reasons for online links between PCs and central resources can be stated in the following terms:

1. The satisfaction of the growing ranks of WS users. These users call their need to tie workstations among themselves and into the mainframe *critical.*
2. The reduction of processing loads on the mainframe. This puts the data processing chores where they belong: at the end user sites.

3. With intelligent WSs, the processing job is brought *to the workbench.* This helps to improve communication between the user and the information stored in the computer.
4. The *tailoring of the application* itself to the individual needs of the user, up to the level of decision support and expert systems.
5. The benefit in considerably reducing *response time,* which in turn further improves personal productivity.

So many favorable results are achieved because *computer power is now dedicated to one job.* Therefore, it can do the job fast and well, provided the communications solutions to be adopted are valid.

Chapter

3

What Is Meant by Artificial Intelligence?

" What is most expected to happen is least likely to take place. The unexpected has a better chance." A WALL STREET ADAGE

The Search for Machine-Based Knowledge

Artificial intelligence (AI) is a scientific field concerned with creating computer systems which can achieve human levels of reasoning. More precisely, AI is the branch of information science that focuses on developing computer programs able to perform tasks normally associated with intelligent human behavior.

This is to be achieved through a collection of computer-supported techniques emulating some of the natural capabilities of human beings. Examples are knowledge representation, inference capabilities, problem solving, engaging in dialog, and understanding natural language, as well as speech recognition and synthesis, computer vision, and robotics.

Artificial intelligence can also be defined as a branch of information science whose objective is to endow machines with reasoning and perceptual capabilities. Characteristic of AI is that it:

1. Manipulates symbols rather than numbers
2. Makes inferences and deductions from information at hand
3. Applies knowledge in solving a problem
4. Uses its knowledge and its associated rules to prune the exponential growth occurring in complex real-world situations.

Research is conducted in AI with the dual aims of making computers smarter and examining natural intelligence phenomena of which we presently know very little. But the focal point of artificial intelligence, over the last three decades, has changed with time (as we will see in the first section of this chapter).

In contrast to previous computer generations, the new software approaches exhibit human-like, intelligent capabilities for planning and reasoning. They also exhibit agile man-machine communications performance. By using AI technology, man-made engines perform complex tasks with little human intervention, or even with complete autonomy.

As a result, our self-imposed new goals include the level of employing intelligent computers as active assistants in the management of complex activities. The broader objective of artificial intelligence is to build both:

- *Cooperative systems,* which will closely assist humans in their daily work
- *Autonomous systems,* which can function without human intervention

Both goals are pursued on a dual track: hard-wired AI engines, with intelligence embedded on a chip, and expert systems written for equipment ranging from PCs to large-scale systems.

For the rest of this century the factors contributing to AI will be the fast-advancing hardware technology, greater generality of software tools, increased awareness and expertise in industry, and greater understanding of underlying principles in applying intelligence in problem solution. These factors will be further advanced by a growing list of successes in the implementation of initial offerings.

A major difference between the current AI effort and that of the 1950s and 1960s is that, during the earlier period, researchers tended to rely on search techniques that were not guided by knowledge. Computational logic was successfully used to solve elementary situations and very well structured problems, such as games, but it was unsuccessfully applied to complex problems. The search space of complex problems tends to expand exponentially with the number of parameters involved,* which is why computational logic proved to be inadequate. A new approach was necessary, one that emphasized knowledge rather than search. It led to the field of *knowledge engineering.*

Three Decades of AI Effort

The 1950s, 1960s, and 1970s were decades of AI effort. In the 1950s, research focused on *neural nets.* An outcome of that work is *Perceptron.*

*The game of chess offers an example of the *combinational explosion* characteristic of the number of states in the search space versus their depth. Chess has some 10 to the power 120 possible positions. In original AI chess problems, knowledge in the form of heuristics was used to guide and constrain the search.

Among the AI researchers best known for their contribution in that direction are Wiener, McCulloch, Newell, Shannon, Turing, and Rosenblatt, the maker of Perceptron. Perceptron can be thought of as a self-organizing automaton, a crude model of the retina of the eye. It could be taught to recognize a limited class of patterns, and it reflected the cybernetic ideas of Wiener and McCulloch about abstract neural networks.

The time was right for hardware approaches to brain simulation. Researchers felt that an interconnected system of simulated neurons could be subjected to a training program of reward and punishment. This was supposed to lead to a learning cycle similar to that of the human brain. The approach has since been abandoned, but the AI work is still of a pioneering nature.

Initial problems included games like chess and checkers and the proof of theorems in mathematics and logic. The game tree concept was introduced in 1950 through Claude Shannon's chess-playing program.

In 1955, the Rand-Carnegie team of Newell, Shaw, and Simon showed that chess playing is a problem analogous to proving theorems in symbolic logic. In 1955, the *Logic Theorist* proved theorems. Research produced the information-processing language (IPL) and took the first steps toward a list-processing language.

The Logic Theorist is one of the oldest manifestations of an intelligent system. It processed nonnumerical symbols instead of crunching numbers and was able to prove several theorems in the *Principia Mathematica* (of Alfred North Whitehead and Bertrand Russell).

A major AI milestone was the 1956 Dartmouth workshop organized by John McCarthy, who coined the term "artificial intelligence." McCarthy also invented the list processing language (Lisp) in the late 1950s. But in the 1950s, few practical applications emerged, no business or industrial interests were involved, and emphasis was on basic AI research.

One of the fundamental thoughts of the early 1960s was the then generally accepted belief that a single general-purpose problem solver could attack all of AI's problems if it featured sufficiently powerful inference capabilities. That is in sharp contrast with today's leading thought that AI needs less inference and more knowledge, because *the power lies in the knowledge.*

The 1960s were characterized by emphasis on *heuristics.* Webster's defines heuristics as helping to discover or learn. In a heuristic method of programming, the machine proceeds along empirical lines and uses rules of thumb (empirical rules) to find solutions or answers. Newell and Simon again played leading roles.

The general theory approach dominated; General Problem Solver (GPS) is an example. This was a program for managing general searches, and it was used to solve problems of elementary logic, chess, and high school algebra, as well as to answer questions. GPS made no specific reference to the subject of the problem. The user had to define the task environment in terms of objects and operators to apply to the objects. In this sense, GPS can be credited as setting the stage for *AI shells*, though in its time it was mainly confined to a restricted domain of puzzles with a relatively small set of states and well-defined formal rules.

The 1961 program *Saint*, by Slagle, provided symbolic integration. Ten years later symbolic integration led to Macsyma, by Martin, Moses, and Engelman, which also was concerned with symbolic manipulation.

In 1963, *Sad-Sam*, by Lindsay, used a context-free grammar and a 1700-word dictionary of Basic English to process sentences about kin relationships. *Baseball* was the first simple information retrieval parser written at Lincoln Laboratories, also in 1963. That same year, Weizenbaum's famous *Eliza* simulated a psychiatrist's dialog to illustrate pattern matching.

In fact, 1963 was a prodigious year for the then green field of artificial intelligence. Newell, Shaw, and Simon presented a chess program, and Samuel a program for checkers. Greenblatt produced an improved chess program in 1967. Those same years saw the formation of the MIT group headed by Minsky and McCarthy. McCarthy subsequently moved to Stanford University.

In the same time frame of the early 1960s, Lederberg, Buchanan, and Feigenbaum designed *Dendral*. It inferred the structure of molecules by mass spectographic data and exhibited the first large-domain knowledgebank. *Dendral* interprets mass spectographs by using conventional exhaustive search techniques. It was one of the earliest attempts to apply AI techniques to real problems, and heuristic rules were used to limit the choice of possible structures for evaluation.

In about 1964, Raphael projected a smart question and answer program using trivial databases. Evans had already contributed to the IQ test problem. The *Student*, by Bobrow, attacked high school word algebra problems. Other major contributions were deductive arguments and information retrieval (McCarthy in 1959, Slagle in 1965, Green in 1969).

The first AI computer-controlled robot, a mechanical arm with shoulder, elbow, and grabber, was made by Ernst in 1962. In the mid-1960s, Minsky and Papert engaged in work on computer vision. Later, together with Winston, they introduced the *society of the mind* theory of programs with heterarchies (distributed components).

A body of knowledge was accumulating. As a result, specialization started setting in. In the mid-1960s to mid-1970s time frame, artificial intelligence work began to be subdivided into four major fields:

1. *Understanding natural language.* The best examples are *Shrdlu*, by Winograd (1970), and *Planner*, by Hewitt.

2. *Issues of knowledge representation.* A 1975 publication by Bobrow and Collins summarized the early 1970s state of the art.
3. *Computer vision.* Ongoing projects were exemplified in Winston's *The Psychology of Computer Vision* (1975).
4. *Speech input research.* Leading projects were funded by DARPA in the early 1970s. By the end of the decade, AI products included *Harpy*, with breakthrough in pronunciation representation; *Hearsay II*, with pronunciation graphs and the blackboard model, which was built on the 1967 experience of Hearsay I (integration of continuous speech); *Hwim*, exhibiting segmented lattices; and *Dragon*, of Carnegie-Mellon University.

Looking back 10 to 15 years with today's experience, we can say that *knowledge representation* was the high point of the 1970s. *Mycin*, by Shortliffe (Stanford University), is a good representative example of this effort, although it is not the only one. *Mycin* diagnoses blood infections and recommends antibiotic therapy. Since the system was successful, its inference mechanism was detached from the domain knowledge to produce *Empty Mycin* (EMycin). This is a shell which can hold knowledge from other fields. *EMycin* has been applied to other problems in medicine and occasionally to other domains as well. *Teiresias*, an interactive interface to help in knowledge acquisition, was added by Davis in 1982, and the original *Mycin* knowledgebank has been rewritten to act as a tutorial system, *Neomycin*.

Another development of the same decade was *Prospector*, developed at Stanford Research Institute by Duda, Hart, et al. in 1978. It helps a geologist search for mineral ore deposits. A further development in the same direction was Schlumberger's *Dipmeter*, an adviser to aid in borehole analysis in the search for oil deposits (1984).

In connection with *Prospector*, several independent knowledgebanks pertaining to different areas of geology were built. Hence, this system too can be viewed as a shell. Its inference system has, in fact, been released as a shell known as *Kas*. It has provided the model for a number of shells which are becoming commercially available.

In a sense, *Mycin* and *Prospector* are representative of the late 1970s style of building AI systems. They have a rather simple knowledge representation, a separate inference mechanism, and a way of making the product transparent and easier to build. We will return to these issues.

Goals for the 1980s

By the mid-1970s it had become apparent to the artificial intelligence community that heuristic solutions, search strategies, and limited knowledge representations were inadequate to solve real-world problems. The complexity of those problems is usually such that the ability to generate suitable search space was not present. Projects which leaned more on the expert domain demonstrated that rules based on knowledge were more important than a search strategy. That led to a focus on *knowledge engineering*.

Knowledge engineering is the process of capturing and representing knowledge in a computer system. It includes acquisition, learning, knowledge-directed database specification, and design methodologies. Knowledge-based environments encompass such issues as decision support systems, CAD/CAM, robotics, and VLSI design.

A rule-based system is able to reason about its own search effort in addition to reaching decisions about the problem domain. That calls for a new way of structuring based on four pillars:

1. *A knowledgebank* containing domain facts and rules associated with the problem
2. *An inference mechanism* acting as the control structure for utilizing the knowledgebank in search of a solution to the problem
3. *A global database* keeping track of input data, problem status, and the relevant history of what has been accomplished so far
4. *A dialog engine* able to engage in man-machine communication, prod, guide, extract answers, and present results (Figure 11)

In subsequent chapters we will elaborate on these topics, but it is important to bring them to the reader's attention now because they impact on what will subsequently be said.

Artificial intelligence research, 1980s style, has greatly benefited from development during the last three and a half decades. This reference is valid not only in regard to aftermaths from the same field but also in respect to broader computers and communications perspectives, which can be classified into three main groups.

One group includes *systems concepts*. They range from front-ending (Dartmouth College, 1963) to time sharing (MIT, 1964), packet networks (DARPA, MIT, 1969), and advanced workstations (MIT, 1984). The second group includes *physical constructs*: semiconductors (Bell Labs, late 1940s), integrated circuitry, microprocessors, VLSI, and high-density, low-cost disk drives.

The systems concepts and the physical constructs closely relate to and interact with one another. The same is true of *logical breakthroughs*: operating systems, particularly Multics (MIT, 1964), database management systems, new types of languages like Lisp (MIT, 1959), the eventual merging of hardware and software capabilities into Lisp

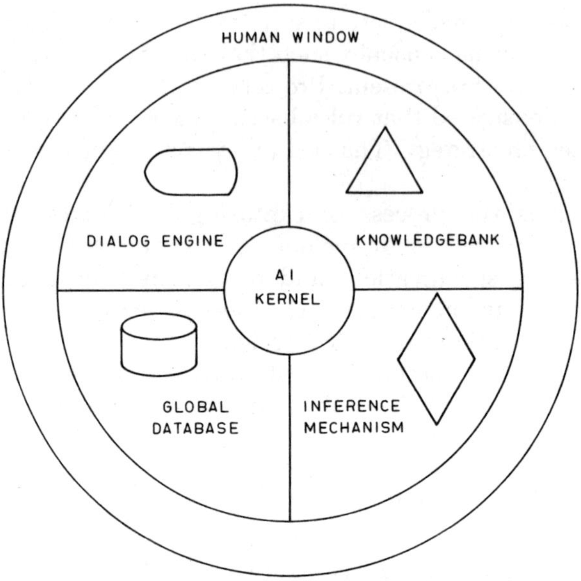

Figure 11 Artificial intelligence system, 1980s style.

Machines (MIT, 1980), and languages such as *Ladder* (by Hendrix) for providing natural-language access to databases.

These references are made because the logical breakthroughs have provided the necessary foundations on which artificial intelligence projects of a new style are being built. We would have been incapable of improving and increasing the system's knowledge, or harvesting the knowledgebank for human use, without the above-mentioned understructure.

An AI system can, then, act as the repository over time of knowledge accumulated by specialists only when software and hardware are available to receive it—and there is an able linguistic interface to facilitate the use of the system.

Against that background, two types of orientation in artificial intelligence work began to appear:

- One stayed on the main track of basic to applied research, along the four lines laid out in the late 1970s.
- The other put its sights on applications development. The guideline has been: "*If we understand the problem, we know how to solve it.*" From this came the expert systems.

It is for those reasons that the focal point of the 1980s has become *computer learning*. Results are nicely represented by *Eurisko*, by

Lenat. Eurisko is a significant development because it extends and improves its own body of heuristic rules automatically. It has also made a breakthrough in very large scale integration (VLSI) design by inventing a three-dimensional AND/OR gate.

If we wish to characterize the last 10 years of AI efforts properly, it will be through the emphasis on *real-world applications.* Working on that premise, computer companies began to develop in-house AI applications such as DEC's R1 (originally built by CMU) and Nixdorf's *Conad.** Both are used to help configure complete computer systems from incomplete order information.

Other applications have been in computer hardware diagnoses localizing faults for repair. Examples are Stanford/Genesereth's *Dart* program for IBM and Savory's *Fault Finder* at Nixdorf. *Diagnostic* applications assist users in recognizing deviations from normal operations in complex physical (for instance, electrical) or logical systems. They are also assessing the causes for the deviations and helping to train the maintenance engineers.

Such applications have an important future, because the principal difficulty in designing large systems is the need to coordinate thousands of interrelated details. The best way to control this complexity is to surround the designer (or maintenance engineer) with an environment of intelligent tools that keep the facts and automatically manage the details.

Another important area is that of *organizational issues* involving technology transfer, planning activities, procurement decisions, and knowledge certification. *Planning* a complex operation such as a space mission or a nuclear power plant requires managing the numerous potential interactions of a large number of variables, a task well-suited for symbolic computation.

Interpretation requires the analysis of large volumes of incoherent and incomplete references to detect a small number of highly significant features. *Symbolic computing* allows the processing of thoughts and concepts in addition to numbers and makes possible the able handling of knowledge-intensive and reasoning-intensive activities.

For those reasons, one of the going forecasts is that symbolic computing will account for 50 percent of all computing in the 1990s. Many tasks cannot be automated by using conventional computing technology and therefore require the capabilities of symbolic computing.

While talking of artificial intelligence, Ted Hoff, the inventor of the microprocessor, commented, "We need to develop algorithms that make

---

* *Twaice* is the tool, *Conad* the knowledgebank. It started with approximately 600 rules and now has 1000.

computers more reasonable. Computers that have more of a personality than just the operating system." Daniel Bricklin, the man who designed the first spreadsheet, once suggested: "People think a new piece of hardware is inherently more capable, but it all depends on the software you are using."

Although software makes the hardware smart, the hardware must become much more powerful to handle the AI programs under development—particularly programs of rules in their knowledgebank. The proposed speed for such machines is based on logical inferences per second (LIPS). We need many LIPS to run complex AI programs. Feigenbaum suggests *10,000 inferences per second* and then adds that the top of the line IBM 3081 gets only 100 LIPS out of a Prolog program. The IBM PC gives 1 LIPS.

There is no exact correspondence between LIPS and MIPS (millions of instructions per second), but some experts tend to suggest that future AI systems will consume between 100 and 10,000 MIPS. We don't yet have machines with such a capacity on one processor. However, because human reaction is slow, AI systems, at their current level of sophistication, can work with what is available—and the decision support variety—on dedicated PCs.

No wonder that project Athena at MIT aims to materialize personal workstations of at least an order of magnitude more powerful than the best available today. A possible growth in demand for built-in intelligence can be expected along the lines outlined in Figure 12 for personal workstations. It is, of course, understood that major breakthroughs in AI will easily eat up the 5 MIPS (even 50 and eventually 500 MIPS) during the coming years. *Intelligence augmented by computers* will most likely be the main trend of the 1990s.

Implementing High Technology

The implementation of modern technology is marked by three interacting trends: (1) increasingly powerful tools at our disposal, (2) greater separation in time and space between planning and execution, and (3) a steadily faster pace of development.

Artificial intelligence is not just the second information systems revolution, *it is the essential one.* Knowledge is now seen as the spearhead of competition. The employment of computer-based, knowledge-intensive processes augments the intelligence level of the user. There are similarities in but also differences between natural and artificial intelligence. These are shown in Table 1, and they are divided into three groups. In two factors AI and natural intelligence are about equal; in six others artificial intelligence dominates. In terms of creativity and being part of our current culture, natural intelligence has the upper hand.

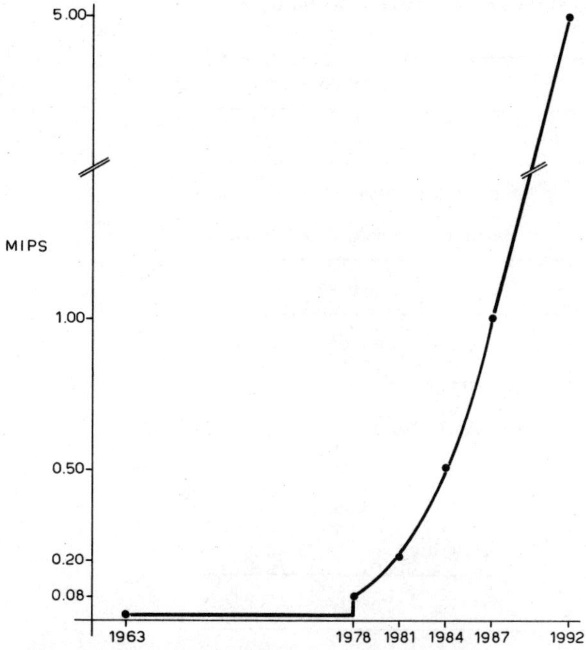

Figure 12 Past and projected increases in millions of instructions per second (MIPS) and built-in intelligence.

There are other issues on the scale. It is easier to interact with an intelligent machine (or person) than with a dumb one. Such an interaction should follow a method, but methodology and rules are becoming our civilization's keywords.

We have seen the links between developments in computers and communications and breakthroughs in AI. Effective application of artificial intelligence requires links to large databases and intensive data communications capabilities. Without a steady flow of data, any AI system will be sterile.

There are constraints to be observed. With AI, high-technology features cannot be bypassed as with traditional DP. Computer power was mentioned as an example. Knowledge systems call for 32-BPW (bits per word) engines, windows, bit-mapping graphics, and expert software.

There are also negative forces working against the use of artificial intelligence in business and industry. For instance:

1. There is disbelief that machines can have intelligence (hence the examples that they can have it).

TABLE 1 Similarities in and Differences between Natural and Artificial Intelligence

Artificial intelligence	Natural intelligence
Equal	
Grows with experience	Grows with experience
Becomes obsolete if not used	Becomes obsolete if not used
Positive	Negative
Outlives the expert's life cycle	Disappears after death of expert
Is consistent	Is irregular
Is permanently accumulating	Is ephemeral, seesaw
Is well documented	Is poorly documented
Is easy to duplicate	Is difficult to transmit
Cost is reasonable	Cost is high
Negative	Positive
Is currently noncreative	Is creative
Is still alien to current culture	Is part of current culture

2. Our prevailing culture has not yet fully adopted the computer, much less the smart machine.
3. Computer experts are still too much oriented toward "data processing." That is a handicap for AI work.
4. Available languages (Lisp, Prolog, Emycin) are not necessarily portable between machines. This creates a detrimental separation between development and end usage. AI projects that do not grow steadily die.

In spite of these negatives, the fields of implementation are expanding. Applications started with medicine and have moved into engineering, mathematics, and the physical sciences. Those are the specialties needed for command, control, and military applications. In them issues relative to computer systems and also programming can be addressed: software specification, design, verification, maintenance, and instruction.

Business and economics are fertile fields for expert systems implementation. So also are natural languages and machine perception. Tax advice, insurance and contract consistency, legal advice, consultancy on investments and other financial matters, and portfolio management are possibilities.

Today a tax advice AI system with 800 rules is operating in America. It solves routine problems but also advises how to take advantage of tax breaks. Business environment scenarios for strategic corporate planning are other examples along the same line.

AI is used in advanced microelectronics and silicon foundries, and among its major contributing fields are speech recognition and answerback. These are well-known applications. Less well known is the use of AI in the development of complex sales tenders.

Knowledge-based systems can diagnose, monitor, analyze, interpret, and consult—and also plan, reason, design, instruct, explain, learn, and conceptualize. This makes them applicable to mission planning, targeting communications and signal analysis, construction, and manufacturing. They can act as equipment design tools, monitor progress, diagnose and repair, and also operate. They can analyze images and make interpretations. They can assist professionals in law, law enforcement, medicine, engineering, accounting, and marketing. They can also be instrumental in education.

Educational applications include instruction, testing, diagnosis, concept formation, and the development of new knowledge from experience. For instance, in a banking environment training may involve:

- Context analysis
- Foreign operations and arbitrage
- Credit application review
- Understanding of market drives

Valid results have been obtained in AI counseling before going into negotiation and in elaborating a tough sales proposal.

Photo interpretation, mapping, and geographic problem solving are areas already served through AI, as are chemical data interpretation, biological synthesis studies, and mineral and oil exploration. Planning and scheduling are fertile areas of implementation and so also are weapon systems: target identification, adaptive control, and all aspects of electronic warfare.

Office automation and decision making are other critical fields in which it appears that AI systems will eventually find use in connection with activities which require professional knowledge. In the process, there will be exposure and refinement of the previously private knowledge in the various fields of application.

As time passes, experience accumulates, and more powerful machines become available, we can expect to see AI systems with thousands of rules. There will also be greatly improved explanation approaches that can say why the system did what it did, advised a certain course of action, and emphasized matters of importance.

For knowledge acquisition, future AI systems may follow multiple viewpoints and have facilities for dynamic fix. For knowledge representation, they may access multiple databases, present problem-solving strategies, determine limitations and bounds, and proceed with autoreasoning.

By the end of this decade, we can anticipate that knowledge acquisition systems will rapidly guide human experts in forming *their* knowledgebanks. One of the projections is that by the end of this century we can see the beginning of systems which nearly autonomously develop knowledgebanks from text, which will herald a maturing information society assisted by man-made intelligent machines.

New AI developments will most likely rest on new fundamental technologies, *biochips* being a precise example. Despite its image as a computer-like device, the human brain more closely resembles an aggregate of chemicals that are constantly interacting. Billions of brain cells (neurons) float in this context of chemical message transmitters.

A serious interest in the possibility of using carbon-based materials for computing has developed only recently in the scientific community, but the work benefits from a convergence of developments in a number of fields. The fields include polymer chemistry, various biotechnologies, and the physics of computation.

So far, theoretical studies suggest that more efficient and adaptable modes of computing than those currently known are possible. Emerging biotechnologies point to the possibility of implementation. Carbon chemistry may facilitate the construction of smaller and faster devices; hence attention has been focused on organic switching devices and conducting polymers.

Champions of molecular electronics say that, by replacing silicon chips with complex organic materials, it will eventually be possible *to pack a thousand trillion bits of data into a cubic centimeter*. By comparison, the human brain uses about 750 cubic centimeters to store the equivalent of about one trillion bits of data. However, human genetic material squeezes about two thousand trillion bits into a cubic centimeter.

Replacing the now classical chips with organic molecules would be revolutionary. But physicists are also working on an idea for improving chips by squashing them into materials so tiny (less than 10 atoms thick) that the electrons in effect move in two dimensions instead of three. These are called *low-dimensional structures* (LDSs). (LDSs can also be used to produce lasers whose wavelengths are tuned simply by varying the thickness of the package. On the other hand, the gamma-ray lasers designed to cripple missiles could also provide the first three-dimensional images of the nuclei of atoms.)

An organic computer built with molecular circuits can cram phenomenal power into a desktop system. Some are saying that it could even lead to synthetic brains. This is an area in which physics and the logical side of artificial intelligence merge.

From AI to Robotics

Even without the developments which are still in an embryonic stage, artificial intelligence work has had significant fallout in business, industry, and the military. The following are two examples of starting with the more theoretical *artificial vision* and moving to the practical and better known robotics.

Image understanding is important in surveillance, intelligence operations, weapon delivery, autonomous navigation, robotics, logistics, and photointerpretation. Natural-language understanding serves in front ends for databases and command languages as well as in text intelligence.

In both these areas, artificial intelligence offers enormous potential for solution of industrial and defense-related real-world problems. There are a number of subjects in which business is gearing up for exploiting the technology to the point that strong interest in AI applications is causing a shortage of qualified researchers.

Artificial vision, to take a specific case, is no longer a simple hypothesis about image understanding. Current research involves many logical questions and answers typically followed in an unstructured way. A challenge with robot vision is how to start extracting information and capturing rules, looking at pictures, and trying to understand. This process involves the technology of analyzing and identifying the contents of a scene from images of that scene:

- *Document processing*: Character recognition, computer understanding of drawings and maps
- *Industrial automation*: Visual inspection, vision for robot guidance
- *Medicine*: Automated blood cell counting, tumor detection on radiographs
- *Remote sensing*
- *Cartography*
- *Reconnaissance*

Many other fields also stand to benefit.

Algorithms for computer analysis of images have been developed in wide variety as the power of available computer hardware continues to increase. Several of these algorithms are finding practical applications.

Major topics covered include feature extraction, segmentation, property measurement, and model matching. Applications to the analysis of images representing scenes are essentially two-dimensional, although three-dimensional scene analysis (including methods of recovering scene properties from an image) is being done.

Templates were used in the early beginnings, but templates cannot solve the vision problem. Light differences and positioning differences, among other problems, make recognition through templates difficult. There is, however, a low-level image processing which focuses on edges and lines and uses segmentation into regions. Major areas of application are:

- Edge extraction and line finding
- Area-of-interest determination
- Clutter discrimination
- Prominence feature detection
- Texture regional analysis
- Shape analysis
- Clouds, haze, and snow and ice detection
- Image enhancement

The approach mostly being followed is to apply mathematical operations which permit more abstract descriptions. Models factor out variations that don't matter, such as lots of similar situations the human eye would rather eliminate.

Other research stresses image sequences, which present a possibility of capturing dynamic developments in a scene by digital imagery. Advances in data storage, processing, and display equipment have made it possible to investigate the automatic evaluation of image sequences versus approaches toward understanding a single image, which essentially captures a static aspect of a scene.

Such work necessarily poses computer power problems and requires mainframe support. That is particularly true of general-purpose solutions and the stage of applied research. When computer vision processes become commodity products, provided that each is specialized, personal computer power may do.

Work on pattern recognition has been going on for more than three decades. The Perceptron was a pattern recognizer (Rosenblatt, 1958, 1962). To this same goal was directed the theory on modification of neural learning theory of D. O. Hebb (1948) and also the mathematical theory of Nilsson (1965). Idealized neurons, threshold devices, the analysis of limitations, and applicable classes of problems are part and parcel of it.

A similar statement can be made about natural language and machine comprehension. From the early 1950s to the early 1960s there was much work on translators. The question-answer process by McCarthy (1958) falls in this field. Natural-language understanding was seen as:

- A vehicle for thought and communications
- A process whereby input of characters helps in inferring wants
- A goal usually achieved through multilayers

General assumptions stressed printed and spoken conversations. This led to the study of speech recognition, two-way communication between man and machine, framing of computer responses, and the use of metaphors. Schank's work on conceptual dependency is significant. It rests on the premise that static situations are represented by states: *HAS*, character owns something; *AT*, indicates where character is; *GOAL*, goal of character; *KNOW*, character knows something.

Artificial speech is another exciting AI area. It should be noted that, despite reports in the popular press to the contrary, none of the current systems have speech input or output (most use keyboards and CRTs) and none are as fast (realtime) as a human being.

Speech understanding involves characteristics of speech sound (acoustic phonetics), variability in pronunciation (phonology), stress and intonation patterns of speech (prosodics), sound pattern of words (lexicon), grammatical structure of language (syntax), meaning of words and sentences (semantics), and context of the conversation (pragmatics). Error and ambiguity permeate all levels.

As for robotics, the real world uses mainly nonmobile industrial robots, though the military is attempting to build autonomous fighting land vehicles. Most existing industrial robots are manipulator arms preprogrammed to perform repetitive actions, often without the benefit of sensory input.

Robot componentry includes robot power systems (drive and actuators), end effectors, and controls. If only internal sensors are used, there is need for careful positioning for repeatability. If external-world signals are used, the robot is more flexible. The latter is also true when the robot is sensor-controlled.

It is the purpose of the vision component to make a robot more flexible by performing a scene analysis. Gerald Barber of MIT has listed some of the capabilities that vision systems should provide for robots. He includes:

- *Location*, as of objects on a conveyer belt (for an industrial robot) or of a geological feature (for a cruise missile)
- *Orientation*, so that the object may be grasped correctly

- *Identification*: which of many objects is the desired one
- *Inspection,* very important for quality control comparisons
- *Error correction* for manipulator positioning, feedback, or navigation

The farther-out goal is the development of multisensor machine perception, that is, intelligent robots able to recognize objects and events from raw sensory data. Such engines would integrate combinational problems encountered in search and be able to plan when confronted with problems of uncertainty in diagnosis. A current example is MSIS.

MSIS interprets sensor information to determine disposition and operation of hostile air defense units. It features an anticipate-plan-interpret cycle. It uses knowledge of location of threats (mobile and interrelated) to identify critical areas of missing information in the anticipate cycle.

MSIS also employs knowledge of potential threats and sensory input to allocate and deploy sensor resources in planning cycles. Knowledge is encoded as production rules to infer probable weapons operation from information such as past status. Critical factors are environmental conditions and distance of things from the aircraft in the interpretation phase.

Artificial Intelligence Markets

According to current projections, the U.S. market for artificial intelligence products will reach over $4 billion by 1990—up by nearly an order of magnitude from the $440 million in 1984. Those values mainly represent software and hardware used for AI applications in the commercial sector; university research and military development installations are in addition to them.

Considerable funds are spent on AI for weapons systems. We will be reviewing the copilot for the Air Force (capable of making realtime battle decisions), the Navy's shipboard computer system for complete management of tactical operations, and the Army's autonomous land vehicle, as well as a ground-launched projectile that can knock out missiles in space.

These weapons systems are in the development stage, but there is also far-out research. In 1985, more than $1 billion was awarded for the Strategic Defense Initiative (SDI), much of it through the Innovative Science and Technology Office (IST). In 1986 this fund will most likely approach $4 billion.

One of the first tasks of SDI was to pull together the best 20 years of past research on antimissile weaponry. That included the development of electromagnetic guns that can fire projectiles at incredible speeds in space and a particle-beam accelerator, known as White Horse, at the Energy Department's Los Alamos National Laboratory. One of the projects is to develop superfast optical computers that use light instead of electrons. IST is also considering biochips which, as described earlier, are circuits made of organic molecules instead of silicon.

Although the budget looks high, there is a significant fallout from weapons research.

- First, in one way or another, 80 percent or more of this money is going to the private sector: companies and universities, whoever masters the brightest minds.
- Second, an American study has shown that every dollar invested in space adds another $4 to GNP over a 10-year life cycle. This increase comprises new products and services brought to the market. *By the early to mid-1990s, it will not be possible to sell products without some AI capability.*

An information systems program based on outwardly impressive achievements cannot be maintained in the long run without AI research. The U.S. Department of Defense has identified artificial intelligence as one of the critical technologies for national defense and for continued economic leadership in the 1980s. The assessment is correct.

Today, in commercial-type applications, the trend is away from the traditional medical and engineering areas and into financial services and business diagnostics. *From banking to investing, the financial services industry will be one of the major clients for artificial intelligence systems.*

Yet, there is no doubt that by far the best clients of the AI business are governments, who rightly see in AI the key to survival of their national industries into the twenty-first century. The first concrete government effort in big money investing came in Japan. In 1978, the Japanese Ministry of International Trade and Industry (MITI) gave the Electrical Laboratory (ETL) the mission of defining a project to develop computer systems for the 1990s. This became known as the *fifth-generation task.* The project formally started in 1982.

The team created under Hajame Karatsu to study prospective functional requirements correctly started with the fundamentals. Its first effort was to forecast the nature of our society of the next decade which the new machine would serve. This gave Japan's Fifth Generation Project (ICOT) a broad scope.

Also in America the government has been the principal source of funding for work on artificial intelligence. The main avenues are Defense

Advanced Projects Agency (DARPA), Innovative Science and Technology Office (IST), National Institute of Health (NIH), National Science Foundation (NSF), Office of Naval Research (ONR), National Library of Medicine (NLM), Air Force Offices of Scientific Research (AFOSR), U.S. Geological Survey (USGS), and the National Aeronautics and Space Administration (NASA). They are listed roughly in decreasing order of expenditure with DARPA and IST the primary funders.

The primary U.S. agent in the advanced technology effort—including AI and fifth generation—is the Microelectronics and Computer Development Corporation (MCC) in Austin, Texas. Established as a joint venture of all American computer manufacturers except IBM, MCC is fast developing as the premier U.S. agency in the computers and communications technology of the end of this century and the beginning of the next.

Ably run by Admiral Bob Inman, MCC is tooled with some of the best brains in the country and is responsible for the *Strategic Computing Project*. Quite evidently, we cannot forget the very significant IBM effort in this domain. IBM is working on artificial intelligence, and it also does considerable research in biochips.*

In Europe, the first AI program funding was *Alvey* in the United Kingdom, which saw to it that England is today a foremost center of artificial intelligence research. In the Common Market, Alvey was followed by the *European Strategic Program for Research and Development in Information Technology* (Esprit) in late 1983. There is also *Eureka*, proposed by the French on a European scale as a counterweight to SDI.

Those are funding agencies, and the first European joint research venture on AI was established in Bavaria by International Computers Ltd., Compagnie des Machines Bull, and Siemens. The plan is to set up a jointly funded institute employing some 50 researchers and working in knowledge engineering. No products are to be developed at the center, and each member is to continue its own proprietary research.

At the same time, both in Europe (particularly England and France) and in the United States there is currently a plethora of start-up firms working in the area of AI. Most of them are focusing on financial applications and planning premises. They bring forward knowledge-based solutions which within a few years will be part of the industry.

As of 1985, the artificial intelligence market divided roughly 3 to 1 between the different branches of AI and the rest. One-third of the AI funding was directed to computer vision. Expert systems accounted for 10 percent of the total (or 40 percent of the 25 percent slice). Natural

---

**ACM Communications*, May 1985.

languages and AI languages together were an estimated 11 percent, and voice recognition represented the balance.

Before too long a consolidation in the AI industry will begin. Start-ups that do not produce marketable products, or that fail to deliver what they promised, will face a shakeout as venture capitalists deny additional financing. But several of the currently small AI companies will become big. That is the way to bet.

Chapter

4

Expert Systems and the Industrialization of Knowledge

"Once the mind is set on something, any challenge can be met."

JOHANN WOLFGANG VON GOETHE

Knowledge and Virtue

Ancient wisdom based virtue on a foundation of knowledge, but without properly outlining which one of the eternal sources of knowledge is the most dependable. If *virtue*, as Socrates said to Protagoras, *is knowledge which cannot be taught*, then there are neither teachers nor students of virtue. But there are *teachers and students of knowledge.*

There are also *virtuous people*. They build themselves up in their social environment in response to societal goals. Since man became a self-conscious entity on this earth, we have labored to improve our geophysical environment—and in recent years even our own molecular and genetic substructures. In contrast, we have done very little to better our logical and ethical structures, which are built on physical premises.

The world in which we live acts both as a catalyst and as an incubator of new ideas. It does not by itself create changes. We also know that, unlike what is taking place with some physical characteristics, neither the acquired knowhow nor our logical assets is or are hereditary. Hence there is the need for expert systems research and implementation to make experience and knowledge transfers a reality.

Expert systems (Esystems) are software constructs that experts in specific fields enrich with their knowledge. By distilling their expertise into sets of laws and entering them into systems, the experts produce applications programs that help nonexperts solve problems in the experts' fields by responding to the program queries.

As such, expert systems are artificial intelligence programs that enable a computer to aid you in a decision-making process. The knowhow of the human expert is used to instruct the computer how to solve a problem or make a decision. The machine can then aid or advise other users in solving the same problem through

- Expert knowledge of the human user
- The computer's ability to store large amounts of text and data and consider all possibilities at high speed

The computer interacts with the user's questions and arrives at a conclusion based on the answers. The user can ask the computer why it wants certain information, and the Esystem will explain its need for data and how the data will be used. Most important, the expert system will say how it arrived at its conclusions; it will not only give advice but also justify the opinion it offers.

At the current stage of Esystems development, intelligent machines are specialist engines addressed to well-defined markets. But the hardware itself is general-purpose (Figure 13), though that may change by the end of the decade as AI capabilities become embedded on chips.

We know from other experiences that software makes the difference; it helps to encapsulate specialist knowledge about a particular domain of expertise. Within such a domain it is possible to make intelligent decisions and achieve dramatic successes in real-life problems.

A Crisis in Data Processing

There is today a crisis situation in data processing. The overriding need for radical changes in software design is being felt. The tools are there. We have fourth-generation language (4GL) methodologies for application development and have a life cycle perspective. But the need for radical changes is not yet a general realization.

In most companies, nobody has done anything significant to alter the way computer systems have been stagnating for over twenty years. In half the Fortune 1000 Corporations 4GL penetration is zero. In the other half, it stands at 20 percent of applications. Only the leaders in information systems give most of their attention to 4GLs and to expert systems research.

The leaders have understood that, to survive, everybody will have to change methodologies. There will be a shakedown among those who don't. Leaders are fast adopting *information engineering* solutions and

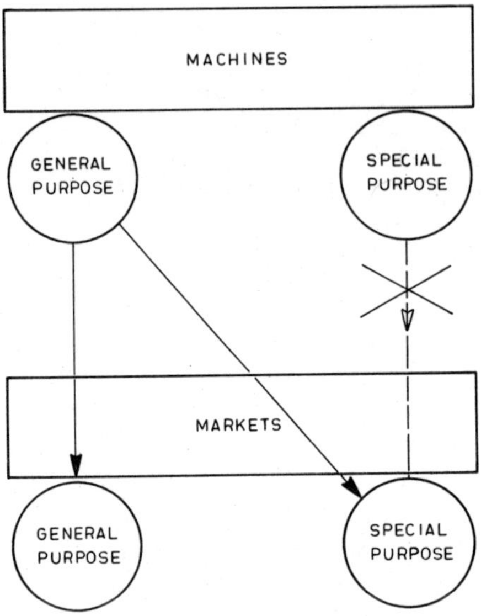

Figure 13 General-purpose engines appeal to special-purpose markets through software implementation.

fourth-generation methodologies. In so doing, they keep their options open to *knowledge-based tools.*

Before the end of this decade, expert systems are projected to provide the *fifth-generation languages* (5GL). There is much more similarity between information systems development and knowledge engineering than anybody has yet imagined, and there are the vast implementation opportunities among end users.

While robotics developments primarily interest defense and manufacturing operations, interactive Esystems are addressed to the ternary sector: banking, merchandising, retailing, and so on. They help in automating the auditing function, support and document investment decisions, and assist in planning, and they are addressed to the professionals. Decision support is a logical development of classical DP—an evolutionary change with revolutionary consequences.

In many professional fields in which Esystems have been applied, productivity improvements reach better than an order of magnitude, well above the 15 to 20 percent obtained through electronic mail (Email). On the other hand, Email is a generalized application whose impact grows with the expansion of the user population, whereas, as stated, expert systems are specific to the areas of implementation. They aim to help the small, well-defined populations of managers and professionals to whom they are addressed.

There is a reason why managers in the advanced segment of the financial services industry are paying increased attention to expert systems and knowledge engineering. They realize that this technology can have far-reaching consequences for their businesses. As a result, questions are being asked and issues are being raised:

- How will AI developments affect my business?
- Do expert systems represent real breakthroughs and hence significant opportunities?
- What applications are possible for managerial services? For the professional?

Answers can be given only if they consider risk and opportunity in financial investments as a unified field. Over the longer term, profitability and the expectation thereof are the driving forces behind managerial decisions. Expert systems can serve in the interests of profitability, but the results will not be a simple matter of course.

Managers and professionals must become educated consumers to gain advantage from expert systems. They must understand the Esystems' possibilities and limitations, as well as their ways of usage, and they must become versatile in knowledge representation techniques.

Precisely because of the importance of Esystems literacy, Nixdorf has instituted two top-level training courses. One is addressed to knowledge engineers and teachers: how to build Esystems. The other focuses on end users and answers the question how to best employ the Esystem in our own jobs.

The usefulness of Esystems is enhanced when we do not make oversight errors, are able to solve routine problems entirely, and can explain to ourselves *why* the expert system reacts as it does. This greatly improves the chances of moving into new areas of problem solving.

We must also appreciate that an expert system is *never finished.* The knowledge changes. Expertise acquired through usage adds new layers. The system must be constantly maintained. This is also absolutely consistent with what is taking place in the whole area of computers and communications. As Figure 14 demonstrates, the focus is steadily moving: from the classical DP of the 1950s and early 1960s, to online transaction processing of the late 1960s and early 1970s and the MIS orientation of the rest of the 1970s decade, and in the 1980s into strategic information systems and hence artificial intelligence.

Not only the computers and communications professionals but also the users must follow in this transition. The performance of an Esystem implementation depends crucially on the quality and scope of the knowledgebank, but it also depends on user interaction. Only when the user

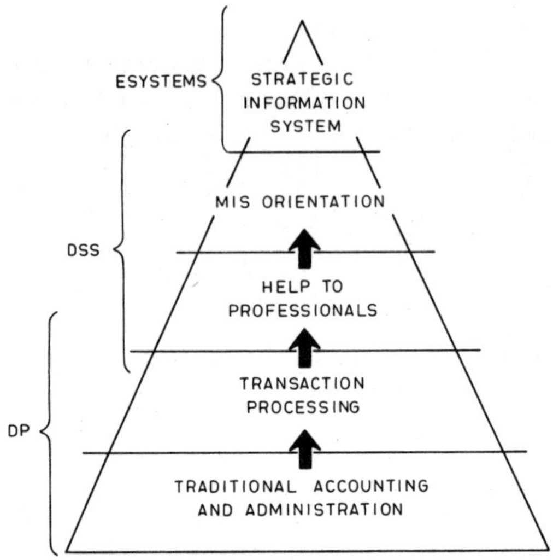

Figure 14 Changes in focus: the transition in computers and communications.

knows what is going on will the Esystem provide a quality of analysis similar to that obtained from highly trained human experts.

Properly implemented expert system services are critical because survivors in a highly competitive environment are the firms best able to provide cost-effective production and delivery of services through the innovative use of information technology. It is, therefore, not surprising that a number of financial service firms are now looking at expert systems as major components of the corporate strategy.

The ability to manage information as a corporate resource is the right formula; improving corporate decision making is the main objective. Therefore, information should be of the highest quality, be available at the right time, and have an intelligence quotient.

Intelligence, in the form of knowledge and expert opinion, is a commodity that is both expensive and in short supply. Expert knowledge is in high demand. That is the background reason why increased attention is directed to the potential benefits that may be realized from recent developments in artificial intelligence.

Layers of Expert Systems Implementation

Expert systems differ from more conventional software, such as decision support packages, in that they use symbolic manipulations rather than numeric calculations in carrying out their tasks. Also important is the fact that they can handle uncertainty and situations in which a strictly numerical solution would be difficult or impossible to achieve.

Esystems can be used effectively in providing commercial customer service, in the analysis of investment portfolios—including yield, risk, liquidity, growth, and security in consumer banking, and in insurance analysis. An example of the latter is designing a life insurance program.

If interest in Esystem usage has reached a point at which business, industry, and finance start developing strategies for potential Esystem application, it is because of knowledge power. Business, industry, and finance need an industrialization of knowhow to remain competitive and maintain a favorable market. The industrialization of knowhow becomes a factor because expert systems let the knowledge of an individual be captured in the computer and be made widely available. Additional knowledge can be added to the software through steady implementation to make the software even better able to solve a problem.

As far as the industrialization of knowledge is concerned, the scope of possible applications is endless. Any area in which a specialist has expertise needed by others is a likely candidate for Esystem use. It is precisely this special knowledge which allows the Esystem to use domain knowledge and reasoning techniques in solving problems. But the industrialization of knowledge can be achieved only by stages, which produces a layered structure in which each higher-up layer is built on the layers below.

There is a macroscopic view in this layering approach, shown in Figure 15, and a microscopic one we will examine later. As decision support systems have been built on the knowledge acquired through data processing applications, plus some other key contributions like modeling, so expert systems are built upon the knowhow gained through DSS.

However, as we will see in subsequent chapters, Esystems, too, need other key contributions. One is significant input in knowhow through robotic logic—itself an outgrowth of artificial intelligence. Another is the interactive dialog procedure, which I would call a *semiexpert system. Inference* and the rules on which it rests form the third key component.

Although inference is indispensable, just as indispensable (if not more so) is the interactive dialog capability. This is the engine behind the question-and-answer sessions we will be talking about in the following chapter. If there were a mandatory choice between good inference but poor dialog and excellent dialog but not so good inference, I would choose the latter.

Always in matters of modeling and forecasting we are better off if we start with an approximate model and then prune it and tune it through steady use rather than start with a seemingly perfect model which accepts no feedback and gives no feedforward. Those who appreciate

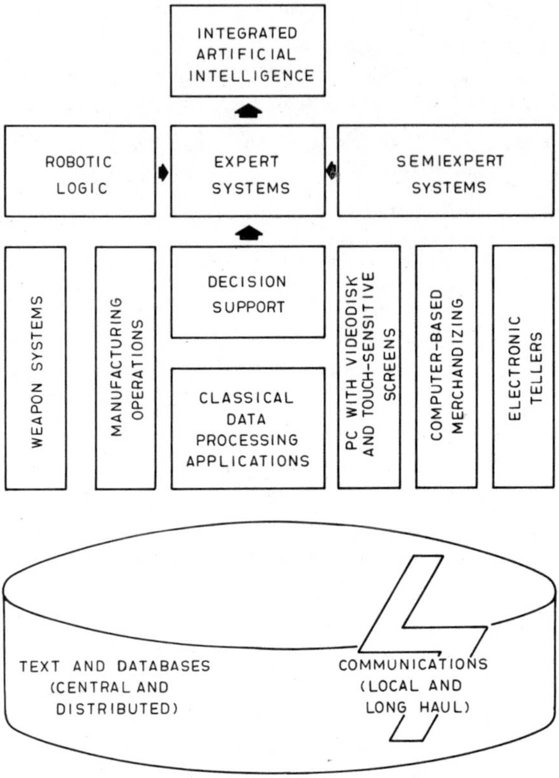

Figure 15 General infrastructure for an expert system.

this fine print know what the arts of simulation, working analogies, and knowledge acquisition are all about.

Now let's focus on the fact that *Esystems have developed from DSSs.* As successive layers, they have interfaces. The interface between a DSS and an Esystem is selective application of available technology to managerial tasks. Change from one layer to the other represents a transition. To be successful, this transition requires a solid understanding of decision processes and ways to improve upon them.

The aim of an Esystem, as of a DSS, is to support, not to automate, the decision process. Therefore, technical design has to match the characteristics of the task, context, and managerial responsibilities.

That is a different way to say that *jobs abiding by firm rules are better suited to Esystem transitions than others.* That statement is almost synonymous with the fact that professional jobs present a better structured environment and hence more fertile ground in which to begin Esystems implementation.

In contrast, the chairman of the board has no precise job specifications. That alone makes it hard to develop a chairman Esystem, though it is not impossible. Say, the chairman assigns to an assistant, who may be a senior manager, the following mission:

1. Develop the criteria to define the order of the day of a board meeting
2. Issue a call regarding budgetary evaluations and also set rules to judge the results
3. Develop issues relative to long-range planning
4. Present certain thoughts on strategic moves
5. Write a list of fundamental financial, marketing, and product choices

The procedure followed by the chief executive officer (CEO) is not necessarily systematic, nor are the above five subjects the same from one board meeting to another. That poses a challenge in Esystems buildup. If we have a procedure which is nonsystematic (and maybe even includes esoteric items), will the knowledge engineer have the authority to make the procedure systematic by weeding out the esoteric items?

That question and similar questions are quite practical. They are *not* academic. The challenge is not just whether the knowledge engineer is pleased or unhappy with the conditions of the mission. The critical question is whether the Esystem developer has the right to change conditions which reflect the CEO's way of doing business. If so, the system will not be realistic; its usefulness will be only theoretical.

Applying expert systems in business is a totally different field than, say, artificial vision. With computer vision, the knowledge engineer will be pleased to make a clone of the human eye, an intelligent engine which can think as well as a human at work. Is the expert good at the job? What is the expert's record? These are questions pertinent to the Esystem builder's mission but impertinent on this level of authority and responsibility.

When we talk of strategic information systems, we have over thirty years experience from data processing, databasing, word processing, distributed data processing, distributed databases, communications networks, and so on, on which we can capitalize. But the field of expert systems is still in its infancy; we don't have such a wealth of accumulated experience. Besides, the chairman's job is not precisely the one we would wish to industrialize.

Now consider a scenario written around professional and middle management functions in which the Esystem encapsulates specialist knowledge about a person's particular domain of expertise. This enables its builder to focus on a very narrow domain and thus achieve success with a real-world problem.

Why Decision Support Leads to Expert Systems

One of the reasons why planning and scheduling activities are among the favored domains of Esystems implementation is that linear programming as developed by Danzig (1953) has been so successful in its area for a good third of a century. It has created and put at our disposal a store of knowledge.

Financial analysis, credit scoring, risk evaluation, balance sheet management, portfolio management, treasury operations, and foreign exchange have been fertile implementation areas for decision support systems, first with modeling and then with spreadsheets. Now the dealer room is one of the Esystem applications most frequently cited by bankers.

To be practical, knowledge engineering needs successful experience with a DSS. Synthesis of truly new knowledge is a very difficult problem. We can get farther if we go step by step, and decision support implementations make good stepping stones.

A workable Esystem in Forex would give a significant competitive edge to a financial institution, and there are attractive results at the decision support level to back up such a project. Table 2 presents the organization and structure of a decision support system developed for Forex operations. The critical facts are:

1. Facts
2. Rules
3. Reasoning methods

At the DSS level, the *facts* are divided into internal and external. The *reasoning methods* are limited to only one consideration. Contrary to that DSS structure, the Esystem is richer in reasoning capabilities. As Table 3 indicates, four items have been added to the reasoning methods. This list will grow with time and experience.

Expert systems in Forex applications are high technology. The use of technology is essential in controlling risk: making expert swaps based on market evaluations, calculating the net exposure of complex transactions, charting and projecting movements of exchange rates, and permitting traders to hedge their bets.

To keep up with the net exposure of the bank as a whole, professionals must evaluate movements of interest rates and currency exchanges. With

TABLE 2 A Forex DSS Built with a View to Esystems

Facts	Rules	Reasoning methods
	Market	
Currency Forex positions	Profit and loss calculator	Spot effect positions
Contract rates	Dynamic equilibrium between Forex and money markets	
Calculating	Line of credit criteria	
	Trade criteria	
	Internal	
Profit centers		
Lines of credit		
Trading limits		
Customers and locations		

hundreds of different types of securities being traded, this work cannot be done with classical DP. An Esystem is the answer.

This is a clear example of what was meant, in the preceding section, by the statement that the implementation of machine intelligence is in successive layers:

- The infrastructure is made of *decision support systems*. The human suggests situations and wants what-if answers. The computer helps evaluate them.
- At the next higher-up layer are the *expert systems*. Here the system suggests and evaluates situations; it gives the proper advice and documents it.
- A still higher-up layer for which we are not yet ready will be *expert systems support (ESS)*. The system will *identify* relevant cases, evaluate situations, and construct documented solutions.

Expert support systems based on artificial intelligence are farther off. But work on Esystems will lead to them, just as effective DSS applications helped in the development of Esystems. ESSs will address much more complex situations than those we are facing today, such as

TABLE 3 A Forex Expert System

Facts	Rules	Reasoning methods
	Technical Information	
Forex rates	Stop loss	Moving average
Deposit rates	High/low	Graphics' curvature
Volume	Capital limits	Support levels
	Fundamental Information	
Inflation rate		
Interest rates		
Balance of payments		
Money supply		
Capital investments		
	Psychological Factors	
Expectation: bullish/bearish		
Sentiment		
Date		
Time		

automatic knowledge acquisition and moving scenarios (Figure 16). The time is not yet ripe for such implementations, though people familiar with weapons projects would say that they are not so far away. The following section will help us see why.

Expert systems can be built so nicely upon achievements obtained through DSSs because, already at the DSS level, managers and professionals obtain valid computer-based assistance. At Bankers Trust, for instance, a PC application in loans made it feasible to sell a loan as easily as selling a security.

The Industrialization of Knowledge

Other references to professional domains further extend the above example. A nuclear power plant automatically shuts down in response to a failure somewhere in its maze of electrical and mechanical subsystems. Is the problem minor, major, or catastrophic? Typically such a problem

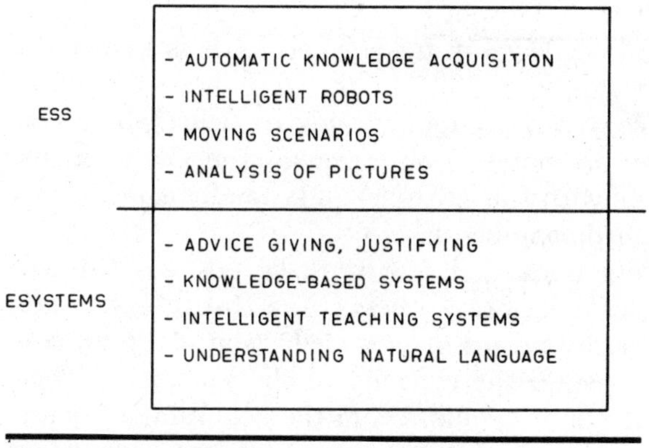

Figure 16 Expert systems and expert support systems (ESS): a layered approach.

would be handled by a human expert. But the expert is not always around. If the expert's knowledge is embedded in an Esystem, however, analysis and subsequent decisions can be tackled successfully by the Esystem.

This is the sense of the industrialization of knowledge, and it opens new vistas. Until recently, computers have been useful mainly in areas where human capabilities are limited. Large computers excel in high-speed calculating and in storing and retrieving large amounts of data. The computers run algorithmic programs: completely defined, step-by-step procedures for solving problems. But such exact computations can solve only a fraction of our problems.

Whether in foreign exchange or in power plant operations, the challenge eventually is to devise machines capable of thinking or, at the present time, emulating the way we employ past experience to solve new problems. Expert systems are said to be knowledge-based because they contain rules of the same kind as those that human experts use when they make decisions in their fields of expertise.

Expert systems are not locked into any specific decision paths. They can pick from alternative possibilities in their searches for conclusions:

- They weigh facts and assumptions.
- They make choices appropriate to each problem presented to them.
- They draw conclusions principally through logical inference, not calculations.

However, as the chairman's example in the preceding section helped demonstrate, it is not true that any ill-formalized body of knowledge is suitable for an expert system. When we say that Esystems use inexact and informal knowledge, that should not be taken to mean that there is some kind of magic key to knowledge in fields where little is known for certain and even less is structured.

Expert system methodology can be applied only to fields which *can* be formulated, even if they are not so well formulated at the moment. That should not be confused with the existence of generally agreed upon theorems or axioms, though it may be of help.

As Albert Einstein once remarked, it ought to be possible through general laws to arrive at the description—hence, the theory—of a natural process. We could do so by means of pure deduction if the process of deduction were not far beyond the capacity of the human intellect. Tradition plays a major role, as it should. From the beginning of quantitative aids to management, computer supports have been identified with personal decision making. On the bottom line, that is the aim of personal computing.

As a matter of fact, the advent of decision support systems was an early warning signal to ossified DP management about the winds of change. But because of inertia and misinformation, in several companies DP did not take up the challenge. That is why in a few years (and in a great many organizations) DSS came into political opposition with DP, a split which has not yet fused.

When DP did not adopt personal computing and the new applications technologies, DSS went into financial applications appealing directly to end users. At the same time, DSS became a dry run for office technology. Like other facets of the office automation (OA) effort, DSS is characterized by fast development; it puts a premium on being able to handle ad hoc needs very quickly.

As experience with DSS further developed, the real challenge became more than just doing what-if extrapolations and experimenting with the financial side of the organization. The challenge is that of a global view studying *why, what, where,* and *how* within an increasingly competitive environment. There is *a natural extension from what-if to why-if.*

Expert Systems in Weapons Development: A Case Study

Domains of knowledge are difficult to capture. But other things being equal, the more that well-funded brainpower works on a subject the better the results we can expect. That is why Esystems in military applications make a valuable case study.

The Pentagon wants brilliant computer programs for battlefield and strategic weapons. And for good reason. Artificial intelligence experts believe the information sciences now stand at a threshold very like the one at which nuclear physics stood in about 1940:

1. In future battles, computers themselves will become the most important weapons in the arsenal.
2. The platforms that carry the computers (tanks, ships, aircraft) will be AI-controlled.
3. The munitions that the computers discharge, conventional or nuclear, will be relegated to the status of accessories.

As an example, new automation techniques may be necessary to help pilots cope with the fire control systems now being designed for the next generation of military aircraft. Pilots of the future may rely on Esystems to help them assess combat situations and take appropriate offensive or defensive actions.

Along this line, significant studies are currently conducted on potential uses of artificial intelligence for fire control and battle management. One item of particular interest is how to identify targets automatically and present the information for a pilot's use. Another involves tactical analysis, including decision making that advises a pilot whether to attack, flee, take a low-altitude route, or apply electronic countermeasures.

The AI project for the Air Force focuses on a "pilot's associate," or silicon copilot, to help operate the electronic warfare equipment. In other words, the system will impart instruction on advanced tactics from more-experienced pilots to aid less-experienced pilots in early days of combat. This is an example of industrialization of knowledge.

For the Army an autonomous land vehicle, a robot tank, will be capable of roving independently. Being unmanned, it can be entrusted with such missions as deep-penetration reconnaissance and weapons delivery. Such an autonomous land vehicle must:

- Plan routes by using digital terrain and environment data
- Devise strategies for avoiding unanticipated obstacles
- Estimate its own position from landmarks and other references
- Update the onboard digital terrain database
- Generate moment-to-moment steering and speed commands
- Monitor its own performance and keep track of its onboard systems

All this should be achieved while traveling at speeds of up to 60 kilometers per hour. It is evident that such an autonomous vehicle will need extremely compact, powerful, and rugged computers, which will run a vision system and an expert system for navigation. Almost by definition, these computers will have to be parallel processors. No machine executing instructions serially is likely to achieve the necessary performance and compactness. There are also knowledgebank challenges.

DARPA estimates that an expert system able to handle this mission will have to contain over 6000 navigation rules and fire at a rate of 7000 rules (logical inferences) per second. By contrast, with current technology, Esystems rarely contain more than 1000 rules or fire at rates faster than 100 rules per second—and that only if mainframe-based.

Not to be lost from sight is the requirement that the vision system should interpret data in realtime from image sensors. That feat will require not only much more powerful vision technology than is now available and also a computer that processes from 10 billion to 100 billion instructions per second. (Today's supercomputers can attain processing speeds of only a few hundred million instructions per second.)

Another weapons AI project is for the Navy: It is for a computer system, aboard the aircraft carrier USS *Carl Vinson*, devoted to intelligence analysis. Its aim is to help the Navy fight battles at sea. The battle management system envisioned would assist the commander of a naval aircraft carrier during conflicts.

The essence of these references is that ongoing Department of Defense (DOD) projects are integrating computer science with military needs as completely as nuclear physics, aeronautics, and rocketry were subordinate to similar needs in the 1940s. Software and hardware projects are ambitious; they include the largest programs ever conceived; and they contain millions of instructions.

Should these programs be successful, machine intelligence may improve conventional weaponry to the point of reducing the likelihood of nuclear conflict. Furthermore, the Defense Advanced Projects Agency (DARPA) expects that lessons learned in the projects mentioned will be applied in a farther-out undertaking: the automated ballistic-missile defense system of the Strategic Defense Initiative, better known as Star Wars.

DARPA is, of course, counting on supercomputers that will provide very capable machine assistance in unanticipated combat situations. This will also call for new techniques, most of which are outgrowths of artificial intelligence. New AI developments are expected to permit computers to recognize objects in video images and converse with humans in natural language.

The scientific ambitiousness of this effort is greater than that of the Manhattan Project, which developed the first atomic bomb during World War II. In the 1986 style, the broadest objective is to develop machine intelligence able to adapt to unpredictable situations on the spot. Such an ability will be critical for autonomous weapons systems.

Although these high-technology examples come from weapons systems, the lesson to retain is that, in the longer term, generic technologies benefit not only the military but also all science-intensive industries and the economy at large. Countries that are leaders in the information revolution are going to be the dominant economic forces of the twenty-first century.

Let's, however, be clear on this matter. Breakthroughs don't come by accident. Advanced-technology missions are accomplished if we have clear objectives, a concentration of talent, a presence of time pressure, properly funded projects, an abundance of supporting resources, and a conducive environment.

Chapter

5

Knowledge Engineering

"It is impossible to make something foolproof, because fools are so ingenious."
POPULAR PROVERB

What Is Meant by Knowledge Engineering?

The term "knowledge engineering" has appeared on several occasions, always in connection with artificial intelligence and expert systems, but the detailed definition has been deferred to this chapter. *The object of knowledge engineering is the development, production, and distribution of intelligence through man-made systems.* Knowledge engineering is the applied-science side of artificial intelligence.

The top challenge in this applied science effort is *knowledge representation*: from knowledge *acquisition* to the development of *rules* and the facilitation to be provided by the *interactive use* of those rules. The latter is known as *knowledge utilization.* Knowledge representation is presently a rather manual process of working with experts. Therefore, we seek automatic methods for transferring and transforming knowledge into computer representation.

Robert Jastrow (formerly with NASA and now professor of astronomy and geology at Columbia College) says that someday researchers will discover that intelligence can be as at home inside metal and plastic as it is in a shell of bone.

The sort of personality that such silicon- or biochip-based intelligence may assume can only be guessed about. At this early stage of development, it is not one of the outstanding research or sociological projects. Our focus is on *knowhow* and its transcription into intelligent machines.

Webster's says the term "knowhow" was first used in 1838. Knowledge engineering deals with knowhow which is inherent in the development of several processes, the most important being:

- Learning systems
- Knowledge-directed specifications
- Design methodologies for rule-based systems
- Symbolic computing approaches

Just because many tasks cannot be automated by using conventional computing techniques, they require the capability of symbol manipulation. Symbol manipulation calls for valid, tested approaches provided by knowledge engineering, which is also instrumental in constructing inference paths for decision, explanation, and justification.

Knowledge engineering describes the process under study and outlines its rules. Such work reflects the often neglected fact that there is a fairly close correlation between the kinds of knowledge existing in an organization and the sort of problems faced in conducting the organization's business. Much of the work on knowledge engineering involves the acquisition of knowhow. It starts with the capability of extracting knowledge from experts, mapping it in computer-based form, and then using it.

Although Esystems are, as has been stated, the first business and industrial implementation of artificial intelligence, pure AI is only a small component of an expert system. The big parts are:

1. Solving in an able manner the man-information, interactive dialog interface
2. Engineering the system to fit the organization through approaches leading to logical manipulation
3. Addressing the crucial issue of data management
4. Training and adapting the organization to use the Esystem successfully

Items 1, 2, and 3 provide the logical infrastructure of the expert system and are reflected in Figure 17. If any one of them is missing or is incomplete, the functional capabilities will be diminished by that much.

Dialog management is a vital component of a successful Esystem, as emphasized in the preceding chapters. The product is for the end user, who should be able to communicate with it in an easy, friendly, but also effective manner.

With regard to item 2 of the preceding list, knowledge engineering develops the rule-based structure. This, along with the appropriate methodology, constitutes the *knowledgebank.* Like a human, rules can cope with incomplete and uncertain information. Ambiguity-tolerant software is a new, and practical, implementation of artificial intelligence in industry.

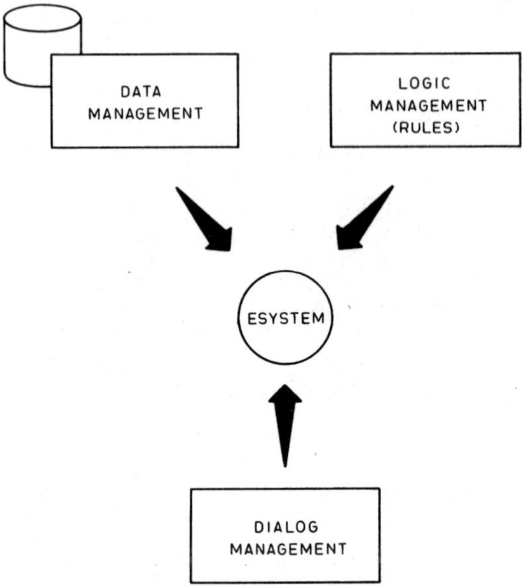

Figure 17 Logical infrastructure of an expert system.

The emphasis on the knowledgebank is important. Thanks to the knowledgebank, an expert system works with equivocal data but produces valid judgments. Knowledge engineering makes the difference by providing the rules and their update through automatic learning features, which are still in a research status.

The importance of able data management is known from classical information systems activities. Although the database of an Esystem is not in the business of knowledge representation, it is the vital element in providing the uninterrupted flow of data on which the expert system is going to work. And there is increasing emphasis on smart databases.

Architecture of the Expert System

We have seen that a focal point of knowledge engineering is the development of a computer program that uses knowhow and problem-solving approaches on a level of skill comparable with that of human experts. To do so, it needs:

1. A *knowledgebank* which contains facts, rules, and situation patterns
2. An *inference engine* able to make decisions within a given domain

3. A *language* in which the rules will be written (for instance, Lisp, Prolog, EMycin, Rosie) and also in which the man-machine communication will take place
4. A *shell*, which includes the inference engine, knowledge manager, and user interfaces
5. *Environment* of other pieces which can be put together like an Erector Set (a kit of parts)

The logical components of the parts kit can be assembled to meet needs. The role played by the aggregate is that of making expertise more widely available within a specified domain.

The knowledgebank stores rules reflecting reasoning paths employed by the expert, and therefore by the system, in solving a specific problem. The inference engine controls the process of invoking the rules that pertain to the solution of the problem posed to the system. An *explanation generator* may be used to present how the system arrived at its conclusion. Rules must also be incorporated to work as knowledge acquisition tools. Typically, they should reflect techniques used to extract knowledge from the domain and subsequently represent it in the system.

The knowledgebank and the inference engine are considered to be the two key architectural components. The *theory of knowledgebanks* is addressed to knowledge representation, knowledge models, recursive data models, object-oriented models, knowledge indexing, and transformation. *Knowledgebank management* involves constructs and languages, constraints and the administration of rules, meta data management, and extensible data dictionaries.

Usually there is an absolute distinction between knowledge and control. Reasoning on large databases and knowledgebanks is a field encompassing inexact approaches, deductive databases, logic-based query languages, semantic query optimization, and a constraint-directed reasoning course.

An integral part of *natural-language* access is question answering, the ability to obtain extended responses and cooperative behavior as well as explanation and justification. Intelligent database interfaces with expert systems include database communications, knowledge gateways, knowledgeable user agents, browsers, and videotex.

Examining the architecture of an Esystem means to look at the way it is (or will be) designed to handle problem complexity and problem structure. Such an examination helps to deduce data and control strategies appropriate to handle those factors.

Knowledge engineering has evolved techniques which can be utilized in developing suitable expert system architectures. The architecture selection and use depends on:

1. Purpose and domain
2. Approach to be taken
3. Knowledgebank and its rules
4. Global database and data communications
5. Control strategy and rule interpreter

The system-building architecture is shown in Figure 18. It relates all parts which combine to create conditions necessary for the development of an expert system.

Organizational Information as a Knowledge Network

After we strip off the scientific shell and apply software engineering approaches, it becomes apparent that expert systems are nothing more (and nothing less) than a new, advanced programming technology. As such they should be sensitive to organizational information flows.

Because of greater dependence on communicating databases and decision support systems, the modern organization faces the challenge of managing more complex aggregates of people, software, and machinery than ever before. Computers and communications will store, transport,

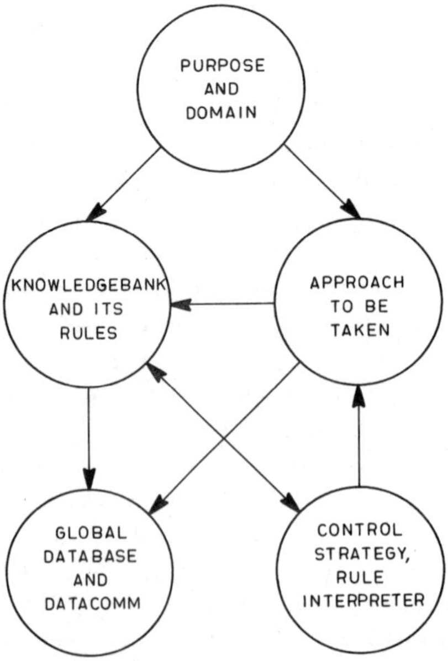

Figure 18 A system-building architecture.

and present vast amounts of text, data, graphics, image, and voice messages.

- These will refer to our clients, our markets, our products and services, our competition, and our suppliers.
- They will talk of the habits, backgrounds, and preferences of those people—and the profitability of our operations.

A new challenge we now face is how to use that information to discover new business opportunities. Even when we have the information, it is going to take quite a while to learn how to use it properly. From that comes the wisdom of implementing expert systems to help us do the job. This is an organizational challenge, and it affects top management; some mighty careers are engaged in the process.

Although more classical software and hardware components will have significant roles to play in terms of *functionality* and *throughput, we need machine intelligence to effectively handle and distill* increasing volumes of text, data, and other information elements transmitted over wires and handled through computers.

A problem lends itself to expert system implementation when its solution has a high payoff, thus warranting advanced-type applications. This is all the more true when classical approaches to obtaining results have not worked so well.

A further major category of AI implementation consists of *problems which can be solved only by expert knowledge.* This evidently presupposes access to the right expert able to formalize his or her knowhow and, with proper assistance, express it in the form of rules.

Still another class of problems for Esystems methodology includes the problems which have, not unique answers, but a number of acceptable solutions. Management problems are a typical example of this class. Management problems change rapidly: new facts are being introduced for a given situation or references are constantly changing. Problems falling in the area of constant development are also an excellent ground for Esystems implementation.

These fertile area definitions are properly reflected in the nature of expert systems. The latter are generally not considered to be finished once they are brought into use. Instead, they tend to continue their development by updating their knowledgebank, inference, and processing methods to reflect changes in their domain of expertise.

Just, the same, with expert systems we need computers and communications networks to carry large information volumes from origin to destination. Networks must cover a broad range of services to be supported at different organizational levels, at whichever layer each service belongs. A network is:

1. A well-defined collection of services
2. A controllable structure, through a network control center (NCC)
3. The means of tying systems and components together
4. An intelligent carrier assuring effective information interchange

The knowledge network of a company able to live with the technology of its times is a good paradigm of expert system application in the knowledge engineering domain. In this sense, a factual and documented study should *start with organizational prerequisites leading into the information system aspects*—not vice versa.

Figure 19 suggests levels of association in dataflow description:

- Actors
- Functions

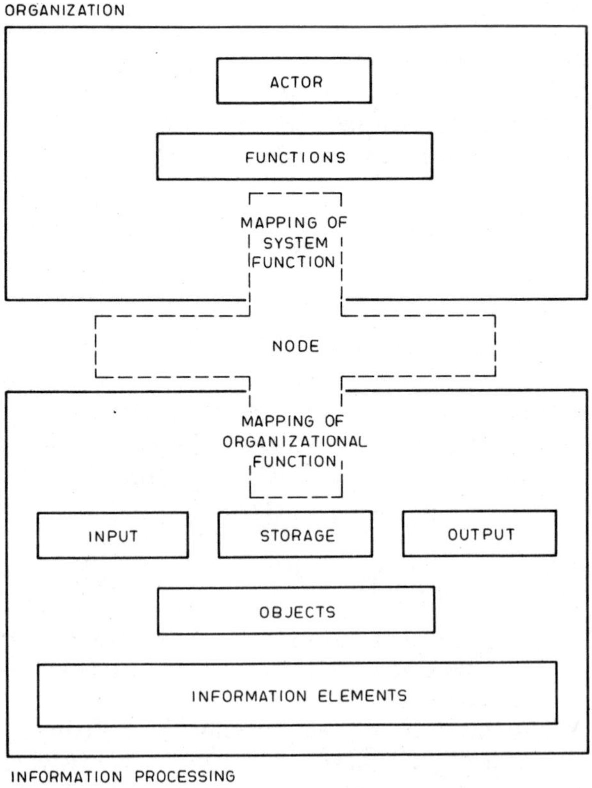

Figure 19 Actors, functions, and nodes in a knowledge network.

- Nodes
- I/O per node
- Information elements (IE)

The needed interface in the implementation system is supplied by common nodes. The nodes are both *function-* and *system-oriented.* The actors and functions are organizational.

The actor may be a manager, professional, or clerk. Depending on the assignment, the person will have one or more functions. Authors and functions can be represented in an author-function matrix. The matrix can be altered without affecting the information system, but information system changes will impact on the matrix.

The link between organization and information system will be provided through a function-node matrix that maps the system structure into the organizational structure. Within the prevailing flow, the input, output, and storage will be composed of information elements (IE). These are typically regrouped into callable *objects* (forms, envelopes).

Examined from the viewpoint of a knowledge network, organizational information is prepared, transmitted, accepted, and processed in the form of documents. The term "document" refers to user-created information that flows through and between office systems. In the broader sense, this includes messages and other kinds of information not ordinarily thought of as documents.

Document handling refers to user-oriented information flowing between office systems. It includes:

1. Creating
2. Formatting
3. Integrating
4. Revising
5. Distributing
6. Receiving
7. Reading
8. Comprehending
9. Processing
10. Extruding
11. Filing
12. Retrieving

A knowledge information network has greater need for formatting than other types of office services have. Formalisms are necessary to assure compatibility among dissimilar office systems and procedures. Knowledge engineering must see to it that identical understanding of knowledge streams is being interchanged.

This further emphasizes the need for an *architecture*, that is, *a set of design principles able to define the relations of and interactions among various parts of a knowledge network.* A different way to make that statement is that knowledge systems must be architectural. They cannot succeed if they are approached in a haphazard, unplanned way. The use of a *systems architecture* permits a stable basis for planning and gives a common direction in both the development of distributed computers and communications and the intelligence built into them.

The freedom provided by system architecture permits companies to be customer-oriented rather than product-oriented. From supply to sales and service delivery, the companies can tune their information flow to market demand and adjust their knowledge flow accordingly.

In the more classical information systems implementation, the proper systems architecture makes it possible to integrate software and hardware from many manufacturers and assures that technology will be made to work the way people work. That's why correct choices are so important.

In knowledge-intensive applications the need for multiple vendors is magnified, which underscores the wisdom of *institutionalizing system research. In implementing a system architecture*, we should:

- Employ design principles
- Define relations between components
- Build intelligence into the components
- Assure the interaction of attached devices

This is assisted by the fact that, in its higher layers, an architecture defines the level of functionality we are after. Describing is not enough, because describing is not defining.

Example with the Pentomic Organization

In Figure 1 we saw the pentomic organization* defined in three layers: strategic planning at the top, functional management (R&D, marketing,

*The term "pentomic" was invented by the U.S. Army after World War 2 to signify the five pillars on which the U.S. forces were based. These were the technological breakthroughs of the time. In the sense used in this book, "pentomic" reflects the five pillars of an industrial organization as identified in Chapter 1 and Figure 1. Etymologically, the origin of the word is Greek: *pente* means "five."

and human resources) as the middle layer, computers and communications as the lower layer and the infrastructure.

The infrastructure should provide organizational information for the upper two layers. Yet, in 33 years of experience with computers this has rarely, if ever, been appreciated. The most important people in the organization were the worst served in terms of data processing: *more than three decades of disgrace.*

Let's not repeat the same errors with knowledge engineering. The information should be tuned to *serve, above all, strategic people and strategic products.* The strategic project is the product on which *our* organization depends for its survival.

- It is typically longer-range.
- It views future needs, not only present ones.
- There is a commitment to its continuation and development.

A strategic product is part of the future cost of staying in business. A *tactical* product is a shorter-range product able to help in doing business today. It is part of the current cost of operations.

Within a properly integrated knowledge network serving the pentomic organization, strategic planning should be given the role of devil's advocate on current business plans. Even if our company is doing well today, it risks becoming another "big brown industry" if there is no regular shake-up.

Strategic planning should be provided with the proper information to use the momentum of products and services doing well at the present time in order to *put the next big income earners in place.* This, too, is a function to be assigned to the knowledge network. The search for new opportunities is closely tied to refining current plans, developing new products, and capitalizing on market growth. That is why we need a computer and communications infrastructure based on high technology.

Information systems is a strategic product in many industries, for instance, banking. There should be a close *coordination between strategic planning and the direction to be given to the knowledge network.* But how can the work be done? Here is a list of suggestions. Knowledge engineering should:

1. List the entities involved in the pentomic organization (internal departments) and the major external entities interacting with *our* organization
2. Characterize the organizational entities according to information need factors such as domain (market data, financial data, news), interest

strength (primary responsibilities, for-your-information, no interest), communication type (memo, report, data records)

3. Examine communication nodes to see what information need attributes they serve and possess
4. Prepare a decision tree to determine department routing for any communication, based on information need attributes
5. Convert the decision tree into a set of production and distribution rules to make the decisions on a consistent comprehensive and fully automated basis

In the preceding section on organizational information as a knowledge network procedural suggestions have been included to help evaluate and score communications.

The goal of Figure 20 is that of an exercise. It represents the central operations of a leading financial institution which integrates three groups under one head: marketing, treasury, and operating proper. Responsibilities are outlined under each box. The careful reader will appreciate the knowledge network linking the three nodes, for instance, credit functions, funding, and processing.

As a consequence of careful analysis, matrix relations can be defined:

- Node/object identifying whether the information element in each pigeonhole (slot) is input, output, or storage (I, O, or S)
- Object/IE matrix able to clearly define every information element involved in the operation

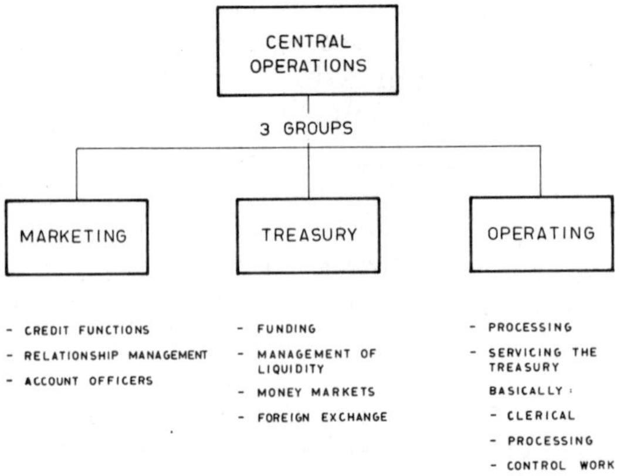

Figure 20 Responsibilities and indicators in central operations of a financial institution.

This macroscopic view of the system leads to the microscopic view through the issue of *forms*. The aim of the forms is the proper presentation of IE and objects, whether for input, output, or storage and further retrieval.

A matrix representation can be effectively used in mapping domain knowledge, an activity generally considered to be the cornerstone of the success of Esystems programs. Domain knowledge can have many forms, including:

- Descriptive definitions of domain-specific terms
- Elaboration of individual domain objects and their relations to one another
- Criteria for making decisions in specific situations

It is precisely because of this emphasis on representation and domain knowledge that systems using artificial intelligence approaches to achieve expertise are often referred to as being knowledge-based.

Finally, it is very important to understand the concept of *meta knowledge*. Meta knowledge is knowledge about knowledge.

Knowledge sources usually transform entries at one level of abstraction into entries at another level. Some knowledge sources operate bottom-up. They aggregate several lower-level entries into a smaller number of higher-level entries. Other knowledge sources operate top-down; they explode compound knowledge sources into their components.

Meta knowledge handles knowledge about:

1. Representation of objects (through schemata)
2. Representation functions (function templates)
3. Reasoning strategies (by means of meta rules)
4. Inference rules (rule description)

Meta knowledge avoids the rigidity of always having to apply a hierarchical structure for abstraction. It provides for flexible structures, and for that reason it can make a significant contribution to expert systems development.

Frames and Languages

Since the language which we use forms our mind, to project domain-specific knowledge properly, we need appropriate linguistic supports for representing the knowledge domain. Basic criteria for knowledge representation include expressive power, understandability, accessibility, and descriptive characteristics. But no currently available knowledge representation language is by itself able to meet all four criteria.

This is considered to be one of the stronger reasons behind the development of semantic networks. *Semantic networks* are object-oriented representation languages on *frames*. Linguistic approaches through the use of frames provide the knowledge engineer with an easy means of describing the types of domain objects to which the Esystem is addressed. Consequently, frame-type prototypes can be used to create a default description of an object, thereby assuring a structured representation.

For instance, one frame might represent a computer and another a whole class of computers. Constructs can be prepared in a frame language organized into taxonomies.* Taxonomical constructs permit a knowledge engineer to describe each group as a specialization of a more generic family. At the same time, a group can have a further specialization (expressed in classes of objects).

In that sense, knowledge is partitioned into discrete structures (frames) having individual properties. Frames can be used to represent broader concepts or specific issues. They help describe classes of objects, address individual instances, and describe components of objects. Frames can be joined together in a hierarchy characterizing common properties and their transmission. They can also be used to incorporate inference methods and complement (or at times substitute for) the other methodological approaches in the development of Esystem products: rule-based constructs and logic programming.

The use of frames has prerequisites, namely, design classifications and the implementation of taxonomical solutions for properties or other characteristics. Four design classifications can be distinguished for frame definition purposes. The first is *presentation*, which includes scroll (for output by the specialist), multipage (division of scroll into groups of pages), page, page composition (stepping stones), windows, overlays, and dimensioning.

The second classification has to do with the *scope* and is best expressed through menus, which are themselves subject to routing and indexing. Menus are routing pages. There also exist utility pages for identification, help, and prompting. These are distinct from the information-carrying infopages.

The third classification has to do with *content*. It includes text, data (tabular), charts, icons, graphics conversion, and eventually voice (editing) and moving images. The fourth classification centers on the desired *security level*. It includes corporate resources (highest security),

*See also D. N. Chorafas: *Databases for Minicomputers and Networks*, Petrocelli Books, Princeton, N.J., 1982, chaps. 14, 15, and 16.

divisional resources (security defined by usage), and microfiles (desk-level databases). This classification is quite important in connection with an expert system's global database.

Let's now consider the taxonomical perspectives necessary in knowledge engineering. Webster's dictionary defines *taxonomy* as the science of classification, the laws and principles covering the classifying of objects, and classification, especially of animals and plants, into phyla, species, and so on.

In knowledge engineering implementation, different families, groups, or classes of items (and information relating to those items) have distinct classification needs. Because a taxonomical classification may not reach the necessary level of detail for all families in a classification matrix, a solution which I have applied is to use *further definiens.*

Taxonomy extended by further definiens permits us to reach the level of detail at which we have an unambiguous link between classification and identification for every object. We cannot assure nonambiguity in treatment without identification. But homogeneous identification has the proper classification as a prerequisite.

Once all slots (pigeonholes) in a correspondence matrix are properly filled, the *dataflow* and *presentation* considerations are addressed to the question *what.* It is equally important to evaluate the *process* or transformation requirements. These answer the question *how.*

Expressed through interconnected frames,* *what* and *how* provide a rich structural language for describing the objects referred to in Esystem rules. They present a layer of generic deductive capability about objects that does not need to be explicitly dealt with in the rules.

Taxonomy can also be used to partition, index, and organize a system's production rules. This simplifies the job of the knowledge engineer in understanding, constructing, and implementing rules. The engineer can better control when and for what purpose particular collections of objects and rules are used in the Esystem.

Dataflow and frame approaches can be used all the way from prototyping to actual Esystem building. Frame-based prototypes containing necessary but not sufficient conditions have been used to conclude that an item is not a member of a family, group, or class—though they cannot be employed to conclude that the item *is* a member.

In this process, we require a natural way to augment descriptions for proper classification to include sufficient conditions for determining membership. When rules are used for that purpose, the family, group, and class taxonomy can provide a guiding structure for designing and

*See also D. N. Chorafas, *Interactive Message Services*, McGraw-Hill, New York, 1984, chaps. 9, 10, and 12.

organizing rules to be used in successive refinements of classification strategy.

Furthermore, it is wise to assure a guiding structure for designing and organizing the rules that specify sufficient conditions for membership in a slot system. This is characteristic of the matrix representation at each level of reference: family, group, and class. Interconnected frames can then be used to provide a means of indexing by invoking rules that deduce attribute values for the situation under study and the objects which it involves.

Tools for the Knowledge Engineer

We said that in a linguistic sense expert system projects can be approached in one of three basic methodologies: frames, rules, or logic programming. The latter uses predicate calculus as the representation language. To some researchers, this is appealing because of its expressive power and well-defined semantics. However, language constructs are very fine-grained and do not always provide adequate facilities for domain experts.

As an example of tools able to assist knowledge engineering to overcome conceptual barriers of finer programmatic interfaces, the Technical University of Berlin has under development a project able to describe rules and methodologies in natural language. Its orientation is that of knowledge acquisition.

The first vital component of this expert systems tool is the *translator*. It interprets statements made in a natural language into symbolic language, including semantics and syntactics. In one of the subsequent parses, the translator converts to symbols and then reduces the resulting strings of symbols into a smaller group.

Syntax is analyzed by parsing. *Parsing* identifies:

- What function each element in a sentence performs
- Whether the input sentence is complete and grammatical

Parsing is specific to a particular grammar the rules of which govern the parsing process.

With expert systems, parsing converts syntax to a form usable by the computer. It breaks a sentence down into components the system can identify and to which it can assign functions. Semantic analysis focuses on the meanings of words and phrases. It proceeds by associating words and their roles in an input sentence with information about the problem domain. Such knowledge constitutes a background context against which new input can be interpreted.

By using stored knowledge of descriptions about objects, events, and

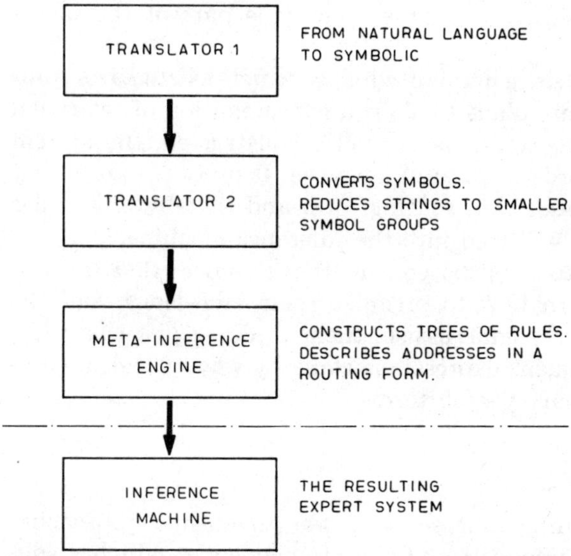

Figure 21 From natural language to the meta-inference engine and the inference machine.

relations, the computer constructs a representation (parse tree) that reflects the relations among the parts of the sentence and can be used in drawing inferences, for example, from known "ifs" to deduced "thens."

The second vital component is the *meta-inference engine*. Its object is "inference about inference." It uses knowledge to construct a tree of rules.* The latter reflects nodes and linkages in a proper definition of knowhow. The meta-inference engine is not a compiler. It is a structural entity able to reflect on logical sequences leading to conclusion on the ordering of rules (Figure 21). This helps structure the knowledgebank.

Organizational logic is as follows:

- IF <premise> is an acceptable proposition, proceed to the conclusion.
- THEN <action>, but check whether a similar entry exists in table form, already classified and placed in position.

A backward-chaining methodology has been adopted. Entry can be made at any point of a tree structure, and the user can ask for review of all the hierarchy above the entry point. When a new rule finds its position in the structural tree, it can declare all other rules it has used

*A matrix solution is also feasible.

and present them as *justification*. This activity is part of the meta-inference engine.

The system capitalizes on a human window which existed from another application. There are plans to allow a concatenation of relational tables as an alternative to trees. As currently constructed, the system can accept some 2000 words in natural language. It produces an output that describes rule addresses in a routing form and thereby links rules together. Such an output will feed into the inference machine.

This expert system tool is based on the premise that professional experts should learn how to organize their knowledge, and the translator—meta-inference engine assists them in doing just that. The assistance and the subsequent expressions come by way of logical commands rather than in binary yes/no terms.

Serving a Purpose

The object of the preceding four sections was to outline approaches feasible in knowledge engineering and the methodologies which result. That having been accomplished by positioning the expert system effort within a business context, it is advisable to look into an inventory of domains already covered by Esystems and associated methodologies.

The first and foremost reference is purpose. The broadest statement that can be made about *purpose* is that of generating plausible representations within the domain for which the Esystem is intended. But that is not a unique reference.

- At Stanford University, the function of AM, by Lenat, is *concept formation*. The purpose is discovery of mathematical concepts.
- At Carnegie Mellon, the function of R1, by McDermott, is *design*. The purpose is to configure VAX computer systems from a customer's order of components.
- At MIT, EL, by Stallman and Sussman, has the function of *analysis*, and the purpose of steady-state analysis of resistor-diode-transistor circuits is to determine voltages and currents.

Table 4 outlines the function and purpose of some of the best-known expert systems. The second most important reference in an architectural construct is the approach to be taken. The AM approach is to start with elementary ideas in set theory. AM establishes a search space generated from these ideas and then chooses the most interesting conjectures and pursues that line of reasoning.

The R1 approach is different: It is to divide the problem into ordered subtasks, correct mistakes in order, put components into CPU cabinets, and then put boxes into unibus cabinets and components in boxes, put

TABLE 4 Functions and Purposes of Expert Systems

System	Made at	By	Function	Purpose
Dendral	Stanford	Feigenbaum, Lederberg	Data interpretation	Generate plausible structural representations of organic molecules from mass spectrograph data
Metadendral	Stanford	Buchanan, Feigenbaum	Learning from experience	Generate set of fragmentation rules (of form used by Dendral), given sets of known structure-spectrum pairs
Mycin	Stanford	Shortliffe	Diagnosis	Diagnosis of bacterial infections and recommendations for antibiotic therapy
Noah	SRI	Sacerdoti	Planning	Robot planning by assigning time ordering to operators in a plan
Molgen	Stanford	Stefik	Design	Designing molecular genetic experiments
SYN	MIT	Sussman, Steele, Dekleer	Design	Circuit synthesis; determining values for components in electrical circuitry
Kas	SRI	Reboh	Knowledge acquisition	Supervising interaction with an expert in building or augmenting an Esystem knowledgebank (implemented for Prospector)
Guidon	Stanford	Clancy	Computer-aided instruction	Teaching facts and problem-solving strategies in diagnosing and treating meningitis and bacterima, or pulmonary function analysis (uses Mycin or Puff knowledgebanks)

panels in unibus cabinets, lay out the system on the floor, and do the cabling. R1 solves each subtask and moves on to the next one in the fixed order.

EL uses assertions in the database to trigger rules creating new assertions. It assumes operating states for transistors and diodes, introduces variables for parameters such as voltage at one node in the circuit, and then uses electrical laws to symbolically compute parameters at other nodes. EL makes conjectures when no further rules are applicable. It observes contradictions and revises conclusions dependent upon the results which it obtains.

The approach Dendral has followed is to derive constraints from data and generate candidate structures. It then predicts mass spectrograms for candidates and compares them with data.

Mycin represents expert judgmental reasoning as condition-conclusion rules. This is done together with the expert's certainty estimate for each rule. The system chains backwards from hypothesized diagnoses to see if a diagnosis is supported by evidence. The approach is to evaluate all hypotheses exhaustively. Treatment is matched to all diagnoses with high certainty values.

Since the next section is devoted to the knowledgebank and its rules, we will not elaborate on the knowledgebank at this point. In terms of a global database, the Esystem may feature cooperative knowledge sources sharing a common blackboard. It may be an inference network model or a goals- or data-directed system; it may be template-driven or model-driven. Its orientation may focus on distributed problem solving.

An important issue is the control strategy:

- For AM, the control strategy is to plan, generate, and test.
- R1 is data-driven; there is no backtracking; and the keyword is "match."
- EL uses forward reasoning, employs guesses when needed, and does relevant backtracking. The basis is priority-oriented, queue-type control.
- Dendral uses forward chaining.
- Mycin employs backward chaining through the rules.

Other control strategies are least commitment (Noah), constraint propagation and heuristic search (Molgen), event-driven, exhaustive search for each state and state-triggered expectation (VM), forward reasoning with chaining representations (SYN), combination of top-down and bottom-up processing (Hearsay II), and network editor and grammar-driven command language (Kas). We will return to these issues.

Chapter

6

Knowledge Management

"Dumb luck beats careful planning—but that is not the way to bet." POPULAR WISDOM

What's the Sense of Knowledge Management?

Knowledge management rests on simple foundations: completeness, power, simplicity, and integration. The *knowledgebank* which we construct must be complete. The rules and methodologies which it contains should complement but never contradict one another.

Knowledge management should assure a *complete* development and implementation environment designed for use in a specific function of a business enterprise requiring expert systems support. This is written in reflection of the fact that the most striking aspect of developments in artificial intelligence does not lie in any specific announcement; instead, it lies in the mood. For the first time there is a consensus that AI is a technology *applicable to the solution of real problems.*

Unlike idealized situations, real problems require complete solutions, whether we talk of isolated instances or of a broader range of applications. Real business problems also call for *powerful* approaches. Trivia have no place in this connection.

Powerful solutions are trademarks of well-done expert systems. In a business environment based on human expertise, the word "expert" typically indicates a person with extended knowledge in a well-defined (hence, limited) applications domain. The expert system can do no less.

Next to completeness and power comes simplicity. *Simplicity* comprises ease of learning and ease of use. It is heavily affected by integration. *Integration* means ease of moving among the various functions of a product offering while making different components appear to be similar to the user. Such components typically use similar protocols, identical subroutines, and common files.

That is a prerequisite for the global database of the expert system. It is also just as important for the knowledgebank and the repository of rules and methodologies—and also of facts about the subject, its definitions, relations, and controls focusing on a specific problem solution.

Each combination of the inference engine with another object in the knowledgebank becomes a unique application. Together, these vital components act as a real-world model of the expertise for the specific domain. This further underlines the importance of knowledge management.

Motivation for developing knowledge management solutions and tools arose from observing the difficulty with which expert systems are built. A case in point is knowledge acquisition. Another important area is expert systems research. There is need for an easy way to build Esystems that can be implemented in selected problem areas and can run efficiently. We must be innovative in our work; otherwise, the software and hardware we produce will be hard to cost-justify.

Knowledge acquisition, system research, and innovation in applications are the keys, not hundreds of thousands of logical instructions per second supported by the machines which we are using. Don't listen to the people who tell you: "An expert system needs 100,000 or more logical instructions per second. Otherwise, forget it." These are guesstimates for military projects with computer vision and complex robotics activity, not for business applications.

Very high speed computers are necessary when intelligent engines run other machines such as weapons systems. *When an intelligent machine interacts with a person, a PC will do the Esystems job well, provided our rules are right.* Besides, at the current state of the art, what we have available for business applications are *adolescent expert systems* with a little less or a little more than 100 rules in their knowledgebank. It will be years before these adolescent systems reach the age of maturity in business, yet they can already be of help.

The Knowledgebank*

A *knowledgebank* contains *facts* and *rules*. Facts (or assertions) are short-term information. They can change rapidly during the course of user interaction. Rules are longer-term information. They direct the

---

*Expert systems literature usually refers to a *knowledgebase*. However, that word tends to be confused with "database," which is now an established term. Furthermore, the same literature often refers to knowledge-based systems, which makes the word "base" awfully ambiguous.

Esystem on how to generate hypotheses from what is presently known or create new facts. The performance of an expert system critically depends on the quality and scope of the knowledgebank. It is closely related to the methodology and dependability of the knowledge acquisition process, as we will see in the following section.

The theory of knowledgebanks concerns knowledge representation, knowledge models, recursive information elements, object-oriented models, knowledge indexing, and transformation. *Knowledgebank management* involves architectures and languages. It aims to:

- Identify constraints
- Develop rules
- Handle meta data and extensible dictionaries

A knowledgebank schematic is shown in Figure 22. It represents the broader definition of this subject.

Knowledgebanks form a field encompassing inexact reasoning, inductive and deductive approaches, constraint-directed reasoning, logic-based query languages, semantic query optimization, and natural-language access. Integral parts of natural-language access are question-and-answer sessions, extended response sequences, cooperative behavior, explanation, and justification.

How does this approach differ from conventional database methodologies? The first and most important difference is that *a knowledgebank is more creative*. Information in a database is normally passive; either it is there or it is not. By contrast, a knowledgebank's facts are active. The rules which it contains try to fill the missing information.

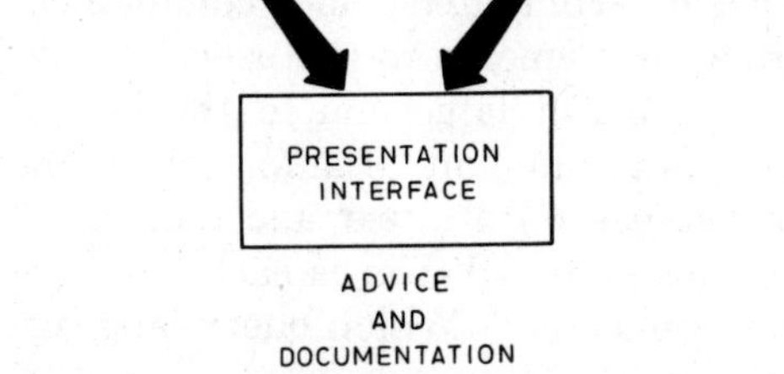

Figure 22 Component parts of a knowledgebank.

The second major difference is that the classical database relies on other subsystems, such as data communications, for its needs. But the knowledgebank includes *intelligent interfaces* for communications, knowledge gateways, knowledgeable user agents, and so on.

Some knowledge engineers look at this subject in a different way. They say that, in a certain sense, a database is a knowledgebank. That is not precise. No doubt some databases contain information representing knowhow about specialized subjects, but that is not enough for a database to be a knowledgebank.

Knowledge must be represented in one of a small number of special forms if it is to be part of a knowledgebank. In general, those forms must allow the information to be used actively rather than merely stay there passively as in a database.

A classical database contains information elements such as names, accounts, levels, and labels. It also includes sequencing and content identification. Its validity depends on its completeness and also on how well we build it, control it, and access it.

Another issue is how we enter data into the database. That is one of the most critical aspects of a modern computer system. Success or failure will almost always be determined in the central core of our business information center, which accounts for the discussion we had in Chapter 2.

Classical databases get smart as a consequence of their database management systems. A DBMS is a sophisticated set of software modules created for a single but critically important function: to build, maintain, and provide accurate access to our data.

DBMS software provides all of the structured organization. The necessary seek and search identifiers are known as data manipulation language (DML). The software modules that actually carry out the required search, find, and retrieve functions are the access methods. Combined, they assure the tools needed to accumulate, store, retrieve, and interpret the text and data contained in the database.

Databases need to communicate. Data communications disciplines (which we have reviewed) bring unlike technologies together into a smoothly working aggregate. Protocols and layered structures help to marry two dissimilar technologies—computers and communications—and so bring required information elements to the user.

This concept is vital to expert systems at large and to the knowledgebanks in particular. There is a large amount of information the Esystem needs to know: In which database(s) are text and data held? Which authorization procedures are necessary? When is each database available? What's the procedure for connecting? Which query language is being employed?

One of the important pieces of knowhow the Esystem must possess is what to do when things go wrong. The answer, which should be coded in the knowledgebank, is easier to give if the expert system has been split into several modules each of which is responsible for carrying out one subtask. That, however, requires well-designed rules able to specify how each module might make use of the others.

Equally vital questions are the organization and structure of the memory elements. To borrow a taxonomical classification, *semantic* (or generic) *memory* contains the facts we know, arranged in a hierarchical network. *Episodic memory* encodes experience.

Concepts in an episodic memory are related to each other by their occurrence in the same episode. In this way, relations between objects are much richer than in a semantic sense. Also, in episodic memory, an object is defined by its function, that is, its role in different operations or situations.

If the encoded information elements in the database, and the rules in the knowledgebank, are well organized, memory search can be directed to only the most relevant items. There is an analogy between this process and remembering in human beings. Similar statements can be made about understanding and reasoning.

Even when we have completed it, a knowledgebank is not yet ready to be run. We first have to use a *compiler* to translate it into optimized language statements so that it will be accepted by the system. An example is the consultation shell. When the compiler is invoked, it first asks for the name of the knowledgebank file. Then it proceeds with syntax checking. That is essential for any serious expert system development, just as it is for conventional software.

As we will see in the appropriate chapter, the shell should offer a well-designed display that makes good use of color, graphics, and other attributes. It should provide a catalog of available knowledgebank sections and their filenames, and it should also make possible the saving of a log of any session for restart, recovery, auditing, or other use. Since this is typically done interactively, the session should proceed with a series of questions. Responses tell the system how to go about searching for an answer to the problem we want to solve.

The user should also be able to request help at any time during a session by typing, for instance, a question mark in response to any system question. Hence, one of the knowledgebank modules should be dedicated to this task. Choices should point to convenience. For instance, one user constructed a knowledgebank by creating columns to represent the four independent factors allowed for each example and the possible decisions that could be made. Then, the user listed the various items in the appropriate columns.

An important requirement for the preparation of knowledge-based software is that the designer must have as fully transparent an environment as possible to work with. Then the focus can be on the selection, organization, and formulation of the knowledge components.

Knowledge Acquisition

Literature on expert systems abounds with references to "knowledge acquisition bottlenecks" and "knowledge acquisition problems." Esystem experts make the same references, but neither they nor the journal articles are currently ready to advance solid approaches. Even so, a solution can be found.

Let's start with the fundamentals. Somebody is considered an expert if he or she has:

1. A large knowledge domain in the form of facts and rules
2. Individual experience generally not found in the literature of the domain or going beyond what is currently available

His or her knowhow may work on the basis of analogies, heuristics, or other judgments or through individual decision criteria that experience taught the expert. The expert's knowledge supports the choice of promising problem-solving strategies. If they turn out to be unsuccessful, the expert goes back to the point from which the strategy failed and tries an alternative course.

That is the way our minds work when we are experts in a given field. On the one side is the networking of minor judgment through which we can reach a major judgment. On the other side are what we call facts, which largely rest on our observation of text, data, images, and other conditions.

The physicist's method involves as a foundation the use of general postulates, or *principles*. From them conclusions can be deduced. Hence, the work falls into two parts:

- First discovering the principles
- Then drawing conclusions which follow from the principles

Once this formulation is successfully established, inference follows on inference. Most important, the process often reveals relations which may extend well beyond the area of the reality from which the principles are drawn.

With Esystems we need something quite similar to the physicist's method, but we are at a disadvantage. We don't have the long centuries of methodological developments on which to draw. We must either invent methods or convert and refine methods from the physical sciences to apply to the *logical sciences* of knowledge engineering.

One way to extract knowhow is empirical. The knowledge engineer watches what the expert does and records it. An example is how the expert doctor's eyes and mind scan the x-ray. Where they stop. What they observe. What is recorded. In this process, the analyst observes the action and asks for an explanation of the *doctor's* logical steps. The analyst follows this process all the way, including how the doctor comes to a conclusion—and what the conclusion is.

In commenting on knowledge acquisition for YES-MVS,* an IBM Esystems specialist has said that getting the knowledge is the biggest problem. That is all the more true because each console operator has had a private method. That is typical of projects that require more than one expert to develop the rules. The knowledge engineer must record each expert's logic and then integrate.

There is no guarantee that two different experts will have the same way of approaching the subject, the same methodology. Even if only one knowledge engineer works with only one human expert, there will be different people in support roles—software and hardware specialists among others. The coordinating task is present.

The coordinating task exists in the physical sciences also, but, by contrast, the world of phenomena uniquely determines the theoretical system. That is not true in the logical sciences. In the physical sciences, a fact is a fact in spite of there not being a clear logical bridge between phenomena and their theoretical principles. Leibnitz described the situation in the physical sciences as preestablished harmony. Perhaps preestablished harmony exists in the logical sciences also, but it has not yet been framed as such.

Expert systems can be used to facilitate the framing process. For instance, Teiresias supervises interaction with an expert in building or augmenting a Mycin rule set. To do so, Teiresias uses a model of the Mycin knowledgebank to indicate whether some new piece of information can be integrated with what is already known. It uses this information to make suggestions to the knowledge engineer and to the expert.

These are examples of knowledge-acquisition systems that are interactive, that involve semiautomatic ways to guide the expert to the right sort of knowledge to introduce into the Esystem. There are also experiments in automatic knowledge acquisition, that is, in extracting knowledge directly from data. An example is Metadendral.

---

*Yorktown Expert System. It is an Esystem structure acting as front end to MVS to relieve many of the console operator's functions.

Metadendral was an attempt to model the processes of theory formation. Its "meta" level is addressed to knowledge acquisition. It accepts as input a set of known structure-spectrum pairs of interest to Dendral. The output is a set of general fragmentation rules.

The intelligence built into Metadendral is akin to a plan, generate, and test approach.

- The planning process interprets each spectral data point as a fragmentation. It collects evidence for similar processes and bond environments.
- Generation creates a space of plausible rules of mass spectrometry constrained by evidence and user-supplied context.
- The test phase checks the plausible rules and uses all the evidence, positive and negative.

This test procedure generalizes the rules to improve support from the evidence. It seeks a better fit between rules and evidence and thus improves the overall knowledge acquisition process.

In a way, the rule-oriented structure of Esystems facilitates automatic acquisition of new rules as well as modification of existing rules and thus moves toward autonomous learning. As an example, AM, designed by Davis and Leant (1982) for discovering mathematical concepts, begins with elementary ideas in set theory.

AM employs a generate-and-test control structure. It searches a space of possible conjectures that can be generated from elementary ideas in set theory. It chooses the most applicable conjecture and pursues that line of reasoning. It has been successful in "rediscovering" fundamental notions of mathematics.

Eurisko, a recent Esystem, explores how a program can devise new heuristics to associate with new concepts as it discovers them. But although the results from the references outlined in the preceding paragraphs are impressive, in the majority of cases there are no automatic aids and whether the work stands or falls depends on the expertise of the knowledge engineer.

In refining task expertise, two different types of knowledge must be learned:

1. Domain knowledge used by the reasoning process
2. The reasoning process itself

Refinement of any type of knowledge requires an explicit representation of the knowhow that can be examined, structured, recorded, accessed, and changed over time. Refinement based on experience requires a way of keeping track of experiences associated with the applicable knowledge.

Therefore, an explicit mapping of both the reasoning process and the domain knowledge must be developed.

This requires the formulation of decision rules after obtaining a good comprehension of the way the expert's mind works. As stated, that is no straightforward matter. Often the knowledge engineers find it difficult to describe the steps in reasoning that the expert uses to make decisions.

The Computer-Based Interview

Analysts with experience in the field tend to believe that some of the difficulty is due to the lack of a structured methodology. Developing an Esystem to perform an expert's task means organizing a body of knowledge well enough to represent an expert's reasoning, which in itself is a formidable task. Also the knowledge engineer sometimes finds it difficult to understand the terms used by an expert, and vice versa.

This is written with the understanding that, as long as the process of knowledge acquisition remains manual (or nearly so), the most evident method is the *interview* with the expert. Observing and recording how the expert operates is really a subclass of this process as rare as the case in which pure observation suffices—without involving questions and answers.

In short, the most popular method of knowledge acquisition involves the interaction of:

1. A knowledge engineer who knows about the tool
2. An expert who knows about the application domain

The role of the knowledge engineer is to interpret the expert's answers to questions with respect to knowledge as such and the method of knowledge representation, to integrate the expert's answers into the growing knowledgebank, to draw analogies to help the expert structure (or remember) important aspects of the *expert's* own knowledge in the application domain, and to pose counterexamples which seem to violate the expert's hypotheses. As a devil's advocate, the knowledge engineer should raise conceptual difficulties and let the expert react.

However, a word of caution is necessary. *The interview should not be purely manual. It should from the start be computer-based.* Nothing should be done without computer support. The examples given in the preceding section on semiautomatic knowledge acquisition are revealing. If no Esystem is available to do it, the job can be done nicely with a fourth-generation language, as we will see in the following chapter on the human window. There are plenty of 4GLs from which to choose.

Also available are expert systems *shells*, as we will see in the appropriate chapter. And we should have accumulated experience on *prototyping*, a most important and vital approach to doing systems work. Whichever specific 4GL or shell is chosen, *prototyping should be the goal of the interview.*

Another approach which has been used focuses on sharing knowhow among experts. One possibility is holding *group discussions.* From experience, I see it as an inefficient solution if done in a manual manner with classical recording. The recording by itself is insufficient for gaining an understanding of its contents and mapping them on a support, though it may be helpful in rare cases.

Here again, chances for success are improved if computers are used, as through teleconferencing. Experience with this approach is still thin, but the approach is worth trying. It produces a permanent record which is good because both the original contributions and the annotations are available. Computer conferencing leads to distributed type group meetings.

Still another approach which has been attempted for knowledge acquisition is holding a knowledge competition. Stefik, who led the team that designed Loops (1983), found it to be effective. Others do not think so. But, again in special cases, it is a method worth trying.

In a research project by Zimmermann and Zysno (1982) a hierarchy of criteria was developed for the evaluation of creditworthiness of customers. Fifty credit applications were evaluated by a number of credit managers of banks, and the manager's judgments were modeled by a four-level hierarchy of criteria.

Another method that has been tried is establishing a first draft of knowledge acquisition and then giving it to different experts individually to criticize it and improve upon it. Here, too, there may be merits but also digressions. This is not the sort of thing one will do with every project.

A better approach than generalized commentaries is to involve the expert in feedback, as by taking the emerging Esystem back to the expert for comment. This will elicit more of the expert's knowledge and help in tuning the contents of the knowledgebank. An even better approach is to provide a good user interface to help the expert follow precisely how the Esystem works, particularly in the early stages of knowledge acquisition. Thus the expert can see exactly where the Esystem is diverging from his or her own thinking and take the appropriate corrective action.

The Role of Misinterpretation

There is ample room for misinterpreting what an expert says when the analyst has little understanding of the domain. This danger is more pronounced when the analyst is interpreting esoteric protocols from the expert in the process of solving a problem. The information may be incomplete, and a lot of interpolation may be necessary.

At the same time, managers and professionals talk much more freely about what they do if the discussion is with someone who understands what they are saying. The knowledge engineer who is a novice in the particular field may actually inhibit the expert. The need for preparation is evident but not always appreciated. It is wise for the knowledge engineer to read about the domain beforehand to understand the basic concepts and jargon. The engineer should meet the expert more than halfway, use the same terms as the expert, and then do any translating that is necessary.

Obviously, the matching is more effectively achieved when the expert and the knowledge engineer are the same person. For instance Pecos, by Barstow (1979), is a system built by a professional programmer to capture his own expertise. Interestingly enough, the Pecos designer suggests he found explication of his own knowledge a far from trivial task.

A great deal of work, Barstow says, was spent in identifying the important concepts in the domain, which were not immediately apparent to him. After the identification had been made, a conceptual framework came in a flash of insight and several pieces suddenly fell together.

In a way, it all comes back to the interview stage, where there is another subclass: the black-box approach. Typically, the expert gives descriptions of reasoning at a shallow level. The expert may tend to approach this state in the course of getting more experience. In this case the reliance is more on memory and less on intermediate reasoning.

In any case, the knowledge engineer should not reject the expert's first descriptions of reasoning. Instead, the engineer should impress on the expert the need to justify conclusions. The justification should help reveal the circuitry within the black box. The knowledge engineer should also guard against internal processes to avoid developing misleading models. No one has reason to believe that one's own first conceptualization is complete or correct. The engineer may:

- Misinterpret the expert's reasoning
- Be overly keen on production rules
- Fail on the details
- Incorrectly comprehend the expert's explanation of the principles of the system

Besides, even an expert who can easily articulate what is done can be wrong. That's why it is sometimes wise to observe the expert actually solve a problem and check that both the information and the logic used are those the expert claims to use. That being said, there is no doubt that in developing an Esystem we must get the best experts we can find. Only then is knowledge acquisition worth its cost. *True experts generally know more about their domains.* Furthermore, they are better than the average professional at applying and using their knowledge effectively.

Last but not least, any knowledge acquisition effort should be subject to a serious, well-done process of consistency checking. This should flash out faults in what will be used to build the knowledgebank. Faults may be due to deviations from the existing pattern, logical inconsistencies, or other difficulties such as misunderstandings.

Complex computer programs naturally tend to have errors; hence they need thorough testing, debugging, and certification. The credibility of the Esystem will be increased if the system is thoroughly tested—as it must be. Thorough testing makes a program not only correct but also intelligible and understandable. The user will ultimately be responsible for applying the results the system gives him or her—and would like to be sure of a good start.

Structuring Expert Systems Research

A research effort can be structured only when we have a conceptual model on which to build. The conceptual model should start with ways and means to effectively extract the rules that experts use and proceed with developing problem-solving methodologies for dealing with those rules.

Structuring the early stages of a process should always focus on end use. Unlike human experts able to introspect about their knowledge, expert systems require reasoning models. Such models will themselves:

- Be based on the organization of experience
- Be subjected to incremental learning and refinement of both reasoning processes and domain knowledge

From that comes the theory that knowledge acquisition may fall into distinct stages:

1. Getting the relevant facts and associated procedures
2. Refining the facts and procedures and providing linkages
3. Building up a prototype
4. Structuring the domain
5. Extracting the first working model

6. Testing, debugging, and refining further
7. Experimental application

If we wish to obtain valid results, each of these steps should be well understood. The right representation should be chosen for it. Relations between parameters should be detailed. In short, we should know what we are doing.

Although our design work should reflect the greatest care, it is just as important to get a system working as soon as possible. That keeps both the expert and the knowledge engineer interested. It also acts as a focus in eliciting more knowledge. Good advice is to *get a system built as soon as one area* (or even one example) of the expert's behavior is understood. That can be done successfully if we have established the guiding concepts and integration methodology beforehand. Figure 23 gives an example of the latter.

Knowledge will be built up incrementally on the basis of experience. Facts that once were unrelated become integrated through repeated occurrence. Reasoning processes can be refined through use. By noticing failures, successes, and differences, as well as similarities among implementation cases, our ability to deal with the Esystem is enhanced. Reasoning processes, the knowledge used in them, and incremental changes of reasoning processes filter through the refinery of actual experience.

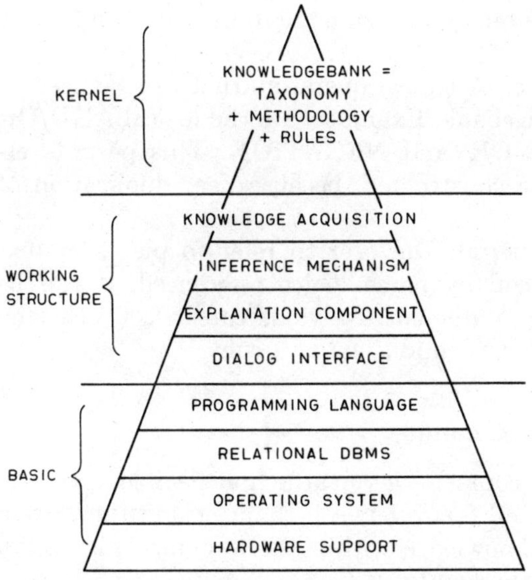

Figure 23 An integration methodology applicable to expert systems.

If the evolution of the Esystem itself requires introspection and examination of the knowledge used in solving problems, that is just as true of the stage of knowledge acquisition with which the whole process starts. We must move forward in formalizing the knowledge acquisition phase, and we can do so if we demonstrate to ourselves in concrete terms our own understanding of that phase.

Explanation facilities can be of a traceback type, in which the rules themselves represented in an understandable form or standard text associated with the rules are or is played back on request. Such explanations presuppose a knowledge of the application area on the part of the person requesting them.

Knowledge representation is an interactive process. It is also the single most important factor in determining how powerful an application we can build with an expert system. The language should be versatile and sophisticated; it should support both numeric and string variables of several distinct types.

The application can set the variables by querying the end user. The main types of variables are facts, strings, numbers, categories, phrases, and if-then statements. They exemplify the methods that knowledge engineering systems offer for differentiating among the various characteristics of a problem.

Major methods of knowledge representation are AI programming languages, actor systems, inference nets, frames, semantic nets, production rule systems, and logical constructs. The latter are often divided into predicate, modal, temporal, nonmonotonic logic, and fuzzy logic.

Quite important is a full set of logical operators that can be used in creating rules in the knowledgebank. Examples are the logical AND/OR operators, the EXCLUSIVE OR, and NEGATION. This permits efficient knowledgebanks to be constructed, because near duplication of rules is avoided.

A phrase parameter may permit the user to refer to pieces of text related to the current problem by name. Once referenced, it can be automatically inserted in any statement. Its value can be set either by asking the user or by proving the conditions of a rule.

Approaches to Knowledge Exchange

The chosen variables should comprise a versatile and flexible aggregate for passing knowledge back and forth between the user and the system and also for processing the knowledge within the system. This ability to communicate concepts is the key to:

1. Offering worthwhile advice and results for real-world problems

2. Constructing efficient knowledge systems that can run in the smaller memory space of microcomputers

The knowledge engineer must specify facts and ranges; for example, the values permitted for numerical parameters may be set in a range declaration. The number types may include positive integers and both positive and negative floating-point decimals. The designer may also specify that number parameters be calculated, deduced from a rule, or asked of the user. Such parameters may be qualitative features that can take any number of specified string values. The consultation shell will build a menu of the listed category options and ask the user for selections.

An expert system must be interactive. It should be able to give advice during, rather than only at the end of, a consultation session when the user has answered all the program's questions. In either case, the system should guide the user step by step through the consultation procedure. These are design characteristics with which the knowledge engineer must be familiar. But perhaps the most challenging job the engineer will be asked to do is carry out a valid organization of the knowledgebank and the global database. For such work there are no precise guidelines, but examples taken from accomplished Esystems projects can be of help.

To organize the knowledgebank, AM uses elementary ideas in finite set theory. Heuristics are employed for generating new mathematical concepts by combining elementary ideas and also for discarding bad ideas. The knowledgebank of R1 is structured around the properties of some 400 VAX components. There are rules, based on the state of the system, for determining when to move to the next subtask. There are also rules for carrying out partial configurations to a total of 800 rules.

The knowledgebank of EL employs rules that represent general electrical principles, make conjectures, and decide what to forget when contradictions occur. SYN, an MIT Esystem which uses ideas of EL, contains electrical laws in its knowledgebank. It also has rules for changing slices and other rules for creating appropriate slices.

The knowledgebank of Dendral is built around rules for deriving constraints on molecular structure from experimental data. It also includes rules for predicting spectograms from structures and procedures for generating candidate structures to satisfy constraints.

It is interesting to observe the differences present in Metadendral, which, as stated, is an Esystem tooled to help in knowledge acquisition by other Esystems. Its knowledgebank contains rules for interpreting spectral data and summarizing results, generating candidate fragmentation rules from the evidence, and generalizing or specializing candidate rules to fit the evidence better.

With nearly the same objectives, but building on the Prospector knowledgebank, Kas takes a different approach. Its rules focus on:

- Inference networks for expressing judgmental knowledge
- Semantic networks for expressing the meaning of the propositions employed in the rules
- Taxonomical networks for presenting basic knowledge among the terms of the domain

Knowledge of various mechanisms, as well as consistency rules, is employed in Prospector for representing and using knowhow.

The knowledgebank of Mycin includes rules that link patient data to infection hypotheses, combine certainty factors, and are oriented toward treatment. In contrast, the *global database* of Mycin includes:

- Patient history and diagnostic tests
- Current hypotheses
- Status
- Conclusions reached thus far
- Rule numbers justifying the conclusions

The last item in the list exemplifies the differences in content between the knowledgebank and the global database. To carry this example further, the global database of Metadendral includes:

- User-supplied context
- Known structure spectrum pairs
- Various input data

The global database of Dendral has mass spectrogram data, constraints, and candidate structures. That of SYN has the circuit, the slice being considered, and a set of deduced values.

A manual design of very large scale integration (VLSI) chips is impossible. Only through the use of high technology is it possible to produce chips with, say, 30,000 gates, because a chip's nuts and bolts are invisible to the naked eye and the unassisted human mind. However, it is not yet true that the more automated a system is the better understood it has to be. Here is where expert systems have their day in computer-aided design.

Another Esystem oriented to engineering design is EL. It contains in its global database facts about the particular circuit being analyzed.

These are represented as assertions in an associative database. Also represented are the history of conjectures used, the conclusions dependent upon the conjectures, and the status of the problem.

The global database of R1 includes:

- Customer order
- Current task
- Partial configuration of the VAX state

AM has in its global database plausible candidate concepts.

In a nutshell, the difference between the contents of a knowledgebank and the contents of a database is that *information in the knowledgebank is contained in a program, which itself exhibits intelligent behavior. Information in the database is accessible in computer storage.* The latter is the classical approach; the former is Esystems oriented.

Chapter

7

The Human Window

"Where you stand on an issue depends on where you sit." POPULAR WISDOM

Conversing with an Intelligent System

In a macroscopic sense, the architecture of an expert system is composed of five modules: knowledge acquisition, knowledgebank, communicating database, rules of the inference engine, and explanatory interface. Having treated the first three of these in the chapter on Knowledge Engineering, it would have been proper to proceed with the inference engine, but ...

Had this book been written for knowledge engineers, that would have been the thing to do. But it is written for business people, and the preceding chapter is already heavy with concepts. There is no point to moving immediately into logical inferences and mathematics. Better now to talk of the *human window.*

The expert system is built for the end user: the manager and professional in the domain of its applicability. The human window is necessary for the user to communicate with the intelligence inside the machine. There is a lot to be said about interacting with Esystems. First, *it is much easier to converse with an intelligent system* than with a dumb one. Second, conversation with an expert system eventually arrives at *assessment.* This takes place through questions and answers exercised on both sides.

Third, interacting with Esystems should definitely account for the fact that the systems are symbolic machines rather than traditional DP-type computers. Fourth, the human window must be designed in the context of widespread man-machine interaction made possible by the development of man-machine interfaces.

Research and development on the design of human windows should lead to a better understanding of man-machine interaction and therefore improvements in the construction of interfaces. Fifth, what we are asking from these interfaces is a subject in full evolution, because Esystems implementation changes its focal point with experience.

When expert systems implementation was limited to a few users in the medical field, where it started, interfacing requirements were more restricted. As implementation moved toward scientific subjects, interfacing requirements automatically broadened. This broadening momentum increased as Esystem usage expanded toward geology and engineering (Figure 24).

But the movement which really brought the need for formal human window approaches into perspective was the spread toward financial issues. Investment advisers, loan officers, foreign exchange dealers, and financial analysts have different interfacing requirements than all the Esystems users who preceded them in man-information exchanges.

An excellent Esystems study by British Telecom referred to the Smith and Baker recommendation that a good user interface be incorporated in the prototype because it could help considerably in the later stages of development. The Dipmeter Advisor system has 42 percent of its code devoted to the user interface. This interface is graphical, and it has proved to be most valuable in test and user acceptance.

Managers and professionals belong to multidisciplinary fields and need support from equally multidisciplinary work teams. Serious work on the design of human windows should bring together researchers from many areas, including psychology, organizational theory, electronics, and computer science.

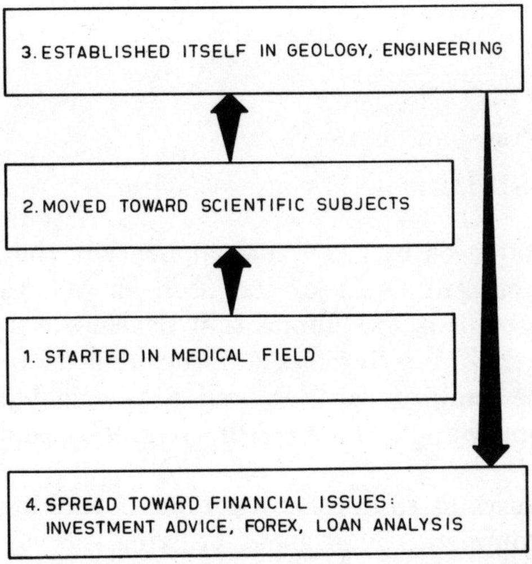

Figure 24 Successive steps in expert systems implementation.

Such research should be primarily concerned with the human user of the Esystem and with the technologies that support the interfaces written for that user. The technologies include image analysis and speech processing, though today they focus on question-and-answer sessions. We definitely need to raise the level of user interface design in terms of innovation and methodology. While adding to current solutions, we also need to improve our capabilities in pattern analysis to make possible the use of advanced speech and image techniques in the user interface.

The Expert System Asks for *Your* Response

The human window for business-oriented expert systems is typically a question-answering model applied in topic domains. Its queries are translations of user goals that involve assumptions about what is said and not said.

To perform their task effectively, such interface mechanisms need relevant facts, keep options for further information and exploration open, and explain themselves in complete answers. The explaining is done in English through comprehensive sentences and also icons (that is, known objects), menus, prompts, and help screens.

This is sometimes called "natural-language programming," but the term is ill-defined. Every vendor uses it as he pleases, and it often leads to confusion. Whether natural or supernatural, the man-machine interface language must be such as to permit the users to:

- Modify their queries as more information becomes known
- Move on to new goals
- Keep traces of solution paths
- Record responses they give to Esystem queries
- Record the explanations and justifications they are receiving

New dialog solutions must be influenced by the actual application; they must reflect the mentality and current needs of the user, as well as the needs to be reasonably expected as the application develops. An example of valid dialog design is the *Bank Services Advisor*. This semi-Esystem helps select appropriate banking services, and it is oriented toward the typical banking client who is unaware of computers and communications.

The system asks a series of questions to develop a profile of banking requirements. It then makes recommendations about utilizing services of the bank. The interaction which follows is about a phone transfer service for the payment of bills.

```
Do you want our new phone transfer service?
   >> Yes.

How much will you deposit initially?
   >> 1000.00.

How many deposits do you expect to make each month?
   >> 2.

What is the average amount that will be deposited?
   >> 800.00.

How many cash withdrawals do you expect to make each month?
   >> 3.

What is the average of each ATM withdrawal?
   >> 100.00.

How many automatic transfers (e.g., pay loan)
do you expect to make each month?
   >> 4.

What is the average amount of each automatic transfer?
   >> 100.00.

How many checks will you be writing each month?
   >> 10.

What will be the average amount of each check?
   >> 50.00.

In the worst case, your balance during the month could
become as low as XXX.XX.
Do you approve this worst case minimum balance?
(If you say no, you will be asked to enter a
different figure for minimum balance.)
   >> No.

Practically, what do you think your minimum
balance will be?
   >> YYY.YY.

A combination of checking and savings accounts
may satisfy your needs best. Do you want such
a combination of accounts?
   >> Yes.

(Considering best savings account . . . )
A time deposit account may be appropriate for you.

Such an account requires you to leave your initial
deposit in the account for a specified time period.

Do you want a time deposit account?
   >> Yes.

What is the longest period you would consider
for a time deposit account?
   >> 6 months.

Recommended account: Time Deposit
This account is . . .

Recommended account: Money Market Checking.
This account is an interest-bearing checking
account . . .
```

Capable man-machine interfaces must have extended portability and must use multiple senses: touch, vision, speech, and advanced graphics.

Solutions should be tested with tools available in applied experimental psychology.

Designers of human windows need to know about people's problem solving, dialoging, explanation criteria, and phrasing in a clear, crisp, comprehensive but also laconic way. After all, the man-machine interface is a new milestone in a history of communications which has seen:

1. The spoken word in the estimated time frame of 40,000 to 50,000 B.C.
2. The written word in about 3500 B.C.
3. Book printing in 1450
4. The post in about 1800, but the penny mail 50 years later
5. The telegraph in 1835
6. The telephone in 1876
7. The typewriter in about 1890
8. The calculator in about 1905 but the computer in 1946

Each one of these milestones has had a permanent effect on the way we communicate. At the same time, it has greatly influenced the way we think.

Man-machine interfacing is a language, and the language we use forms our minds. No wonder that this has attracted due attention in serious research projects. Britain's Alvey Man-Machine Interface (MMI) program, for instance, has allocated 70 percent of its 650 research workers to the human interface, 17 percent to pattern analysis, and 9 percent to displays. Other matters absorb only 4 percent.

User interface design includes interactive techniques with emphasis on developing ways of using new workstation architectures and input devices. This work is oriented both to the end user and to the expert developing the knowledgebank. Another key issue is integration methods for combining two or more applications (domain independence) or interactive capabilities (multimedia interaction). The same thing is true of technology evaluation, including analysis of alternative hardware and software architectures for interactive systems.

At the same MMI project, the human factors team works on cognitive processes of the individual user, with particular reference to the perceptual, problem-solving and decision-making processes involved in using interactive knowledge systems. This work includes evaluation techniques for objective measurement of human-computer performance.

Work also takes place on usability characteristics and determinants such as training, environment, hardware and software design, and user support. Person-to-person interaction, for instance, the voice messaging system, also is studied.

Emphasis must also be placed on the organizational consequences of tools and techniques for facilitating and evaluating the use of expert systems by groups of users. One of the possible organizational consequences is fatigue, which increases error rates.

Higher error rates may occur because of fatigue after extended video use. Fatigue can be brought on by:

- Poor resolution of the characters on the screen compared with characters printed on paper
- The flicker of the characters that occurs if the screen is refreshed (usually some 30 times a second)
- The glare that can result from reflections in the glass screen
- The natural tendency to look downward at material that is being read, whereas video units require the user to look somewhat upward

These are examples of the details which need to be studied if we wish to provide able solutions to the design of the human window.

Using Fourth-Generation Languages

The past three decades were the age of systems development. In 1985, however, we entered a new age of systems research with emphasis on expert systems, and in 1985 the fourth-generation language (4GL) population was preeminent.

There are many groups of languages under the 4GL heading, and the most important groups have a database management orientation.* They can be expected to dominate the scene for a few years. As Figure 25 suggests, by the end of this decade they will give way to a new generation (5GL), the emphasis of which will be knowledgebank management.

Whether we talk of the third, fourth, or fifth generation of programming languages, the role of the language is to enhance what we can do with the human window beyond pure and simple programming of the computer. That is not to say the latter job is unimportant. Computers and communications store, transport, and present vast amounts of text, data, graphics, image, and voice messages.

- They refer to our clients, our markets, our products and services, our competition, and our suppliers.

*See also D. N. Chorafas, Fourth and Fifth Generation Programming Language, vols. I and II, McGraw-Hill, New York, 1986.

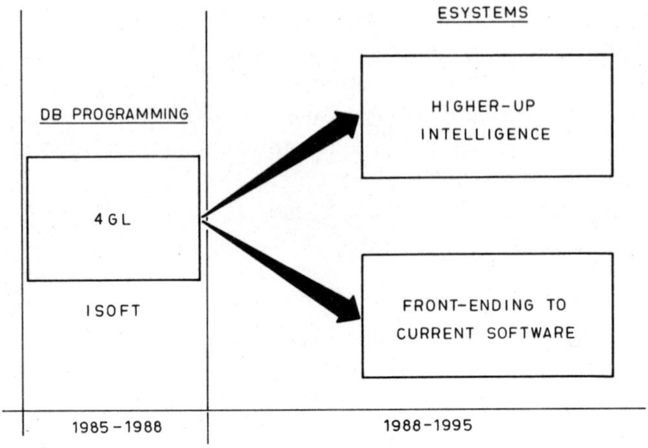

Figure 25 From fourth-generation language programming to expert system applications.

- They have to do with the habits, backgrounds, and preferences of clients and competitors and the profitability of our operations.

But a new challenge we now face is how to use this information to *discover new business opportunities.* Although we may have the information, it is going to take quite a while to learn how to use it properly. This is an organization challenge, and if affects top management. To answer it effectively, we need human window capabilities.

At the current state of the art, fourth-generation languages are ideal for semiautomatic knowledge acquisition. They support:

1. Interactive procedures
2. Database management
3. Prototyping capabilities

The results they offer lead to the automation of system analysis and design, as well as coding and testing. Fourth-generation languages provide high-quality object codes and make greater productivity by computer professionals feasible, but they also appeal to the end user. The user can learn some of them, such as integrated software, in a day's time.

The 4GL orientation is toward multifunctionality, a polyvalent approach, and structured development. Sure enough, there are different levels of sophistication in programming with fourth-generation languages. The lower layer is that of a *linguistic interface* that provides the programmatic linkage between the *back-end functions* of a relational DBMS and the *front-end tools.*

Typical examples are SQL of IBM and Quel of Ingres. Both are query-type data languages. From a programmer's viewpoint they are much more efficient than, say, Cobol, but they are less efficient than programming by forms and by example.

Quel and SQL are examples of *one-dimensional programming* (1-DP). Other query languages (and 4GLs) also follow this approach:

```
PRINT 1984-JUNE-ACT SALES, 1983-JUNE-ACT SALES
    (1984-JUNE-ACT SALES/1983-JUNE-ACT SALES)
    (2000 ITEMS * AA - ZZ)
WHERE (STORE = ATLANTA OR STORE = COLUMBIA)
```

Another example of one-dimensional programming, done through a more sophisticated language but in a similar programming mode, is:

```
SELECT <Article> from <Inventory>
WHERE <Status = Replenishment Level>
```

Some query systems present a dichotomy between form operations intended for the end user and database operations. Database operations follow a relational query language, which, after all, is the job of the linguistic interface. A better approach is to use the form's level to query the database, that is, to formulate database queries by filling forms.

Two-Dimensional Programming

The filled forms are formats the system should try to find in the database. Such an approach can achieve a completely uniform interface. By contrast to the linear, one-dimensional programming structure of the simple query, languages working by form and by example are based on the technology of *two-dimensional programming* (2-DP). Two-dimensional solutions are more than a programming methodology.

1. There are methods of database creation, management, retrieval, and presentation.
2. The methods permit the use of very few entries.
3. The entries express the equivalent of a lengthy conventional language program.
4. The entries manipulate the database directly, without any need for the programmer to specify what is to be done.

Furthermore, users with no knowledge of formal programming language can, after about two days of training, formulate 2-D programs to retrieve, modify, define, and control the database.

Retrieval is based on simple table selection. Suppose the task is to list names of all employees who belong to factory A, their salaries, and the starting dates of employment. To begin, the user is presented with a blank table skeleton on the screen:

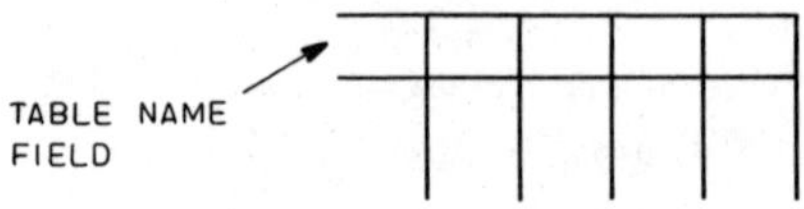

The user keys the appropriate name into the table name field—DEPT (factory department)—and may now either type in the column headings or let the system generate the headings automatically.

Having established the column headings, the user can program within the 2-DP frame by making entries:

DEPT	NAME	SALARY	DATE
		P.	

These entries will be needed for cross-referencing between fields. Let's assume the user needs the names of employees and the salary amounts, but only for the employees managed by Mr. Uri, who is responsible for factory maintenance. This query involves a scan of both the DEPT and the EMP tables.

For this job, two 2-DP frames are displayed on the screen and the name fields of both tables are filled in. The formulation of this 2-DP query takes the shape:

DEPT	NAME	SALARY	DATE
	N̲		

EMP	NAME	MGR
	N̲	URI

The element N̲ in both tables causes the listings in the NAME fields of the tables to match: Employees working for Uri will be selected from the EMP table and listed on the DEPT table.

Redundant columns will be erased with a special function key. Since the user can scroll the screen left, right, up, and down, information elements (IE) do not need to be displayed simultaneously on the softcopy. This permits the user to handle programs with many tables, each of which can have a number of columns.

Cross-referencing can take place within a column. We may, for instance, want to list the names and amounts for maintenance technicians who spent more than the standard time on the systematic maintenance of equipment in Department C.

One of the significant facilities of two-dimensional programming is data exchange between tables. To collect information in various tables and place it in a new, user-created table as an output report, we must map an example element from the base tables to a new format.

To create an output table containing the names, amounts of fringe benefits, and managers of employees at a certain date, we construct:

DEPT	NAME	AMOUNT	DATE
	<u>N</u>		

EMP	NAME	MGR
	<u>N</u>	

EMP 1	NAME	AMOUNT	MGR
	<u>N</u>		

The output table is composed by mapping data from the base table. Its headings do not need to correspond to the headings of the original tables.

Now suppose that, once these tables have been created and framed in pages, we wish to preserve them for future reference. They can be named, stored, and retrieved as infopage information. Access to infopages can be either direct (through number and keyword) or by means of *menus.*

Menus are tree structures which provide automatic routing to the infopage we need. The user is presented a master menu from which a first choice is selected. This brings up a second menu, and so on, until the infopage sought for is located.

Menu management may improve the handling of events by sorting the events. Commands can come from any input device if the content of a menu window which displays a keyboard layout is pointed to. The literature of some vendors speaks of menu systems as being natural-language programmed, but, as remarked earlier, natural-language programming involves much more than that.

Introducing Management Graphics

Experimentation and guidance on the design of human windows is necessary because, as experience with interactive programs has made clear, application programmers have great difficulty in defining the user interface. They often sacrifice user friendliness for efficiency. They think of concentrating on algorithms without being aware that they are defining a user interface at the same time.

Expert systems application means dialog. It should be regarded as a distinct system component. Both the application proper and the dialog aspects deserve concentrated attention, and they should receive it. Figure 26 diagrams this concept of distinct but interrelated component parts which make up a presentation system. Just as the lack of data flow or the absence of logic management (inference, rules) will not make a functioning aggregate, so the Esystem will be incomplete without the proper dialog management capabilities.

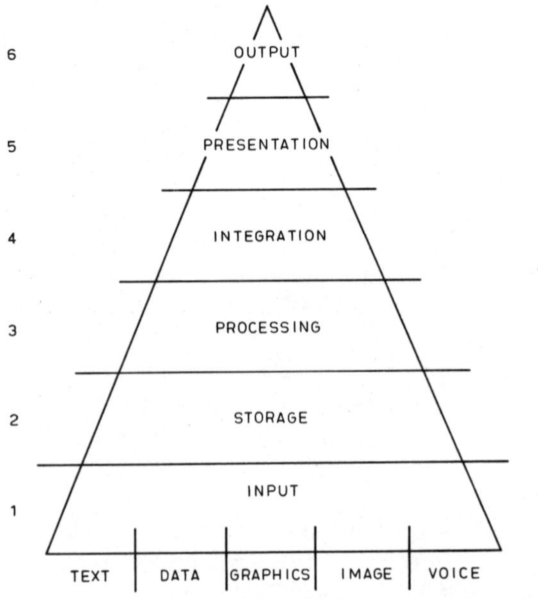

Figure 26 Distinct but interrelated component parts make up a presentation system.

The end user, whether making an inquiry or getting an input from the Esystem to which a response should be made, is communicating with a process run on the machine. This process addresses the input/output device. The dialog phase starts at this point. User advice, echo, error messages, and correction features must be provided and be adjustable during a working session. Adjustability can be realized on several levels in order to provide control as soon as possible. Useful features include a system echo indicating input device–dependent data, a standard echo visualizing input data, and a command echo displaying the output meaning of the man-machine exchange.

To provide for a user-friendly interface, echos can be give in icons, which we define as familiar objects. The same thing is true of certain menus and other user inputs. Graphics are the manager's and the professional's shorthand. A study of trends in demand for different types of business applications systems has interesting implications for the future of online graphics. Middle- and senior-level managers were surveyed to determine the mix of solution types currently at their disposal and their demand for additional services. The study showed that:

1. Traditional transaction processing comprises 90 percent of the installed base.
2. Online query systems with some analytical capability constitute 6 percent of the base.
3. Flexible, decision-oriented systems for management support (including PC-based) are at the 4 percent level.

But times are changing, and the demand is shifting. As this study suggested:

4. Current requests for transaction processors are dropping to 50 percent.
5. The need for query and analysis is at 20 percent.
6. The largest growth is shown by demand for meaningful decision support systems, which stands at 30 percent. The systems are mostly run on intelligent, interactive workstations.

In this quantitative reference is embedded the critical role of online graphics. More information can be presented in a graphic comparison of two trends, *and* the information can be rapidly comprehended.

- The manager who wants to explore and learn more about decision making must be able to make comparisons and easily comprehend the results to maintain idea development.
- The manager who has to wait for 2 hours to read tabular data, or wait days for batch turnaround, is restricted in making decisions.

Without graphical systems support, the extent of idea exploration and development by most managers and professionals is minimal. Too few alternatives are considered and evaluated. Only priority crises can force managers to analytically explore semistructured alternatives manually.

Since these facts are now becoming known, we can expect to see not only more analysis tools but also more graphics. That is a challenge for expert systems. First, there are the programming and analysis facts. The demand for inquiry, analysis, and DSS is so overwhelming that lack of trained designers and programmers is already constraining the growth rate.

- Extremely user-oriented graphics software packages must be developed to relieve this bottleneck.
- Such generic packages must interface all hardware and software with full labeling and prompting for managerial use.

Expert systems can make a significant contribution in this area. They can act as front ends to existing software to automate the task of manually preparing the interfaces, which comes from the Paleolithic Era of computing.

Second, the design of the Esystem itself should profit from graphics approaches. It is inexcusable to design new systems which do not incorporate a significant quotient of graphics presentation. Two-tier systems which look to the future in terms of inference and to the past by emphasizing text and tabulations are devised only by schizophrenic system researchers. (Rejoice, there are many of that kind.)

We also have the graphics languages to do a good job. They start becoming commercially available with:

- Built-in editor
- Calculation routines for diagram details
- Ability to output with three different graphic machines (screen, plotter, printer)
- Enrichment of the diagrams with headlines, dates, and explanatory text
- Scaling capabilities and division of axes of reference

The desired diagram is defined in the dialog, the input being made with functional commands. The result is available on the screen and can be changed in an interactive manner. Stored in files, graphics are callable at any time. The design validation process, full debugging aids, and other tools are included in a package.

Dataland Project at MIT

Most important, we have research projects with results surely worth integrating into the expert systems effort. A first-class reference is some of the output of the Architecture Machine Group at MIT* under Negroponte, Bolt, et al.

In a media room about the size of a personal office, one entire end wall is all screen: A longer than 4-meter-diagonal sheet of plate glass, which can be backprojected upon by a color TV. The user sits in an armchair in the room's center, and small joysticks are mounted on the arms of the chair next to touch-sensitive pads.

The system surrounds the user with sound. Automatic speech recognition and synthesis for speech output facilities are present; they enable user and system to talk to one another. A keyboard is noticeably absent.

The monitor to the user's left bears an image of *Dataland*, a personal world of data belonging to this user. Dataland is not a map of the data; *it is the data.* The user can travel over to the data, retrieve it, project it, and then zoom in to activate it for perusal. The user can change position on Dataland by scrolling or touch the desired item on the Dataland display monitor and ask to be taken there: "Take me to the map at lower right."

Combined with expert systems, Dataland-type implementations will most likely first appear as high-technology electronics support for top-level managers and then filter down to organizational echelons as prices for quantity lots fall. At the same time the spaces used will become richer and more involved. For example, we can expect three-dimensional spaces wherein the learned user will find different shapes of spaces useful and compelling with contents radically different to suit *personal* needs.

Graphics solutions will by all evidence precede automatic speech recognition, whose current offerings have troublesome operating features and limited vocabularies. But there will eventually be voice recognition add-ons for personal computing and communicating requirements.

Significant work is currently being done on *speech processing.* This includes speech recognition: pattern matching by template extraction, integration of statistical models into speech recognition systems, and speech synthesis. Examples include methods of text-to-speech conversion, achievement of intonation patterns, and speech transformation algorithms to reflect age, sex, or style of delivery.

Current technology permits voice input under certain conditions: when there is a stream of commands—not just one or two, when there is a possibility of selection of named objects, and when hands and/or mind

---

*Now merged into MIT's new Media Laboratory.

are busy with other occupations. There are also *drawbacks*, the main one being vocabulary followed by training user and machine.

Until more advanced systems become available, we must satisfy ourselves with the systems we have and offer a *user-friendly input.* At the 1985 Hannover Fair, Nixdorf did a test on input media. It involved 1000 users, with the learning effect balanced out. The input media were:

1. Graphic tablet
2. Hand-actuated mouse
3. Foot-actuated mouse
4. Track ball
5. Keyboard
6. Joystick

The graphic tablet was judged to be the best input medium by a factor of 2 over the next in line, the hand-actuated mouse. Next to last came the keyboard. The joystick was least acceptable even if for some obvious tasks it led the list.

A Role for Interactive Videodisks

There are other processes which in their specific areas of implementation are reaching maturity and can be integrated into an expert systems concept with visible effects on the human window side. One of the most promising is the *interactive videodisk* (IVD, optical disk), which makes gigabyte memories possible at low cost.

Automotive manufacturers and their dealers have entered a new era of communication by using interactive videodisk systems. The systems are applied to a wide range of sales, promotional, and training tasks. The entire videodisk system can be moved conveniently to wherever a dealer needs it: in the showroom, workshop, display window, staff room, or even off the premises at special functions.

Customers of the Swiss travel agency Esco can now benefit from a new way of selecting their holiday destinations. They look at previews of different resorts. The interactive videodisk previews show much more vividly and effectively than a brochure ever could all the attractions, surroundings, and available facilities. In that way they form a valuable sales aid, as well as a new customer service.

Once the destination has been chosen, a direct videotex telephone link with the travel agency's central computer shows realtime information on costs, weather conditions, available dates, and flight bookings —in fact, everything needed so the final selection can be made on-the-spot. This new service has been introduced at the 320 Esco travel agency offices throughout Switzerland, and about 90 percent of the available holiday destinations are already featured on interactive videodisks.

The German Popular Banks have applied a similar interactive videodisk system with videotex connection to real estate sales and holiday bookings. The system was developed by Frankfurt's Betriebswirtschaftliches Institut für Kreditgenossenschaften together with Philips. Banking applications have profited from optical disks in more than one way. An *electronic teller* is composed of ATM, PC, optical disk, line discipline, presentation screen, and touch-sensitive screen with menus (Figure 27). A similar unit can serve as a retail sales–POS system.

Information storage is not expensive. Each low-cost videodisk ($15 for the disk and about $1000 for the read-only unit) has sufficient capacity for 54,000 individual picture frames per side. Each frame has an individual code number by means of which it can be located instantly when required. The frame can store information such as menus and infopages or be part of film sequences, still slides, or text blocks, all of which can be combined in any order according to the desired form of information presentation.

Videodisks uniquely offer outstanding audio and video reproduction quality. The system works in special replay modes like freeze-frame and slow motion, which are used extensively in demonstration-type programs. And there is the inherent durability of the optical disks themselves,

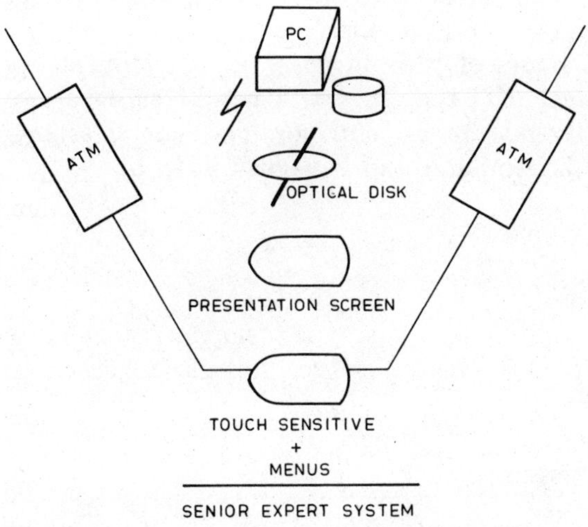

Figure 27 Electronic teller: a test area for expert systems.

which are not subject to wear or other degradation no matter how often they are played or handled.

In many organizations today, interactive videodisks perform a number of valuable functions: in training—for example, technical, sales, product—and also in the presentation of financial and sales strategies, competition comparisons, and new promotional actions. By using the optical disk's motion picture integration capability, the material shown can be backed up by personal messages from senior executives. This feature, which is today often used in commercial videodisk applications, can be employed to enrich an expert system's human window.

AT&T has developed, for the Ariel information network multiple-videodisk architecture, remote information stations, use of live two-way video and audio, a system for overview of services, and language and editing tools. It has videodisk-based electronic catalogs that employ the system for electronic publishing, digital data encoding, and authoring.

Sony has developed interactive videodisk procedures for training material composition, program design, script modifications, and production chores. The latter include the use of optical disks in computer-aided design (CAD), manufacturing, sales training, and service training and as an information database.

At New York University, by using an IBM PC and a videodisk player, Bress has put together NYULIVE, a 1-hour interactive program to help teach the basic rules of evidence to the students participating in a legal services clinic. Through two monitors, one of them for images and voices from the videodisk and one for the instructional questions and text generated by a microcomputer, the program can solicit and record a student's comments, answers, and questions.

This system saves Bress hours of time in coaching his clinical law students for a simple but real trial that they will handle as a part of their training. As a result, he anticipates that more law schools around the country will be using this computer-and-videodisk program:

- As an adjunct to courses on evidence
- For clinical legal services programs

Expert systems have a crying need for this type of support to enhance the human window. We have to blend advanced technologies together; we cannot always be reinventing the wheel. Remember that mathematics, though a very important part, is only a part of the Esystem. Equally important parts are user interfaces.

Let's recapitulate. Interactive videodisks really became active in business applications in 1984, though they started being used in entertainment electronics in 1979. An IVD system combines the flexibility of computers with the vast storage capacity and high-quality pictures of laser disks. Enriched with videotex connection, it becomes a communications device.

With current technology, optical disk supports feature permanent recording. Data, text, graphs, images, and sound are permanently etched on the disks at a factory and can't be changed by the user. But a personal computer attached to the video player can overlay timely information on the video image. The aggregate becomes a valuable tool that answers the need for expert systems to communicate with end users effectively.

Chapter

8

The Inference Machine

"The light at the end of the tunnel may be the headlamp of an oncoming train."

A RAILROAD EXECUTIVE

Changing Meaning of the Word "Machine"

The word "machine" is Greek in origin, but it once had a different meaning than it has today. In ancient times, a machine was any instrument or artifice. The word was connected to neither the technology nor the intended use of the object, whether that was production, transformation, transport, calculation, or communication.

The meaning has changed, yet from the ancient use of the word to the modern there is a connective link: "Machine" identifies not only the instrument but also the process, which is reflected in the evolving sense of the word. We can trace the history of technological evolution by following these successive meanings.

Concepts can acquire content only when they are connected, however indirectly, with sensible experience. But while science as a functioning system is the most objective process we know, science in the making, as an end to be pursued, is subjective and psychologically conditioned by our wants.

In the origins of scientific development there is always a key idea which eventually becomes the background reference. This is the abstraction and idealization of physical reality. It is a necessary process toward maturity, which uses mathematics as an exact science and also as a means of description.

By being a formal system of signs and rules, mathematics offers the possibility of translating in quantitative form factors and variables which, in their origin, were qualitative in nature. We no longer say "cold"; we say it is 32°F or 0°C. We don't say "go slow when driving in the city"; we say "the limit is 30 mph or 50 km/h."

To effect this translation into generally understood quantitative expressions, which have become part of our culture, it was necessary to have a quasi-revolutionary change in mentality. Three instruments have been vital in this change:

1. The advent of quantitative thinking based on metrics, as opposed to vague qualitative expressions
2. A translator system able to transform the apparently nonquantifiable qualitative expressions to the precision of single numbers
3. A mathematical structure, serving as an instrument for calculation, which permits the manipulation and control through numbers of the relevant facts of nature

The first relevant facts of an awakening science were those related to physical concepts and their variations, such as mass, force, speed, acceleration, and temperature. Logical constructs came much later. Let's, however, not fail to appreciate the transformation. Without new concepts we wouldn't have developed anything else. Without the translator we would have had no measuring instrument. Without the mathematical structure, calculation would have been impossible. The history of scientific and technical discovery teaches that as humans we are rather poor in creative imagination and independent thinking. We need a framework within which we can act and produce.

The New Empire of Logical Entities

Inference is the lesser known understructure of the larger domain which includes decision making and, as well, scientific thought. Inference is both an act and a process: How to use approximate reasoning strategies to arrive at a valid estimate of a situation while having uncertain data and imperfect rules.

It is existence and reality we wish to comprehend. To do so, we have to establish connections between the facts of experience. They must be such that we can predict further occurrences from those already experienced. Some think the full accomplishment of this task is the only end of the scientific effort.

Seen as the greater system which has incorporated science, technology has been born from steadily evolving concepts, the links we establish between facts and experience, the prediction capabilities we provide ourselves with, the measuring instruments we develop, and the research we do for the improvement of our instruments in order to obtain greater accuracy and precision in our endeavors.

Modern machines are the descendants of the basic idea that inside nature, within an aggregate which supposedly contains chaotic, uncertain, and nonquantifiable elements, there exists a subtle numerical code which is precise and unitary. To control nature and put its forces at our disposal, the machines which we make must be just as precise. Technology is given the task of making them precise.

Science provides us with theories. The main attraction of a theory lies in logical completeness. If any one of the conclusions drawn from a theory proves wrong, the whole theory must be given up, because to modify it without destroying the whole structure is impossible.

It would not be the first time that happened, nor will it be the last. Our theories must change as we become better able to *comprehend reality*. Precisely the same thing is true of managerial and professional decisions—and therefore of the inference mechanisms to which this chapter is devoted.

As managers, professionals, scientists, and technologists, we are always on the lookout for the simplest possible system of thought which will bind the observed facts together. The *simplest system* is not the one which the average man will have the least trouble assimilating. It is the one which contains the fewest possible mutually independent postulates or axioms.

The special aim we must constantly keep before us is *logical unification*. Let's always recall, as Einstein observed, that the content of logical, mutually independent axioms represents the remainder which is not comprehended. Logical unification was first applied as a principle in the field of physics, and hence in the physical world. That happened not in ancient Greece, Egypt, Babylon, or Rome, but in our current civilization during the last two centuries. The concept did not exist in the ancient world, and that for no strange reason. The prevailing thought among ancient philosophers was that nature could not be mathematically expressed but the dimensions of the earth could be.

Hence, there was the development in Egypt (and this for taxation purposes) of the first great mathematical concept, that of *geometry*. Based on the evolving unitary laws and the metrics supporting them, Euclid subsequently developed the first *systems concept* on earth.

The fact remains that ancient thought did not retain the numbering system as applicable to the physical sciences. Many centuries passed before mathematics, in the algebraic sense we consider it today, turned into a larger systems reality, and many more centuries passed before an aggregate of laws of thought became part of our nature.

We should appreciate this step-by-step evolution. Geometry was and is a great mathematical system. It gave birth to other developments such as trigonometry, which made possible the study of celestial bodies. But geometry is not directly applicable to physics and chemistry, nor can pure logical thinking carry us far without the appropriate mathematical understructure.

Pure logical thinking cannot yield knowledge of the empirical world. Our knowledge of reality starts with experience and ends in it. Galileo (1563–1642) saw this and brought it forward into the scientific world of his time, thus becoming the father of modern science.

A system of theoretical physics is made up of:

- Concepts
- Fundamental laws, which are supposed to be valid for the concepts
- Conclusions to be reached by logical deduction

Not only must these conclusions correspond with our experiences but the system of laws itself must be describable—and also described—in a formal manner.

For formal descriptions in the physical world we needed algebraic approaches and differential calculus. We have them thanks to centuries of steady effort. We have also experienced their culmination in the peak of physical achievement: the splitting of the atom. It would not have been possible without mathematical breakthroughs.

The great system of algebra is not necessarily applicable in the logical domain, which needs mathematical approaches suited to its own requirements. The laws of thought are not the laws of physics. The structure of any system is the work of reason. Empirical contents and their mutual interaction must find their representation in the conclusions of a theory. In such a representation lies the value of and justification for the whole system.

Today in the implementation of laws of thought we find ourselves at a stage quite similar to the one in which physicists and chemists lived and worked after the alchemy years had ended and serious work began to be done in the sixteenth century. The new Galileo Galilei is not yet known. What we do know are some basic logical equations. They are four in number and easy to remember:

1. Inference + knowledge = intelligent system
2. Context + information = knowledge
3. Rules + methodology = inference
4. Algorithm + data = computer program

They are written in a layered form, the upper layers being the more important and feeding on the lower ones.

There is a relation between knowledge engineering and data processing: The former has capitalized on what was achieved by the latter. That having been done, knowledge engineering moved onward. But there is also a stratified correspondence which is explained in Figure 28.

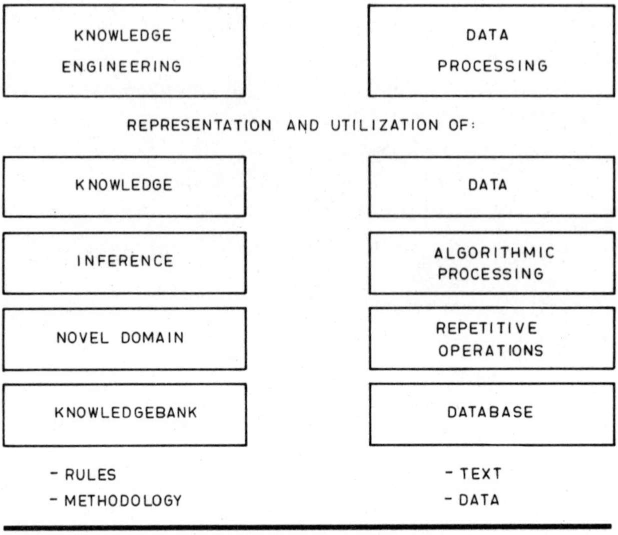

Figure 28 Knowledge engineering compared to classical data processing.

In the world of logical entities into which we are moving we will most likely have the same experiences with the physical sciences. The distance in thought between the fundamental concepts (including their laws) and the conclusions (which have to be brought into relation with our experience) will grow larger.

But we can learn a lesson from the past. The simpler the logical structure the smaller the number of logically independent conceptual elements to support the structure. When the number has become small, idealized logical inference will be reaching maturity.

Models and Modeling

The logical inference engine is a high-level interpreter. That contrasts it to the better known mathematical model which, in the general case, is a simulation of real entities. However, because experience so far has been heavy with modeling and light with logical inference, I start with the former concept.

We try to make for ourselves, in the fashion that suits us best, a simplified and intelligible picture of the world. We then try to some extent to substitute this cosmos of ours for the world of experience, and thus to overcome it.

A reference model may be drawn of a complex system and used to evaluate performance, study failure probabilities or uptime, or represent the interaction between subsystems given normal and/or exceptional operating conditions. Figure 29 is a reference model of a system for computer-aided design.

A model of reality is a theory which represents things themselves and not merely the probability of their occurrence. Various models can be used to describe and reason about a physical system. For instance, we can construct a functional model which bases a prediction of its behavior on the functioning of its components.

To construct a functional model, we may assume that the components work correctly as prescribed and that controls are the way they should be. Once the model is in place, we can run the system it represents on a computer and study its behavior with reference to a variable we can change at will.

Reference models can be very helpful. By working interactively on the computer, a complete but not necessarily processing-efficient model should be drawn up. This will aid the designer in determining, for instance, database structure and functional modules for the prototype. Important elements of such a model are:

1. System context
2. Information elements
3. Essential functions
4. Functional specifications

The system context shows where the system will obtain and deliver information. The definition of the information elements can be used to

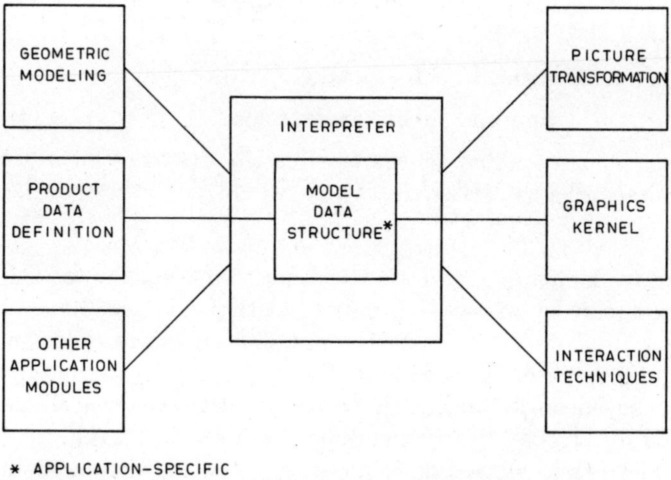

Figure 29 Reference model in a computer-aided design environment.

create a database structure outline. The designer need not be concerned with the possibility of the schema requiring changes as new needs and/or possibilities are discovered during prototyping.

When we are able to experiment with a reference model, information elements and data tables can be added or deleted online with little effort and no loss of stored information. The essential functions refer to what the system must perform to deliver required information when it is necessary.

A functional model may be represented in the form of rules, constraints, or degrees of freedom or complex programs which simulate the device in great detail. In fact, because of this property, functional models have been an active research topic in artificial intelligence for some time.

A somewhat different way to look at a system is through a causal model. Here the task is to represent the causal connections between various properties of system components. The causal model does not need to know how each of the components actually works. It offers a more abstract view of a machine. This is effective for diagnosis, particularly in cooperation with a functional model.

Through the power of abstraction, models provide insight into important characteristics of complex systems. Therefore, they can be used to help in:

- Rigorous, tractable characterization of, or approximation to, engineering systems
- Insights into complex products requiring analysis and/or testing
- Evaluation of different alternatives in allocating resources and their aftermaths
- Experimentation possibilities in a financial environment
- Optimization in production and inventory systems
- A high level of abstraction that makes feasible the discovery of individual differences and inconsistencies which would not otherwise be apparent

Insights obtained by modeling lead to better understanding, the testing of theories, and a consistent, well-structured design. Models have a potentially strong impact on management decision in many fields of implementation and in practical direction.

Models can be based on deterministic or probabilistic criteria. They can use heuristic rules, focus rules, inspection rules, or solution rules. All of them have been tried at some time in artificial intelligence, and some of them with expert systems. We have defined heuristics. In the case of focus rules, a grouping takes place into rule sets which are associated with context. Inspection rules establish an interface between heuristics and deep reasoning. They associate a number of observable symptoms with a causal network.

In contrast, solution rules associate symptoms directly with solutions and make a distinction between primary and secondary symptoms. The aim of deep reasoning is to find explanations for anomalies by using the causal network.

Backward reasoning is based on a couple of principles: First, if the effect of a property is normal, then there is reason to believe that the property itself is normal. Second, if the effect of a property is anomalous, the property may itself be anomalous. In this sense, the deep-reasoning algorithm starts from an anomalous property, and then the causes of the property are investigated until observable facts are arrived at.

Backward reasoning hypothesizes a conclusion and works backward from "thens" to find antecedent "ifs" that support them. Whether in forward or backward reasoning, the Esystem may make use of *backtracking*. This means that, when the system reaches an obstacle, for instance, a dead end in a search, it backs up and tries to follow a different line.

This procedure has a major impact on the need for *explanation facilities*. Because many Esystems explore different states, follow alternate search paths, use a number of rules, and so on, it is not immediately obvious to the user just how the expert system reasoned. It is therefore helpful to arrange for a facility to explain and justify the system's reasoning. In that way the user can evaluate how the Esystem is working. Simple explanations consist of listing the steps taken through the problem space; others include the reason for taking those steps; and still others incorporate the justification procedure.

A quite important issue in computer-based reasoning is the fact that, unlike people, Esystems assume they operate in a closed world. They work on the hypothesis that their knowledge of the domain is complete and adequate. The man-machine dialog examines properties the system has (or thinks it has) under control. Queries are posed by the system to the user about these properties:

- If they are anomalous, an explanation has been found.
- If they are normal, the explanation for the original anomaly lies in other domains and must be investigated.

This man-machine communication is the core of expert systems design. That is, the machine queries the user; the user answers the machine; and the machine uses the user's answers to build its knowhow, understand the situation, reach a conclusion, give advice, and document the advice.

Models also pose requirements. They demand that collected data or observations from existing implementations (or simulations) be used to drive the model. Alternatively, people cognizant of the situation respond to the model's demands. This is the sense of interactivity.

In classical experimentation, as cannot too often be repeated, valid data represents 80 percent of a model's success. At the same time, the algorithmic part, if it is done hastily, haphazardly, and imprecisely, will produce misleading and grossly incorrect results.

A similar statement can be made about the equation:

$$\text{Inference} + \text{knowledge} = \text{intelligent system}$$

The inference engine is very important, but knowledge is even more important because it constitutes the key to success.

In classical modeling, say, engineering work will be modeled in terms of text and data in databases containing records created and manipulated by computer-aided design. Such models typically involve

- Procedural steps
- Operands (units of information)

They emphasize the task-oriented nature of office work. Each procedure is designed to perform a particular task. The models also identify important and often unpredictable roles played by component functioning.

With expert systems, and artificial intelligence at large, the frame of reference is somewhat different. There is no procedural component—whether we talk of heuristics or of the second-generation inference engines. But there are operands which we must define and supply to the intelligent machine.

The Sense of Logical Inference

First the fundamentals. We said that the knowledgebank contains rules:

- Tens of rules for simple expert systems
- Hundreds of rules for Esystems of middle complexity
- Thousands of rules for Esystems of great complexity, for which we have as yet neither the technology for development nor the necessary computer power in logical instructions per second (LIPS)

An educated guess is that a system with fewer that 10 rules is in the DSS category, one with 10 to 50 rules is a simple Esystem, one with 50 to 200 rules is above average, and one with 200 to 800 or 1000 rules is rather sophisticated. That's about where we stood in 1986, but not everything depends on the number of rules.

Beyond 1000 rules we sometimes talk of *expert support systems* (ESS). Figure 30 integrates these observations into a layered structure, which includes the evolution from DP (first batch, then realtime) to Esystems and ESS. The dashed line divides the Esystems into classes. It is wise to decide on which side of the dashed line a new project is to be.

This issue having been settled, the next critical question arises: *Is "rule" synonymous with "logical inference"*? Some knowledge engineers say "roughly yes," but that is not quite accurate. Indeed the rules are used by the Esystem to make logical inferences. But there is also the methodology to account for. Hence the third fundamental equation is written as:

$$\text{Rules} + \text{methodology} = \text{inference}$$

The components of a full-fledged expert system, says Richard Forsyth, are (1) the knowledgebank, (2) the inference engine, (3) the knowledge acquisition module, and (4) the explanatory interface. Forsyth adds: "All four modules are critical. While a knowledge-based system may lack one or two of them, a truly expert system should not."

We have spoken of the knowledgebank, its inference engine, and also the human window. The knowledge acquisition module is actually a *knowledge acquisition method*, and there are other methodologies embedded in the knowledgebank.

The general presentation of a rule written in literature (and in the expert systems) is:

```
IF <hypothesis> THEN <action> ELSE <other>
```

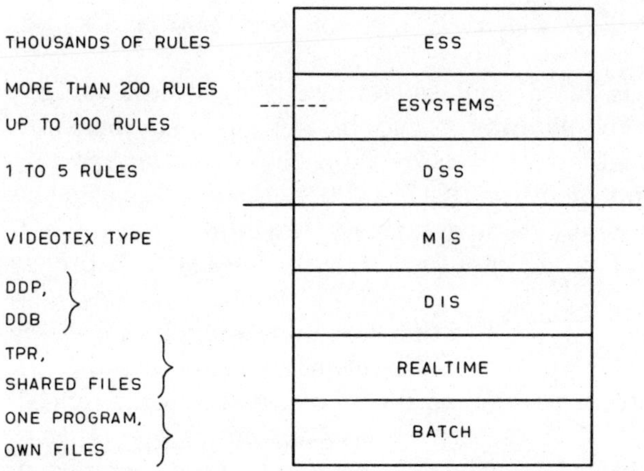

Figure 30 A layered structure in expert systems applications development.

But this is only an example, not a rule on rules. There are many ways of expressing rules. Some have to do not so much with the ingenuity of the designer as with the language we are using. The language we employ forms our mind and guides our hand:

- *EMycin* (a shell) allows simple rule description. It does not involve a pattern machine.
- *Lisp and Prolog* permit the expression of more complex structures, including pattern machines.

In short, there is no well-known standard to say "as a rule, this is a rule." As an alternative, the concept of logical inferences is used, which is a process description approach. As such, it has embedded in it the methodology.

Rules and methodologies are used for a problem-solving paradigm. The methodology organizes and controls the steps taken to reach a conclusion, solution, or consultation. One commonplace but powerful example is the chaining of if-then-else rules to form a line of reasoning.

- If the chaining starts from a set of conditions and moves toward some even remote conclusion, the method is called *forward chaining.*
- If the conclusion is known, or is a goal to be achieved, but the path is unknown, we work backwards. This method is called *backward chaining.*

Forward chaining is a rather natural direction for problem solving when data or ideas is or are a starting point. Hence, it has been used in expert systems for analysis, design, diagnosis, concept formation, and similar activities.

Backward chaining is more applicable when a hypothesis or goal is the starting point. In planning situations, for instance, backward chaining works from goals to subgoals by using the action side of rules to deduce the condition side of the rules. A different way to make those statements is that forward chaining involves reasoning from data to hypotheses. Backward chaining tries to find data to prove or disprove a hypothesis.

Pure forward chaining may lead to unfocused questioning in a dialog. Pure backward chaining may tend to be relentless in its goal-directed activities. Another problem with forward chaining (without appropriate heuristics for pruning) is that we derive everything possible whether we need it or not. A problem with backward chaining (without appropriate heuristics for guidance) is the handling of conjunctive subgoals.

Alternatives in Chaining Solutions

There is as well *sideways chaining*, sometimes called the *rule value* approach. It uses neither forward nor backward chaining, which tends to concentrate on data and hypotheses. Instead, it addresses itself to evidence:

- For each item of evidence it assigns a value. This is the value of the rule in the process of inference.
- Then it first asks the question with the highest value.

The Esystem concentrates on asking questions which seem important to it. Based on the answers, it continuously modifies its ideas of what questions are important. In a way, that is how human experts behave. The problem is how to define an important question. That is done by calculating the value of each item of evidence. One weight can be the sum of the maximum probability shifts which can be induced in the population of hypotheses currently in the knowledgebank.

We can also use a *combination* of *forward and backward processing*, particularly when the search space is large. One approach is to search both from the initial state and from the goal or hypothesis state by utilizing a relaxation type of solution to match an intermediate point. Let's always recall that neither forward nor backward chaining is problem-free.

With *forward pruning* not all successors are searched. Search is made in the more promising branches to a deeper level. Much depends on how far the node is from the finish—an approach known as best-first search and hill climbing. A distinction is also made in terms of optimistic-pessimistic (marginal) forward pruning.

Notice should be taken of the *alpha-beta procedure*, also called backward pruning. It features a modified depth-first generation. It produces results equivalent to depth-first minimax, but it creates a smaller fraction of tree. The algorithm is:

- When max-position $\leq$ alpha; alpha cutoff
- When min-position $\geq$ beta; beta cutoff

To attack a conjunction, we must find a case in which all interacting subgoals are satisfied. Such a search can often result in a combinatorial explosion of possibilities if appropriate domain heuristics and suitable inference schemes are not found for all types of problems to achieve an efficient Esystem.

Inference that proceeds from greater abstraction to less abstract (more detailed) statements, is *model-driven*. Vander Mees has said that God is in the detail. Detail means clarification, concretization, and definition. When we are moving from more abstract to less abstract symbolic statements, we are generating expectations: The problem-solving behavior is *expectation-driven.* This too is a fundamental concept in expert systems research. Sometimes a problem-solving approach is to work from the bottom up: from the details (specific problem data and definitions) to the greater levels of abstraction. An approach in this direction is said to be *data-driven.*

If we choose our next step on the basis of either some new information or the last problem-solving step which was taken, we are responding to events. This activity is said to be *event-driven.* The event-driven methodology is similar to forward chaining, except that the situation (or data) is evolving over time. As a result, the next step is chosen either on the basis of new information or in response to a changed situation resulting from the last problem-solving step which was taken.

Knowledge engineers consider that an event-driven approach is appropriate for realtime operations. It is also applicable to dynamic planning problems. Furthermore, since the expert system must reason with uncertainty in knowledge or data, numerical techniques can be utilized. Alternatively, uncertainties can be handled by incorporating a form of backtracking.

Numeric procedures have been developed to handle approximations by combining evidence. Mycin employs certainty factors related to probabilities. It uses the range of 0 to 1 to indicate the strength of the evidence. Another possibility is *fuzzy set* theory, which also is based on possibilities. We will return to this issue.

Search Strategies

Search strategies are methodologies for generating candidate solutions and for testing acceptability. For any problem with practical value, exhaustive search is not feasible.

In early artificial intelligence systems, search was heuristic. A new generation of solutions advanced the concept of dependent knowledge to limit search. Different methodologies are necessary when the Esystem is destined to work in a small search space or a large search space.

Small search space is characteristic of straightforward problems, limited problem dimensions, and cases in which a given problem can easily be divided into smaller semi-independent parts. Then a single line of reasoning is sufficient, and the direct approach of exhaustive search can be applicable.

Backtracking is not necessary. Reasoning is often done by elimination.

- Rules generate possible solutions.

- Other rules (tester) prune the solutions that fail to meet preestablished criteria.

This is known as the *generate-and-test* method, and it was one of the earliest methods to be implemented. A good example is Dendral. It runs a plan-generate-test sequence and uses forward chaining. It:

- Derives necessary constraints
- Systematically generates candidates
- Tests candidates against experimental results

The first two steps are encoded as tables of production rules. The second step particularly is encoded as a special procedure. This special procedure is to look at the global database of partially structured chemical compounds. Its production system searches down an AND/OR tree. There is no unstructured formula termination condition. The premises in this tree structure are:

$$\text{Arcs} = \text{rules}$$

$$\text{Nodes} = \text{databases}$$

At least at the database level, the problem is divisible. The arcs provide connecting links.

Complex problems which are indivisible call for a methodology able to handle *large search space*. Exhaustive reasoning by elimination would be topheavy, and therefore it is no longer appropriate. More powerful techniques are necessary.

A hierarchical generate-and-test approach may be effective if means are available for evaluating only partially specified candidate solutions. If so, early pruning of whole branches of reasoning representing an entire class or entire classes of solutions can be done. This greatly reduces the required search.

Another method with large search spaces is the so-called *dependency-directed backtracking*. It means tracing inconsistencies and logical errors to the steps of the inference that created them. Dependency records determine what to invalidate. A conceptually simpler approach is *chronological backtracking*. Its method is backtracking to the most recent choice point and starting on a new logical search path from there.

We have said that if it is possible to divide the problem into noninteracting subproblems, we can obtain smaller search spaces. However, few complex real-life problems fall into this class. Most common is the case of *interacting subproblems* in which valid solutions cannot be found independently. Methodologies have been devised to take advantage of the smaller search spaces associated with this environment. One of them is to find a fixed sequence of subproblems so that no interactions occur. R1, the Esystem for configuring VAX computers, successfully takes this road.

Another methodology is *least commitment.* It coordinates decision making with the availability of information and then moves the focus of problem-solving between the defined subproblems. Decisions are postponed until there is enough information to reach them. For instance, in a planning problem we may assign a partial ordering of operators in each subproblem. We will complete the ordering only when sufficient data on the interactions of the subproblems is developed.

Results with Different Search Procedures

Still another methodology is *constraint propagation.* It represents the interaction between subproblems as constraints. The latter are viewed as partial descriptions of entities or as subgoals (relationships) that must be satisfied.

Constraint propagation can also be viewed as a mechanism for moving information between subproblems. Through the introduction of constraints rather than by choosing particular values, the knowledge engineer is able to pursue a least-commitment approach. *Plausible reasoning* (guessing) is still another method. It is an inherent part of dealing with interacting subproblems. If the guess is wrong, other methodologies such as dependency-directed backtracking can be used.

Another way to approach a large search space is to develop alternative or additional spaces. An example is *employing multiple models.* A complex search can be simplified through the use of alternative models for either all or part of the problem. SYN is a good example of an Esystem which combines the strength of multiple models by using equivalent forms of electric circuits.

Another approach is *meta reasoning.* It works by adding additional space layers to a given search space to help decide what to do next. Examples are the focusing and scheduling of meta rules in Crysalis and the use of a strategy space in Molgen.

There are also approaches to dealing with time in terms of *time intervals*; for example, situational calculus was an early approach by McCarthy and Hayes for representing sequences of actions and their effects. It employs the concept of situations which change:

- When sufficient actions have taken place
- When new data indicates a situational shift is appropriate

Thus situations determine the context for actions. Through the use of frames (discussed in the following chapter) we can indicate what is changing and what remains the same when an action takes place. For monitoring patient breathing, VM employs the situation approach.

Planning premises can be handled through a *time constraint* approach. As a planner Esystem, Noah dealt with interacting subgoals.

The method of least commitment and backward chaining initially produced a partial ordering of operators for each plan. The planner adjusted the ordering of the operators to resolve interferences when interference between subgoal plans was observed. This produced a final parallel plan with time constraints.

A further possibility is a *unification algorithm.* It finds the sequence of substitutions to be made to reduce to clauses that are resolvable. It fails only if no such sequence exists. Resolution with unification can be a complete method of inference.

The examples which we have considered involve *search procedures.* From the discussion it is evident that these are a combination of:

- Evaluation function (generally static)
- Backup approaches
- Search tree solutions
- Chaining possibilities
- Generation procedure(s)

There are also *refinement strategies* resting on algorithms that selectively choose resolutions. Refinement strategies fall into three classes: syntactic, semantic, and ancestral.

Chapter

9

Induction, Deduction, and Fuzzy Logic

"A shortcut is the longest distance between two points." A LESSON FROM EXPERIENCE

A Plan of Action

For the solution of any problem we must have available a plan of action and a set of operators. Each operator executes an activity that might take the program closer to the goal, that is, its solution. In a computer search, we typically try operators until the goal is reached. For instance, a heuristic search will be guided by algorithms for estimating values of operators or sequences of them after an operator is applied. Thus, an operator is rated valuable if it reduces the difference between the current and the desired state or helps make another valuable operator applicable. But we also need the services of a representation system that makes inferences of new facts.

Induction and deduction are methodologies providing for resolution and unification—and thus leading to refinement strategies. The chaining alternatives we examined in the preceding chapter come under this master plan leading to logical inference. For instance, a refinement may be working backwards from conclusion toward hypothesis (backward chaining). We need a methodology to develop a production system. This will typically be an orderly set of rules called production of form:

- Condition → action
- If → then
- Situation → action

Note that action is not restricted to inference. Production usually refers to and alters the contents of the working memory. It could, for example, use predicate calculus. Important is the work flow:

1. Iterate over rules
2. Resolve conflicts
3. Pick which rule to fire
4. Execute and reiterate

Expert systems software does not employ DO and GO TO statements. The whole program is encoded in conditional action.

The second-generation expert system not only uses rules but also has a model of the domain. In this manner, deeper reasoning is possible if the rules are inadequate. A learning component looks at the result of deeper reasoning and abstracts new rules from it. This method is called rule learning by progressive refinement.

Theorem proving, program synthesis, and robot planning are examples of a problem reduction process through the setting of subgoals the achievement of which will secure the overall goal but which require interfaces that are subject to refinement. They also call for an overall strategy so that the subgoals do not conflict with or deviate from the master plan.

Although knowledge acquisition and automated reasoning can be regarded as separate entities, machine learning for them can also be seen as a refinement of earlier expert systems. That is particularly true of the process of learning to adapt rules, algorithms, and strategies based on past performance. Learning can take many forms:

- Whenever error occurs
- When inference exceeds a priori set level(s)
- By being programmed
- By being told
- Through the study of examples
- By means of self-sufficient discovery

To learn, the Esystem may use deductive inference, inductive inference (learning from experience), or reasoning by analogy across the problem area.

A program should not conceptualize the field in a different way from the experts in that field, but it should provide the framework in which experts can contribute their own knowledge. The modules of an Esystem should conform as well as possible to rational human thought processes and thereby produce reasonable and acceptable results when descriptive and formal considerations are properly balanced.

This process is embedded in the refining portion of a problem-solving system. Production rules, general principles, characteristics, circuit facts, assertions, information elements, and a rule interpreter are key component parts. The same thing is true of the methodologies we will examine in the following sections.

Inductive and Deductive Approaches

It has been stated on several occasions that an expert system is based on a rather extensive body of knowledge about a specific problem area. When we say that we have succeeded in understanding a group of logical processes, we invariably mean that a *constructive theory* which covers the processes in question has been found.

Besides the inference methodology applicable in a certain domain (we are not yet ready to talk of pure theories), there exists a concept we can borrow from the physical sciences. It regards a set of what Einstein called *principle theories.*

Principle theories employ the analytic, not the synthetic, method:

- The elements which form their basis (even the starting point) are not hypothetically constructed but empirically discovered.
- Such elements present general characteristics of processes, principles that give rise to mathematically formulated criteria.
- Separate processes, or the theoretical representations of them, have to satisfy the processes and associated criteria.

The advantages of a constructive theory are completeness, adaptability, and clearness. Those of a principle theory are logical perfection and security of foundations. Even at this early stage in the development of inference engines, both theories (or their logical approximations through methodologies) are important in our work. A general theory in the domain of logical processes divides them into two broad classes: *inductive* and *deductive*. Expert systems broadly fall into these two classes:

1. *With* deductive *approaches the rules are assigned in advance by the developer.*

Their environment is fairly stable in characteristic rules, which is sometimes a limiting factor. The basic concept behind a deductive process is presented in Figure 31.

As we will see in the following section on fuzzy logic, today we have the alternative of a machine that reasons from analogy, not deduction,

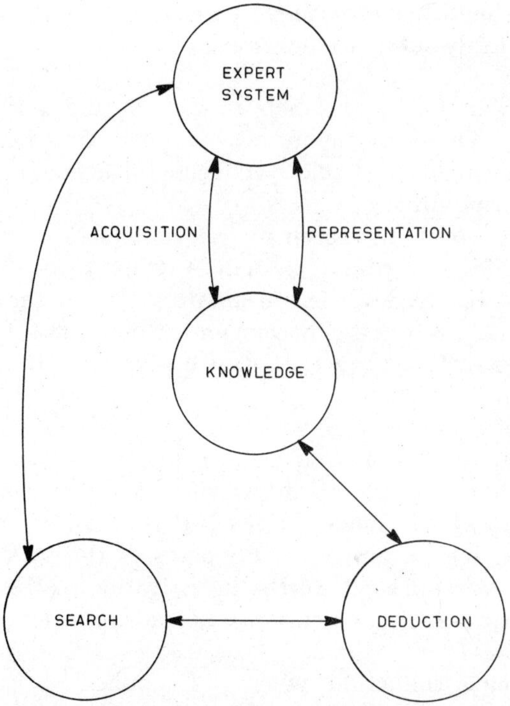

Figure 31 The basic concept behind a deductive process.

and applies experience gained from past situations to new ones. In the process, it formulates new insights and develops new knowledge.

2. Inductive *solutions tend to develop their own rules and methods that they find are appropriate and are in line with acquired experience.* Typically, their environments are not clear or are changed frequently.

Although the objective is to learn from experience, many inductive systems have no deep model which is the source of learning. Instead, operators are proposed to gradually peel features away to arrive at the essential properties of a concept or rule.

By inductive inference is meant the progression from statements describing particular events to a statement of universal form. In an inductive sense, a knowledge engineer would follow five basic steps: observation and recording of all facts, analysis and classification of the facts, inductive derivation of generalizations from the facts, testing of the generalizations, and implementation of the resulting kernel.

Inductive inference can be used to detect and rectify inconsistencies, remove redundancies, cover gaps, and simplify rules, says Michalski.

But there are also problems. The difficulty with *consistency checking* is that many inconsistencies are fairly subtle to detect even by a cognizant person.

Furthermore, if we had to wait for all the facts to be collected, our project would never get going. There are an infinite number of facts. We can then say that only relevant facts should be collected. But which are the relevant facts in a starting project?

We have no hypotheses to guide us in search for relevant facts, nor do we have, in the logical domain, a coordinate system of reference such as the one available in physics. In physics, the coordinate system is the body to which events are spatially referred. The movement of a vehicle is considered with reference to earth's surface; that of a planet, to the totality of the visible fixed stars.

The laws of the mechanics of Galileo and Newton could be formulated only with the aid of a coordinate system. And we also know that the state of motion of such a system may not be arbitrarily chosen if the laws of mechanics are to be valid. We have not reached this point of physical perfection in handling logical processes. Poppes sees the task of the logic of knowledge as consisting solely of the investigation of the methods employed in systematic tests, to which every new idea must be subjected.

In spite of the criticism made, induction, when it is applicable, is a good strategy because it can produce a bank of rules quickly. Also, it accounts for all cases in the database. The knowledge engineer, in contrast, may fail in this respect. Michalski and Chilausky compared machine-induced with expert-derived rules for diagnosing grain diseases. Their finding was that the expert's first set of rules covered only some 80 percent of cases.

Semantic Networks

Together with the methodologies which were covered in the preceding section, the fundamental background processes of induction and deduction assist the knowledge engineer in representing ordinary language and general knowledge in ways a computer can understand. We can build *semantic networks* capable of being incorporated in a computer program that enables the machine to make human-like connections among the concepts it is treating. Expressed in a simple manner, the semantic network is a chart that sets out connections among entities so that a computer can follow from that point on. This enables the system to manipulate the relations among objects and their attributes.

To cope with general knowledge, some designers have tried to use *scenarios* or *scripts*. The idea is that when people think (or speak), they draw from reservoirs of framed references (or stories) which instantly put a piece of information or a problem into a context. So researchers have tried to write some of those stories into a form that a computer can understand. At Yale University, De Jong developed a program which can write a news item. It does so by calling on scripts contained in the computer.

Not everybody agrees with the scripts approach as one of general applicability. A major objection is that there are so many possible scripts that only a few could be incorporated in a computer. They would be more useful, this argument goes, if computers could use them as precedents to understand new situations. This idea has been tested in *Macbeth*, which turns the story into a pattern of causes and effects. A computer working on this track would, in a sense, be reasoning by analogy.

Scripts evolved from another notion: *frames*. As discussed in Chapter 5, a frame is a data structure for describing a stereotyped situation. Frames are an attempt to impose formal structure on ordinary thought and language. The approach rests on the premise that we can reduce whole categories of actions and descriptions to a manageable number of basic references.

At Yale University, working along similar lines, Schank divides all action into two classes:

1. *M-trans*, the transfer of mental information
2. *A-trans*, the transfer of actual (meaning physical) objects

The aim is to allow English language sentences to be recast and represented in a form that a computer can manipulate. The background idea is one of *conceptual dependence*.

Finally, one of the arguments about the design of inference engines has to do with the size of rules. It can be simply stated in these terms: How many conditions and how many actions should there be to a rule? So far, this has been a problem for the knowledge engineer. Rules can always be made:

- Bigger, hence more nearly all inclusive
- Smaller, by inserting intermediate states

Rule size is a function of the level of detail at which an Esystem represents its concepts. Often, papers discussing this choice justify recommendations of a coarse or a fine granularity by the size of rule that it entails.

Barstow suggests that small grain size facilitates the intelligent use of knowledge because the pieces are more understandable. He adds: "If a rule is too big, it's wrong." To the contrary, Lenat and McDermott propose Esystem rules of coarse grain size. Their reason is that in this way each production process will be a meaningful unit. It will be easy for experts in that domain to understand. Waterman also recommends using a high level of granularity. Each argument has a background. This is additional evidence that meta rules—"rules about rules"—are still missing. The skill of the knowledge engineer is decisive.

Fuzzy Sets

Dealing with *uncertain data* is not a problem. It is an opportunity. This is where things start to get interesting, provided we have means of dealing with uncertainty.

The message carried by the statement about uncertain data should be read between the lines. It is important because it traces a division between models and inference engines. A model handles an idealized abstraction. Inference permits us to deal with uncertainty. Fuzzy logic, Bayesian logic, certainty factors, and multivalued logic are examples of the mechanism. Fuzzy sets theory provides a method of obtaining and handling essential subjective—and therefore ill-defined and ambiguous—information. Such information is typical of human cognition and reasoning.

Zimmermann stresses that, to characterize an aggregate system, *we first need a descriptive model, a paradigm.* This paradigm explains and describes the central aspects and their relations in a manner easy to understand. However, the essential features of the paradigm must be represented formally. This bears on the two essential aspects of the paradigm: the *subjective categories* and the *connections.* Here is where fuzzy sets come into the picture. Based on his work at the Technical University of Aachen, Zimmermann suggests that suitable formal representations are given by fuzzy sets for the first class and by connectives of fuzzy set theory for the second class. But what are these fuzzy sets?

The concept was introduced by Bellmann and Zadeh.* They defined a decision in a *fuzzy environment* as the intersection of fuzzy sets representing either objectives or constraints. The grade of membership of an object in the common area of two fuzzy sets—that is, the fuzzy decision—was determined by use of either the min-operator or the product operator. This sounds too mathematical, written for scientists. It does not fit well in a management-oriented book.† Let's take a different

---

*R. Bellmann, L. A. Zadeh, "Decision Making in a Fuzzy Environment," *Management Science*, **17** (1970), pp. 141–164. Zadeh had also published a seminar paper at University of California, Berkeley, in 1965.

†With apologies to the author, whose theory is, however, first class.

look at the issue, necessarily more verbal since we cannot benefit from the precise and concise language of mathematics.

First of all, *fuzziness* defines the following state of mind: We may not know exactly what we want, but we can describe the process of a weighted decision. The *fuzzy sets* are *qualifiers*. Their proper place in an expert system is that of an intermediate layer between known modeling solutions and the Esystems architecture which we have defined. Figure 32 shows this connection.

Let's not underestimate the future of fuzzy sets. An excellent example of fuzzy set application in the banking field is *Raroc* (Risk Adjusted Return on Capital), a system developed and used by Bankers Trust and currently marketed by DEC. Classically, loan officers in the banking industry approve or reject a loan. Raroc resembles a statistical sampling procedure with qualifiers. Rather than simply accept or reject, it establishes levels of acceptable risk with different interest rates applicable by level. This covers the marginal risk till the next level is reached.

Fuzzy sets have in the background a *fuzzy logic*, that is, a logic working with uncertainties. We can always put in some certainty factors, but the system is not given a definite path to reach conclusions. From the work done during World War II at Columbia University in connection with the Manhattan Project, we have a theory of mathematical statistics supporting a three-valued logic:

- Accept
- Continue test
- Reject

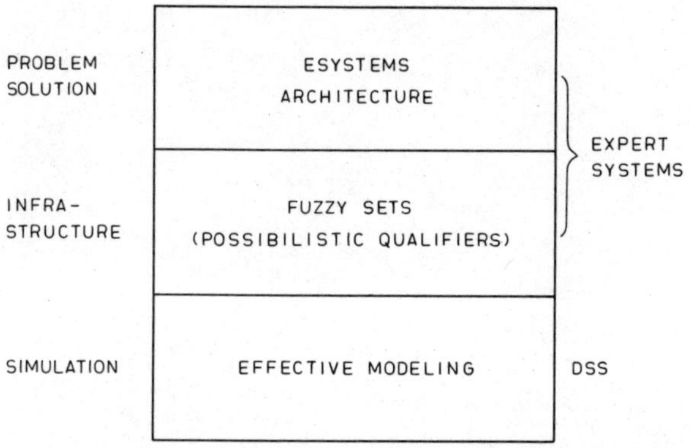

Figure 32 The place of fuzzy sets in an expert system: an intermediate layer between known modeling solutions and the Esystem architecture.

The theory can be nicely used by a goal-seeking, iterative search process. Binary solutions are not necessarily the only foundation of the laws of thought. We have two eyes, two ears, two hands, two feet, but one mouth and twenty digits—which were used in ancient Gaul as the base of a numbering system.

If there is an association to make between type of logic and type of system, we should say that the expert system has an infinite-valued logic and the computer a binary one. Figure 33 makes this point. Fuzzy logic can be three-valued, multivalued, or infinite-valued. The basic issue is that it admits the possibility of the real but unknown values, taking on any position in the interval between *true* and *false*. Usually, the latter are arbitrarily set to be 1 and 0.

Evidently important is the fact that, when defined in terms of their members, sets corresponding to fuzzy logic are not as crisp as typical black and white sets. Objects may be only partly included in a set, hence the term "fuzzy sets." The theory sounds great, and so it is. The trick is to try to deduce the certainty factor. It can be done and it has been done. Raroc is but one example.

The implementation of fuzzy sets may present a significant advantage. To prove a theorem or hypothesis or reach a conclusion, the expert system must show:

$$\text{Premise} = \text{conclusion}$$

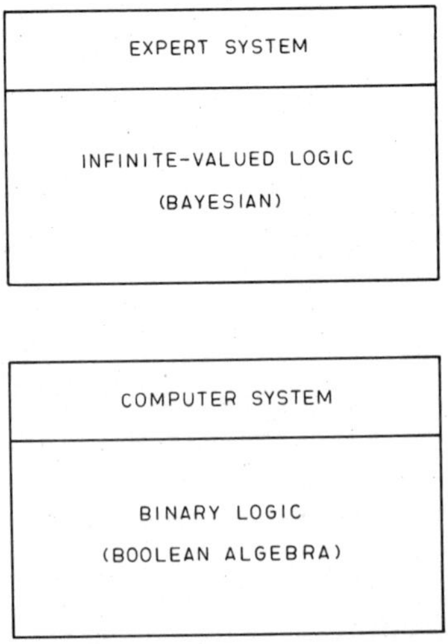

Figure 33 The expert system has an infinite-valued logic; the computer has a binary one.

To do so effectively, it should check all combinations. But by using fuzzy sets, it is possible to define a domain which has high and low boundaries. The domain establishes the extent to which the search must go.

A different way to make that statement is that the Esystem does *not* need to have everything organized in the usual clear-cut, true-or-false steps. Instead, data and decisions can be qualified with percentages that inject an element of probability, from very probable to likely, into the analysis.

Risk-Adjusted Solutions

Classical computer programs are useful in applications that require manipulation of precise data. But expert systems are designed to deal with a more realistic world in which information does not need to be manipulated so precisely—or judgment and evaluation can be only approximate.

By employing fuzzy logic, the Esystem has a greater chance of accurately following a perception prevailing in real life. Such approximate reasoning relies on linguistic variables, qualifiers, hedges, and *noise words*.

- "Cost," "measurement," and "volume" are examples of linguistic variables.
- "Low," "high," and "reasonable" are qualifiers.
- "Very," "quite," and "about" are hedges that can be used with qualifiers.
- Noise words are phrases such as "should be" that impact the readability of policy statements without affecting logical meanings.

A data dictionary residing in the Esystem can contain the names and definitions of qualifiers, hedges, and noise words to be used in a particular application. We can also create multiple vocabularies, each with a specific orientation.

Just the same, we can allow gradations of certainty. This is closer to human nature, and real-life decision making, than we might think. When we are forced to make black and white decisions, we cannot afford to be wrong. If we are wrong, we lose. Fuzzy sets are more forgiving. If we figure something is 70 percent blue, but it turns out to be 50 percent blue, we have not failed as badly as in a yes-or-no situation. Besides, it is not always feasible to package a complex field of knowledge into a series of neat little questions and base the result on only yes-or-no decisions pertaining to each of these questions.

Thus, fuzzy sets are *the* elegant approach not only when uncertainty dominates but also in other situations in which they help overcome knowledge acquisition difficulties. It is, however, important not to confuse process and structure. Figure 34 gives an example.

One of the important areas of fuzzy sets implementation is that of business and scientific problems which cannot be solved quickly through classical methods because of data overload. They range from airline scheduling to weather forecasting. Robotics also can profit, and so can design activities. Hitachi Ltd. has already tested a fuzzy logic automatic control system for trains projected to be used on Tokyo's commuter lines. At Kumamoto University, in Japan, Takeshi has designed an integrated circuit for processing fuzzy data.

There are other fields in which fuzzy logic implementation is expected to have advantages. One is *spatial reasoning*, for example, reasoning about space and object geometry to solve grasping, trajectory, and assembly problems in robotics. Others are *pattern recognition* and *sen-*

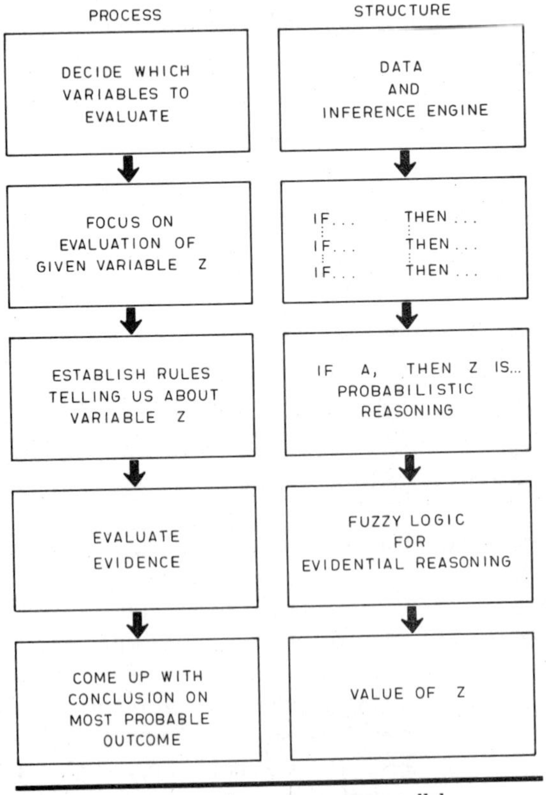

Figure 34 Process and structure run parallel courses. It is important not to confuse them.

sory reasoning about the capabilities of sensors and task requirements to solve sensor application problems and assimilate different sensory modalities.

Another field is *temporal reasoning*: reasoning over time to solve coordination and efficiency problems such as optimal scheduling. And, by extension, *task planning systems* combine spatial, temporal, and sensory reasoning to plan tasks efficiently and mediate their execution.

Financial type management decisions also are open to fuzzy sets. In fact, they may constitute the best example of an applications domain. They feature:

- Uncertainty
- Graded membership in a set of possibilities
- Nonmonolithic logic
- Possibly inconsistent multiple hypotheses
- No requirement for exclusivity
- No possibility for exhaustiveness
- Multivaried logic (true, false, intermediate)

Not only are these the characteristics of fuzzy set theory; they also tell by themselves what fuzzy logic is all about.

As stated in the preceding section, Bankers Trust based its design of Risk Adjusted Return on Capital (Raroc) on the following premise: Typically, when a borrower (company or individual) goes to a bank for a loan, a binary decision is made: "qualify/not qualify." Risk-adjusted approaches are not binary: They stratify and put a premium on risk ceiling by risk level.

Risk assessment aims to quantify dangers so that responsible officers can decide if a particular risk is worth running. Calculated risks covered by premiums *permit*:

- Expanding money and securities trading activities
- Further building up and marketing financial services

But, when implemented in a banking environment, new tools and methodologies also require maintaining and selectively enhancing the quality of services. There is today a growing interest in *service quality control*—just as, in the 1950s, statistical quality control invaded manufacturing.

Developing new information processing products to sustain new goals is a most worthwhile task. The trick with multivalued systems is having management decide where to draw the line between layers. Demands are also posed in information system perspectives:

- Online total committed position of the bank by credit risk
- Online total committed position of the bank by liquidity level and maturity
- Capital exposure data
- Interactive profitability evaluations
- No geographics limitations
- No time-zone constraints

Other demands are mathematical; they have to do with the proper implementation of probabilistic logic within a basically managerial process. The knowledge engineer should do this integration job in close coordination with the professional expert, who will be not only the adviser but also an integral member of the project team.

Machine Learning

Machine learning is an ambitious subject, but the phrase is ambiguous. It can mean something which is much more difficult than that which has so far been achieved with expert systems. Even to approximate machine learning, the Esystem must contain or use a criterion. A system can be said to learn if:

- It is capable of capturing material which is new knowledge
- Its performance improves according to established criteria when the job is repeated often enough

With this in mind, there can be some simple exercises in which an Esystem learns. The first is the case of *playing a game* with a finite number of moves. If winning and losing positions are given as data with appropriate scores attached, a criterion that high scores are better than low ones may enable a program to improve the quality of its play if it keeps a cumulative record of all moves and associated results.

Second, in real-life situations there may be *incremental learning*. Consider as an example a knowledge organization able to take care of cases which fit diagnostic criteria. We may wish machine learning to take this form: In addition to dealing with normal cases, the Esystem must be able to deal with unexpected ones.

This is a typical evolution from novice to expert. It requires humans to learn how to deal with exceptional cases, and it should be through incremental learning in which previously learned knowledge is put to use.

- When it fails, the reason for the failure is established.

- Through this process, previous knowledge can be debugged.
- Next time a similar problem is seen, new refined knowledge is applied to it.
- Hopefully, as a result of learning, the same failure will not happen again.
- Also, when previously learned knowledge is used successfully, the credibility of the rules being used must be reinforced.

The game example can also be called failure-driven incremental learning because the Esystem gains knowledge through a failure-driven process. This approach can be successful if key processes are properly considered. The basic steps are initial action, observing the result, noticing the failure, assigning blame to a specific rule, explaining the failure, correcting the failure, and updating the rule. Notice that next to action and the recording of outcome, the key step is *noticing the failure*. But there may also be an additional response to the action which is unexpected (as far as the Esystem is concerned). Such response must be recognized and further analyzed.

Whether an exception or a violation, a deviation can be explained and recorded only if it is recognized. The data dictionary must be rich for this purpose, the more so because there may be varying degrees of resemblance. A little more sophisticated approach would consider *cause, diagnosis, and effect* by way of prescription given by the expert system. In this case, explaining the failure would be more complex because linkages create a greater number of possibilities. As an example:

- The diagnosis was wrong, and therefore the prescription is unsatisfactory.
- The diagnosis was right, but the prescription was not appropriate to the diagnosis.
- The diagnosis was right, but the prescription did not work.
- The diagnosis and prescription were right, but something new has come up.

In finding the cause of this new deviation, the Esystem may learn to establish that an additional diagnosis has to be made. If it lacks the necessary information to make a more complete diagnosis, then one of four strategies can be followed:

1. Learning by example, or inductive learning.
2. Learning by analogy. This presupposes a large database or, even better, communicating databases and Esystem access to public databases where relevant references can be found.

3. Learning by requesting and taking advice from the knowledge engineer.
4. Learning based on self-made construction of approximate proofs.

Note that not all these solutions are distinct. There is some overlap, but no doubt the most intelligent solution is the fourth one.

As expert systems get more sophisticated, we may see cases in which systems learn by designing and carrying out experiments on their own. This will require the coverage of actions that must be performed further up in a hierarchy of contexts, given that each learning approach must have a context in which to work for any specific field of application.

Against the measure of practical application, *Metadendral* was the first implementation of machine-learning expert systems. It discovered rules of fragmentation in large organic molecules under mass spectrometry by generating possible candidate rules and seeking to verify them. This it did by looking through a library of cases.

As this successful experience documented, machine learning is within the realm of possibilities. The system found new rules that had not yet been discovered by any expert chemists. A series of papers for chemical journals was produced. Another Esystem, Lex, also demonstrated it could improve its problem-solving expertise through experience. It generated selected problems in its domain, solved them, and learned by analyzing their solutions. The method was to represent a plausible range of heuristics and induction to obtain, expand, or shrink the space associated with a given solution procedure.

Developing an expert system that can learn involves several problems. They range from how to learn rules and facts to how to learn new concepts and how to reorganize knowledge itself. However, as experience with intelligent machines accumulates, *learning to learn* will increasingly be seen as a requirement. More emphasis will be put on conceptualization and inference, passing through a stage of guided discovery learning.

Chapter

10

Languages and Shells for Expert Systems

"The other line always moves faster."
A FRUSTRATED DRIVER

The Concept behind the Use of Shells

Increased development and implementation of expert systems is dependent on the availability of adequate programming language shells. Choices are increasingly being conditioned by restrictions: the application area within which the Esystem domain falls, the possibility of and ease in expressing facts and relations pertaining to the problem, and language interfacing facilities.

The emphasis on documentation is repeated with linguistic choices, as is the ability to provide explanations of conclusions, clear lines of reasoning, prototyping capabilities, experience and expertise, and management and extension of the knowledgebank. No single language among those available will be able to do all that is required. This and the ability to provide friendly, easy-to-implement interfaces for the developer have been the reasons behind the development of *shells*.

One way to look at shells is to consider them Esystem toolkits of components. They help the increasing population of users to put expert systems together. But the problem of choice remains, and with it the problem of run time efficiency.

A shell can be quite helpful in developing an expert system for a specific application, provided it is well chosen. This means the characteristics of the application can be properly handled without introducing a great deal of generality.

Correct choice also means the available explanation and interaction facilities help speed up development and make prototyping feasible. As we will discuss in the appropriate section, a prototype is a real-life but not optimized system. It:

- Helps to clear the developer's ideas
- Is valuable for user feedback
- Can be helpful in projecting testing chores at an early stage

But shells also have disadvantages. They add an interface layer that requires its own resident interpreter. They are more general tools, and therefore they are not job-specific in a field based on specialization. Also, different projects in the organization might choose different shells, which would lead to a proliferation of programming languages with an aftermath of confusion from development to maintenance.

A choice of programming language cannot be independent of the purpose for which it is made. The purpose of the choice is dual: First, and better known, is the aim to program the machine. But there is also the underlying goal of providing a well-understood common ground for users, system analysts, and programmers (Figure 35).

The advice which I will give regarding the use of Esystems shell is no different than the one I have given in regard to the employment of high-powered fourth-generation languages, to which I fully subscribe:

1. *If* you have to do 1, 2, 5, 10, in general, only a few copies for PC or supermicro, use shells.

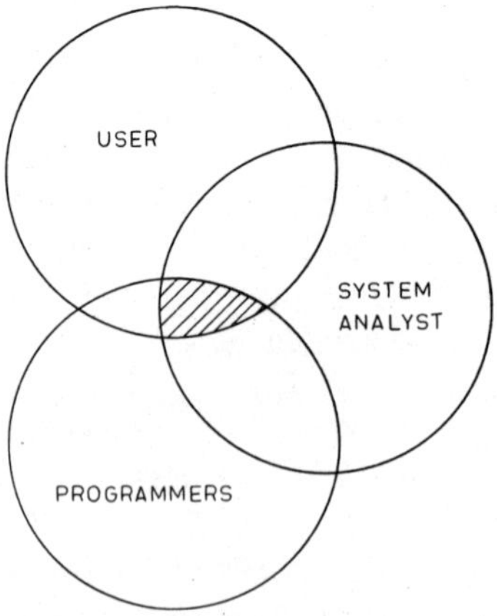

Figure 35 With classical approaches, only a small part of the interests that characterize users, system analysts, and programmers was common concept. With 4GLs we can achieve full coordination. The key is prototyping.

2. *If* you plan to spread the Esystem in the organization (as you should be doing) in 50, 100, 200, 500, 1000 or more installations, don't use shells, and hence compile at run time. Employ a precompiler.
3. However, for early experience, prototyping, and demonstrators, shells are fine. Just make an educated choice.

Waterman and Hayes-Roth have done a first-class study of six shells:* Mycin, Kas (Knowledge Acquisition System), OPS 5, RL1 (Representation Language), Hearsay III, and AGE (Attempt to Generalize). They have compared the shells with each other and also with two Esystem languages: Rosie and Expert. Theirs was a thorough investigation, and it is recommended reading for knowledge engineers. It offers both insight and perspective.

What we really need for the industrialization of knowhow are languages that are based on database programming systems and that have operation on both logical statements and data as a primary goal and calculation only a subsidiary activity. Ongoing technology makes it wise that they should have relational characteristics.

Eventually, as hardware-wired inference chips (an outgrowth of current AI contracts to chip manufacturers) become available, new programming languages will be characterized by a merger of programming features with the hardware inference logic and operating system. That is true of rule editing, databasing, data communications, and flow control characteristics as well.

Lisp, Prolog, and the Others

A number of knowledge representation languages are now available. The most popular artificial intelligence language is Lisp. Designed by John McCarthy, it is, in its original form, the first generation. Second-generation AI languages include Prolog (a French-British development), Planner and Conniver (from MIT), Fuzzy (from Rutgers), and Smalltalk (from Xerox).

I would be tempted to call shells a third generation of AI languages constructed at a higher-up level in a hierarchy of linguistic developments, which would be like comparing a DBMS front-end type 4GL to C, Pascal, or Basic. But then there is a whole group of in-between references to be made. These two-and-a-half-generation AI languages can be subdivided into groups:

*D. A. Waterman and Frederick Hayes-Roth: "An Investigation of Tools for Building Expert Systems," The Rand Corporation, Santa Monica, CA, 1982.

- Antecedence systems (Amord from MIT as an example)
- Frame-oriented systems (FRL from MIT, KL-ONE from BBN, KPL from Xerox)
- Factor-type languages (M-Actors from Kyoto, CSSA from Bonn)
- Production- and logic-oriented languages (OPS from CMU as an example)

Most of the enumerated first- and second-generation programming languages have had some further development. Let's start from the beginning. Lisp has proved itself in over 25 years of artificial intelligence research, but so far it has had no commercial success. It thrives in academic centers because it provides an effective research medium, but it lacks database management capabilities and for long years it has not been standardized.

By 1985 there were too many Lisp dialects. As a result, and to provide a standard ground, university people did a common subset, *Common Lisp*, and the Department of Defense (DOD) contracted to put it on a chip: *Lisp Engine*. The objective is to execute Lisp in microcode. IBM is also known to be working on a Lisp machine. The Japanese Fifth Generation Computer Project is developing a C/Prolog machine, *Personal Sequential Inference (PSI)*, but NEC is working on Lisp.

Lisp is not oriented to the end user, but for the knowledge engineer its advantages are simplicity and reasonable clarity. Given a working knowledge of a few basic facts and rules (and there are only a few), Lisp is a very flexible language. It is also indefinitely extensible.

Such flexibility is a two-edged sword. The knowledge engineer who does not like some of the facilities Lisp provides can write others and incorporate them into a personal version of Lisp. That is not good practice. It is mentioned only as an example of what might (but should not) be done with Lisp.

Flexibility and extensibility derive from native simple basic Lisp operations. The whole language works in small, easily understood chunks. Long, nonelegant junction constructs (familiar to users of other programming languages) are hard to duplicate in Lisp. A good Lisp program consists of a master routine with a number of associated subroutines. Most likely, none of the latter would be more than some twenty lines long, no matter how complex the overall structure.

As stated, the main disadvantage I can see with Lisp is the rather large number of dialects, each with its own pros and cons. All of them are similar, apart from a few very minor differences of syntax, but it is not good to have such variety and hence incompatibilities that make program portability difficult.

At the same time, providing a really common set is no trivial task because microcomputer Lisps are almost invariably written for specific machines and even models. But again that is true of every programming language. The various Lisp dialects available for microcomputers are subsets of the Common Lisp, which runs only on mainframes. There is no generally accepted standard for these subsets, because what one designer sees as a very desirable feature of Lisp may strike another as less relevant. Let's add that programs are written in Lisp to control robots. Research on vision recognition and speech recognition, both subjects related to AI, is done to a significant degree in Lisp.

We have seen that the AI and 5GL computer work in Japan is done in Prolog. European R&D laboratories also work in Prolog. But that is not to say that Prolog is the answer. As Forsyth suggested:* "If the Japanese do adopt it without radical modification (and the signs are that they will not), the West can relax till the end of the century."

The reasons given include very little protection against minor misspellings, the need for the user to understand implementation details of a backtracking mechanism, built-in predicates with side effects, the steady high-speed memory resident in the relational DBMS (the relational DBMS is a key advantage over Lisp and other competitors), and so on. This is written, not to discourage the use of Prolog, but to make prospective users careful in their choice.

Of the other second-generation languages mentioned in the beginning of this section, Smalltalk had an interesting development. It became the origin and basic reference for the Apple Lisa and Macintosh products, with their user-friendly graphics interfaces, pop-up menus, and similar features. But Smalltalk did not make it in the big league of AI language adoption by the expanding user population—though some researchers are in love with it.

I once had in a post-graduate seminar in Berlin a student whose mind was set: "Smalltalk or death." Putting to one side that such a one-track mind is unfit for a researcher, vendors of Esystems will be well advised to stay away from programming languages which are not very popular with users. The market votes with its dollars.

In conclusion, total programming capability is at a premium, but the language which has only advantages has not yet been invented. There are benefits to be obtained by merging the features of OS, DBMS, and programming structure with those pertinent to logical inferences. Some shells do so, but Esystem shells also have disadvantages.

---

*Richard Forsyth (ed.), "Expert Systems," Chapman and Hall Computing, London, 1984.

A valid strategy would be to use a shell for prototyping and then Lisp with a DBMS for run time processing. Some (but not yet many) Esystem development centers also think of passing from the shell to a 3GL like C or Pascal. The idea is interesting. It suggests we can program the machine at three levels:

1. Shell
2. Lisp
3. C

C is more appropriate as a 3GL choice if the Esystem runs on Unix and a relational DBMS like Ingres, Oracle, Informix, or Mistress. Pascal is a better alternative in the IBM world, because IBM is actively supporting it.

Expert System Shells

An expert system *shell* is a programming environment. It includes a number of components the user can apply to build an expert system, and it is mainly a prototyping tool.

Although there should be a knowledgebank for every application, shells are deficient in this respect. They contain *no* domain-dependent knowledge, but they support all the other facilities such as:

- Inference mechanism(s)
- Database access
- Natural-language dialog interfaces
- Procedural interfaces
- Explanation facilities

There are presently available several commodity shells, mainly from small U.S. start-up companies established by university professors but also including a German computer manufacturer. A shell becomes a complete expert system only when the appropriate domain knowledge is added by the knowledge engineer. Thus buying a shell does not automatically produce an Esystem solution, even if a commercial offering may include an elementary knowledgebank facility that can be used as a demonstrator.

Originally, shells were developed from particular Esystems by removing the knowledgebanks. An example is the development of EMycin (EmptyMycin) from *Mycin*. As a matter of fact, Mycin has given rise to a whole family of shells and new expert systems developed by using those shells (Puff, Sacon, Drilling Advisor, Wares, Teiresias,

Guidon). Other examples are Kas, Sage, AL/X, and Microexpert from *Prospector*.

To appreciate the design choices, let's focus for a moment on the last example. Microexpert consists of two programs: a rules language compiler called *Expcomp* and a run time module called *Runexpt*. To create a model, the user first writes the rules in the rules language, which resembles block diagramming. Rules are entered into the microprocessor and written to disk by using the standard UCSD Pascal system editor.

The procedure forms a source file which will be compiled by using Expcomp. This compiler produces two output files rather than the conventional file:

1. The *object file* contains the structure of the model in the form of tables which can be loaded into central memory and used at run time.
2. A *message file* contains all the ASCII text strings from the source.

According to the designers, the reason for the latter is that Esystems tend to contain large amounts of text. It is advisable not to hold the text in central memory, because the result would be to restrict the size of the model which could be handled on a microcomputer.

There are two features of Prospector the designers chose not to implement. First, at the beginning of a session Prospector asks the user for a list of the minerals encountered. It processes this list against a table giving synonyms of common minerals. Cox suggests that, at Microexpert design time, it was thought that this feature was too application-dependent to be generalized. But then he adds: "However, I am now not so sure that this was a good decision."

The second Prospector feature not implemented was the new semantic facility which allows the model writer to introduce new words to specify types of rocks. The designers felt one can get the effect wanted without specifically having this feature in an advice language. Now they have changed their minds and say the feature is a prime candidate for inclusion in future shell editions.

The changes of mind show how dynamic this field of expert systems shells is, but they are to the credit of the microexpert designers. They show how closely implementation is watched. "I eat my words and find them a very nourishing diet," Lord Allanbrook once said, "rather than stay on the wrong side."

On the other hand, the evolution from going Esystems has made some of the shells too limited to specific domains of knowledge. As a result, their orientation may be too dependent on the original Esystem's knowledge representation, their framework may not be suitable for general problems, their control structure may be inapplicable to another expert's reasoning, or task-specific knowledge may even have been included in the inference engine.

Commodity Shells and Toolkits

Historically the first commodity shell was AL/X. It was made available only in 1980, which suggests that shells are still evolving. It was followed by EMycin, Microexpert, and Sage. Since Prolog itself is not suitable as a shell for wider usage, some shells written in Prolog are being developed. Apes and ES/P are two examples currently available.

The use of a list-processing language for writing shells has its merits because many users of shells have expressed a need for the shell source code to be able to tailor the interface to their own requirements. Such tailoring is better done and the results are more efficient when finer programmatic interfaces are used.

Lisp, too, could be used for shell development. We can conceive a layered structure with a commodity shell at the top layer, followed by *toolkit* or arrays, strings, datatypes, DBMS functionality, and so on, and then Common Lisp. At the bottom of such a structure would be a hard-wired Lisp engine on a chip (Figure 36). Some technical literature tends to distinguish between shells and general-purpose linguistic tools developed on the basis of expert systems, for instance, Rosie from Mycin. These are being referred to as *toolkits*.

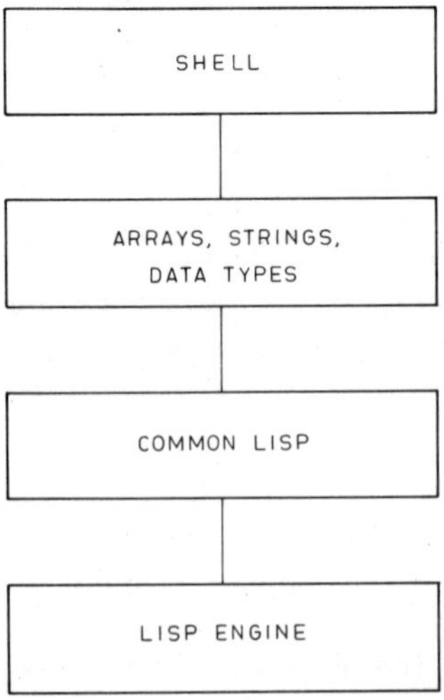

Figure 36 From the Lisp engine to the shell. Layers of implementation.

Age and *Hearsay III* are examples of early attempts at developing toolkits. In Hearsay III, different types of knowledge and different methods of reasoning can be applied almost independently to solve a problem. That approach started with Hearsay I and II, which were developed to interpret continuous speech. They required knowledge of everything from semantics to acoustics (hence, Hear/Say).

Hearsay III is in itself a three-layered structure:

1. At the top level is the user interface.
2. At the middle level is the *knowledge source* link, also known as *blackboard.*
3. At the bottom layer are the different knowledge sources.

The blackboard is a globally accessible data structure linked to independent sources of knowledge which cooperate in forming hypotheses.

Age follows a different design approach. Here, a shell is constructed by choosing:

- A user interface
- An inference engine
- A knowledge representation scheme

and so on. The effect different choices have with respect to the intended use of the shell can thus be determined. That, in turn, helps structure the resulting shell within the domain of the implementation.

The developers of Age isolated a number of inference, control, and representation techniques from some already existing expert systems and reprogrammed them for domain independence. They have added a routine which guides users in constructing their own individualized expert systems. They have also provided two predefined configurations of components. One, the *blackboard framework*, is intended for building programs based on the blackboard model, as employed in Hearsay II. The other is a predefined configuration for building programs that use backward-chaining production rules like those in Mycin.

Figure 37 contrasts the approach of Hearsay III to that of Age. It helps show that toolkits are not monolithic developments. A toolkit may be assimilated to a *development environment.* It presents fewer ready-made solutions than development environments of the shell type, but it has greater flexibility and hence offers more possibilities.

Some offerings provide not only symbolic languages like Prolog and Lisp under one cover but also task-oriented screen editors and some partially working modules in a number of libraries. They are, however, available only on large computers. Also, they are rather expensive.

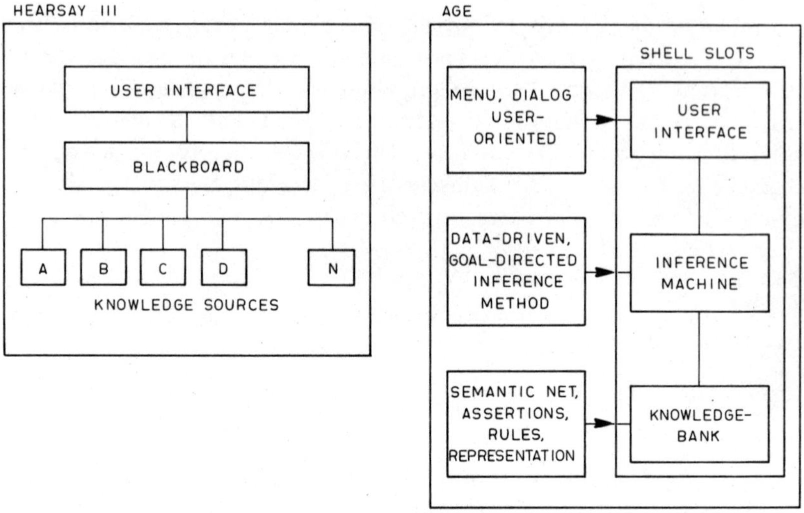

Figure 37 The Hearsay III approach versus that of Age: two different concepts of shells.

Like most artificial intelligence languages, development environments can run chunks of program as soon as we have written them. That is important because, based on this fact, many Esystems are also incremental. We can add rules to our model at any time. The alternative procedure is to produce a system which has a separate rules compiler. In that case, if we have to change our model, we must first edit a rules source file and then recompile our model, as we do if we are using, say, Algol. Microexpert works that way.

There are advantages and disadvantages in both alternatives. The second alternative conforms with compiler tradition. Its proponents say it is also more elegant in a design sense. The first alternative gives faster results and introduces a different concept in program development and maintenance.

Prototyping

First the definition: *Prototyping* is a user-driven approach that is visual thinking-oriented and is able to present a fully functional working model. It is a new experimental way of programming; it produces a code which is easy to change and adjust.

Analysis work done through the use of prototyping tools is computer-assisted. Programming work is done at high speed, but the resulting code is in need of optimization for run time processing reasons. That is why prototyping should be seen within the context of applications and project management (Figure 38)—not as an entity all by itself.

Rapid prototyping of computer applications is becoming a popular system development tool. The formal method of building software systems by using structured analysis and pseudocode has been abandoned by users who deplore its limited capabilities. Prototyping became important as end users acquired increasing knowledge of system development through experience on their own intelligent workstations.

Prototyping techniques do not require much programming expertise, but they do accelerate time scales. Some professions are, however, more open than others to the use of prototyping. Engineers are well acquainted with the idea of building and using prototypes. For over 50 years, design work and associated experiments have included the introduction of prototypes at the end of the design phase. Typically the prototypes are scale models constructed to validate the system specifications.

Simulation has been another approach. First, in the late 1940s and early 1950s, analog simulation with differential analyzers was used, and simulation was practically synonymous with that approach. Then, in the 1960s, with the development of specialized prototyping languages, digital simulation became the focus of attention. The simulations were used to create pilot systems for testing the feasibility of new proposals.

These approaches represented steps in the development process. In engineering applications, simulation languages produced software that

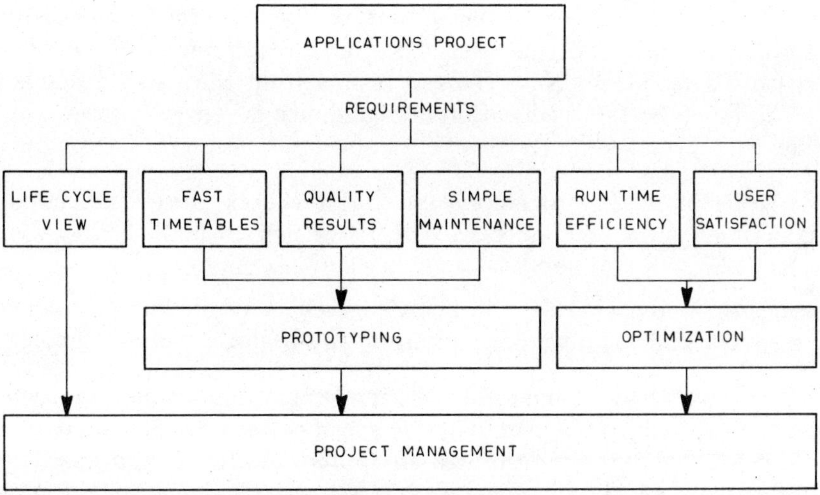

Figure 38 Prototyping should be seen within the context of applications and project management, not as an entity by itself.

was intended to be thrown away when the production version was implemented.

The progress in business and financial applications has been different. There prototyping came in through the use of spreadsheets (first VisiCalc, then Multiplan, Lotus 1-2-3, and so on) in the analysis of financial statements. The developed computer program was typically on a PC dedicated to one workstation, and the frequency of use was not such as to call for optimization. Rather, ease of use was important.

In the general case, rapid prototyping capitalizes on the experience gained through earlier model-making methods. It is further promoted by the fact that it does not require add-on development time or throwaway software.

- Prototyping is the first activity that occurs in a development project.
- It continues through all phases of the system life cycle, even after a refined version of the prototype software has been implemented.

Expert systems shells do provide users with powerful prototyping tools. But, as stated, not all tools apply to all implementation domains. Therein lies the importance of the right tool choice.

Apart from the development aspect per se, prototyping does help improve the communication between the knowledge engineer and the end user. When working model functioning is satisfactory, it is time to demonstrate the system to the end user. With prototyping, changes can be made at little cost.

Since little effort has been invested in it, the rapid prototype can easily be modified to better define user needs and requirements discovered during this early stage. Nevertheless, results from the user's response will be so much better if education and guidance are given to users not familiar with prototyping.

- First, it is important to emphasize that the user is viewing, not a production system, but only an early approach to how that system might look.
- Second, it is advisable for the knowledge engineer and user to agree on a review and approval schedule from the beginning of the project.

The prototyping cycle ends when the implementation of the prototype has been approved by the user, detailed specifications are complete, and all documentation has gone through an appropriate review process. The final acceptance of a project can be expressed exactly in a standard *facts and rules* format of an expert system through prototyping. That is much truer now that basics of Esystems technology are well understood and associated frameworks are being used to assist in projects of software development.

Thanks to computer-run prototyping procedures, we can forget about the need to have design specifications complete, approved, and frozen before development begins. We can also eliminate a good deal of hardcopy output and report formats. A working prototype is more useful than paper records during analysis and design.

In another sense, technical specifications can be derived from a user-approved prototype. This can fully alter our perspective of the traditional life-cycle methodology provided that we don't use this methodology blindfolded but instead:

1. Analyze the candidate applications
2. Determine potential project size
3. Evaluate the probable usage requirement
4. Estimate performance standards
5. Establish user preferences for interface characteristics

We have spoken of the latter in the chapter on the human window. Menus, prompts, help screens, and natural-language approaches are examples of user-friendly interfaces.

Routing trees for menu solutions are an example of an area open to prototyping. Menu selection begins with basic choices of input and reporting. Each level of the menu hierarchy (routing structure) should include an online help facility, prompting, browsing, forward, and return to the preceding level.

Routing capabilities are indispensable in an Esystem able to help the developer conceptualize elements like tables, attributes, and screen that need to be included in the prototype. Icons and menus should invoke the various functions to be manipulated. Routing procedures should permit users to branch to menus such as data entry, analysis, reports, and graphics. Help screens should list choices of reports the user can produce. The appropriate level of menu nesting depends on the size and complexity of the application.

The prototype's structure can be reviewed to determine the functional modules to be developed. There is usually a one-for-one relation between essential function and a module in the prototype. Modules will be invoked at run time from the appropriate menu and should be aggregated by type of function.

It is also necessary to provide the proper training for rapid prototyping. Users should not become uneasy with the transition to rapid prototyping concepts. They should be put in a position to use the tools they have available in an effective manner.

Facilities must also be provided to assure that prototypes can be expanded into production systems. A feature of such approach is the ability to:

1. Create and run the prototype by using menus
2. Employ screen forms that minimize programming effort
3. Easily modify data structures online
4. Have testing procedures available so that a resulting prototype can be used both as a first-phase production system and as a test bed for better testing procedures

In fact, prototyping does not end even after the system goes into production. A flexible, readily modifiable system is in place. Therefore, adaptable and perfectable maintenance requirements can be met by using the same prototype.

Reveal and Exsys

This chapter has carried the message that many expert systems shells are currently available. The objective of this section is not to review all of them but, rather, to appraise some commodity shells and thereby contribute to user orientation. But first of all a warning. Don't ever get involved with a vendor who offers you an Esystems shell on a "me too" basis or get into negotiation with a company with an uncertain future. The supplier has to be solid, and the system offered you must be one of the supplier's strategic products. That is emphasized in Figure 39, which divides all offerings into four main classes. Your goal should be to select from class 1.

Reveal

Reveal (a British development marketed in the United States by the Knowledge Engineering Division of InfoTym, a subsidiary of McDonnell Douglas) has many typical expert system features such as knowledge-based rules and fuzzy logic. It also incorporates a wide range of traditional programming facilities.

This shell can be looked at as a reasonably large scale commodity software product designed to make knowledge engineering accessible in companies already acquainted with decision support applications. It features a wide variety of applications domains. Users can range from the novice to the skilled Esystem developer.

Reveal offers programming constructs such as IF, ELSE, DO, and REPEAT and also special functions: compound interest, mortgage pay-

CLASS 1	STRATEGIC PRODUCT - VENDOR'S FUTURE DEPENDS ON IT - USUALLY DESIGNED AND DEVELOPED BY VENDOR
CLASS 2	THIRD PARTY: UNDER SPONSORSHIP - WRITTEN TO VENDOR'S SPECIFICATIONS
CLASS 3	THIRD PARTY: VENDOR'S ADOPTION - EXTENSIVELY TESTED - SUPPORTED BY VENDOR
CLASS 4	THIRD PARTY: NO POSITION TAKEN - VENDOR KNOWS PACKAGE EXISTS, BUT HE PERFORMED NO TESTS AND TAKES NO RESPONSIBILITY

Figure 39 Four levels of vendor support in commodity software offerings.

ment calculation, and depreciation. The latter can be used for developing business decision support applications. The system is equipped with data management and report generation facilities. They include the ability to interact simultaneously with many external data files.

The default mechanism is the formalism of fuzzy production rules. There is the concept of a *policy*, that is, a collection of zero or more production rules existing as a named file object in the database. Policies may be applied to the current problem context under user program control.

Reveal's inference engine is formed through the structure of program control. This provides a clear distinction between knowledge and control procedures and is the reason why Reveal is said to be targeted toward both Esystems and DSSs. Originally designed for mainframes, Reveal is now offered at the PC level. Portability has been facilitated by the fact that the Reveal development environment consists of a table of data and a program model that describes the relations among the matrix rows and columns.

All Reveal file objects are held in a single host system file referred to as the *Reveal database*. This is constructed along relational lines. Multiple datasets, associated with the same or different programs, can be managed at the command level, without the builder becoming involved in problems of file or records layout.

The program model is equivalent to an inference engine. It is possible to set up variables and constants and also to define so-called *qualifiers*, which are major components in the Reveal context. Allowing the user to create personal inference engine procedures in the form of models is a departure from typical practice. Reveal's design is based on the premise that users should be able to build inference procedures on their own and tailor the procedures to individual applications as they see fit.

Exsys

The Expert System Development Package (Exsys, by Exsys, Inc. of Albuquerque, N.M.) can be used to make expert systems with many rules, conditions, notations, and statistical capabilities. It includes an editor for creating the rules and a run time routine that executes applications programs. The latter is important for designers who want to distribute applications programs.

Exsys Esystems permit the user to interact with the program by asking:

- Why information is needed
- How the software program arrived at a conclusion

The shell will fully explain. It will also support both text and numeric variables.

Exsys numeric variables are double-precision floating points. Arithmetic, trigonometric, log, and square root functions are featured. Numeric variables can be calculated by the software and displayed with the results. Probability features are supported. Exsys knowledgebanks use text presentations and ask multiple-choice questions. The entire knowledgebank must fit into central memory, but it is possible to use the run time module to run it in less memory than the editor needs to create it.

There is an editing module for creating the rules, conditions, and alternatives that make up an Esystem. Its features keep track of the flow of logic and options in the system. They also prompt the user to provide the data needed to set up an application. The editing program permits the user to easily review and change the contents of the knowledgebank. It also links up to the run time module, so the designer can try out changes as they are made. The screen helps to display the established rules and conditions clearly.

Exsys offers *what-if* features that permit the user to readily see the effects of changing one or more of the answers in the Esystem's conclusion.

Thus the user can quickly determine the sensitivity of the conclusion to a particular answer. The same feature allows expert systems models to be created and tested.

Exsys consists of two programs: the *rule editor* and the *run time.* The former allows the user to create, edit, or delete rules. All input to the editor is English text, menu selection, or algebraic expression. Text is entered into the editor only once and then selected or recalled by number. When a new rule is added, it is checked against all of the existing rules for consistency. If there are potential conflicts between rules, the user is notified and can make the necessary corrections.

The run time program runs the rules created with the editor. During application development, the softcopy can be moved left, right, and to the bottom.

- The left side plays the IF and THEN conditions.
- On the right side, alternatives and conditions can be recalled, scrolled, expanded, and edited.
- The bottom displays prompts indicating commands available at the particular functional level one is in.

The editing program lets the user easily review and change anything in the knowledgebank. It links to the run time module, so the designer and/or user can try out changes as they are made. The editing module also makes it feasible to print the contents of the knowledgebank, thus making it possible to make changes based on what one sees on the screen.

Design-wise, Exsys supports backward chaining. It also permits larger problems to be broken into chunks. Rules can then be written in terms of the solutions to the smaller problems. The software can call up other programs, including most spreadsheets and database managers. It can transfer their output into Exsys for analysis or also call up other external programs.

Other Currently Available Shells

M1

M1 is a development tool (by Teknowledge, Palo Alto, Calif.). It is a software construct for exploring practical applications by using knowledge-based rules. So far, it has largely been used for demonstration purposes. These include:

- A Bank Services Adviser, which matches banking requirements with bank product lines.

- A Photographic Adviser which uses information about environmental conditions to recommend the shutter speed and film type to use.
- A Wine Adviser, which suggests what type of wine to serve with different meals.

M1 operates in compiler fashion. It checks the syntax of a knowledgebank each time it is loaded, reports errors, and places a marker as near as possible to the offending text. Among the M1 features are a multiwindow display, an automatic question generation module, presupposition checking, an explanation facility, certainty factors, and the use of variables in the knowledge representation language. Certainty factors can be associated with facts and rules, and that permits the representation of heuristic-type knowledge.

Like other high-level languages, the M1 syntax offers facilities for printing text, using variables, doing mathematical computations, and processing support lists. The latter feature can be used to sum a list of values recorded at various points during a consultation. There is a knowledgebank auditor for tracking conclusions, and there is a knowledgebank browser for listing all rules and facts containing particular expressions. Multivalued as well as single-valued attributes are supported.

The knowledge representation language provides for the use of substitution variables. These automatically take on values through pattern matching during a consultation. Knowledgebanks can be loaded dynamically during man-machine interaction. An overlay capability assures segmentation for larger knowledgebanks than central memory can accept. This shell allows up to 200 rules to be used at one time, enough to create a halfway complex application. More rules can be used via the overlay feature mentioned above.

Small changes can be made from within M1 by means of the add or delete rule facilities. Rules can also be listed by number through the list command. The certainty factor value (F) must be an integer between 0 and 100, depending on the context. This is a key concept in building Esystems with M1. Certainty factors are not used only in hard-coded form in knowledgebanks. The user may answer a question with certainty factors to indicate varying degrees of truth or falsity. M1 ignores propositions that end with a certainty factor of less than 20 percent.

When running through an M1 consultation, the user will see a list of questions and answers. The activity takes place in a special section in memory: the cache. During a consultation, the cache contains M1's intermediate and final conclusions. Each time a rule succeeds, a cache entry records the event for later use. The user can list and change these entries as part of the knowledgebank debugging process or save them to a file for later analysis.

A trace command permits the user to interactively follow what is happening during a consultation. One of the most helpful of the debugging tools that M1 offers is the *instrument panel.* Before starting a consultation, the top half of the screen will be divided into four windows labeled Events, Reasoning, Options, and Conclusions. The usual question-and-answer text appears below the window.

- The Events window, naturally enough, indicates which events are taking place.
- The Conclusions window notes which conclusions M1 has reached in response to input.
- The Reasoning window records how the Esystem inference engine invokes various rules in the knowledgebank. It will show which rule succeeded.
- The Options window indicates the user's responses to the current questions.

The instrument panel is useful, but when a lot of text occupies such windows, it can be confusing. Also, text is sometimes scattered when knowledgebank entries are wider than the windows they occupy.

S1

S1 (also by Teknowledge Inc.) is a different tool. Whereas M1 is PC-oriented, S1 runs on a supermicro. It is designed to assist experienced knowledge engineers in the development of larger knowledge systems.

The power of S1 lies in its integrating strategies for representation, inference, and control. Its knowledgebank is composed of three kinds of knowledge: factual, judgmental, and procedural. Each is encoded in a separate chunk.

- *Factual knowledge*, representing assertions about and relations between objects. It is encoded in a frame system.
- *Judgmental knowledge*, representing heuristic rules of thumb about the application. It is encoded in if-then rules.
- *Procedural knowledge*, which reflects sequences of problem-solving steps. It is encoded in control blocks.

S1 also offers training and professional support to aid in the Esystem development process. The maintenance system built for S1 includes a telephone hotline to assist in product installation and operation.

ExpertEase

ExpertEase was developed by Donald Michie at Edinburgh University. (In 1984, Human Edge Software, Palo Alto, Calif., acquired the rights to produce ExpertEase in the United States.) This is an inductive logic program able to give end users and experts some insight into the problems they work with and the conditions affecting them. The user does not have to write the rules that the program uses to make decisions about data. What the user must do is structure the material so that the program can infer a logic table from examples.

When ExpertEase derives its rules, it ignores factors that are not really important in reaching a conclusion. In that way, it passes expertise on to the people who run the knowledgebank: The ability to infer rules from examples can be useful to people who don't know the logic behind certain conditions, or events, but suspect that events may be related and that the relation is a consistent one.

This shell is written in UCSD Pascal. It features menus and an annotated list of the files. Help screens are available, and requests for help are met quickly. ExpertEase prods the user to list all possible items or numeric values that might appear in each category of factors and in the list of decisions. The user need enter each possible item or numeric value only once.

Typically, after the items or values are listed, the user moves to a second ExpertEase screen that allows him or her to proceed with the examples. Since all the item names or numeric values of the factors and results are already in the program, the user can enter the example quickly and save time and effort by typing just one or two letters of the item name or numeric value wanted. The program will fill in the rest.

Timm-PC

Timm-PC (from General Research, McLean, Va.) is a micro-based expert system which thinks about various ways to solve problems when critical information is inadequate or missing. Its approach is to capitalize on the fact that most real-world situations are not all-or-nothing propositions but instead vary by degrees.

The shell uses pattern-matching techniques that allow the user to differentiate between statements that vary continuously and those that have an all-or-nothing quality. In so doing, it uses a partial match procedure that resembles the nearest-neighbor search algorithm.

Like most other Esystems shells, Timm-PC uses a production rule approach. Knowledge is encapsulated into distinct rules comprised of *if* conditions and *then* results. Its knowledgebank begins with a special declaration section that contains specific information about the attributes that will be used in individual files.

One of the shell features allows the user to link separate knowledge systems. The linking is done by making a direct reference to branching or invoking a rule in another knowledgebank that requires referencing to establish one of its conditions.

Timm-PC chooses a result and estimates its dependability, even when very little information is supplied and the dependability is very small. Each factor of a problem is considered as a coordinate of a *point*. Values supplied by the end user specify the coordinates. The shell looks for the most similar points already in its knowledgebank and makes some kind of choice.

An *inquiry utility* is helpful because it allows the user to review the Esystem's decision structure. A menu asks the user to choose:

- D for decision structure
- K for knowledgebank
- N for number of rules

By looking at the knowledgebank, the user can see a rule by supplying its number or type ALL to see all the rules. The decision structure contains the names of the various choices, names and allowable values of the factors, and help instructions that go with each of them.

Chapter

11

Expert Systems Projects

"All warranties end upon payment of invoice." COMMERCIAL MAXIM

Planning an Expert Systems Project

Expert systems are growing more complex at a rapid pace. When results of artificial intelligence research are adapted to personal computers, we can expect a wide variety of powerful Esystems, natural-language generators, and robot controllers. However, intelligent machines are no be-all and end-all for decision makers. They are specific to functional areas. They are only as good as the rules, hypotheses, and criteria embedded in them. And they should be the subject of careful research projects.

There are many phases in a valid applications development methodology, and three of them are most important. As shown in Figure 40, they are:

- Project management
- Integration studies
- The use of new, efficient tools

Able project management starts with the project structure and the detailed definition of goals, brainpower, and timetables. Successful expert system projects typically:

1. Are small in size
2. Rest on finite domains of knowledge
3. Exhibit a high degree of knowhow
4. Are addressed to well-defined fields

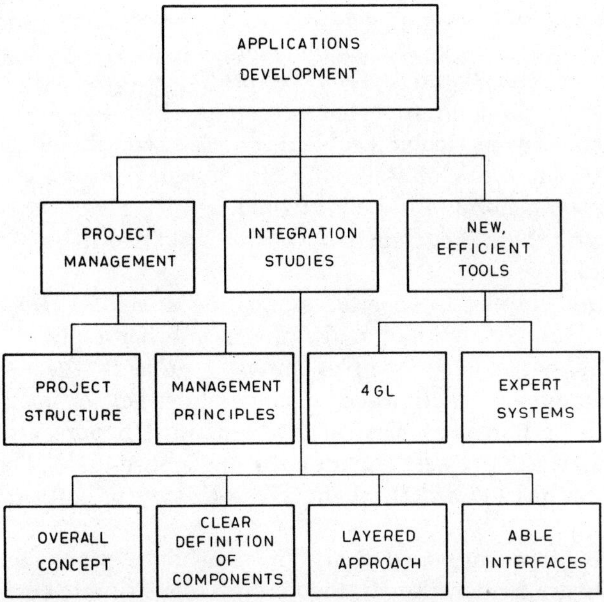

Figure 40 Phases and component parts in a valid applications development methodology.

A key issue in setting up a project is to decide which relevant information should be shown to the end user. A second key is fast-development timetables. The time to develop an Esystem can be very contained. Table 5 presents seven organizational steps and the corresponding times invested in producing a financial adviser system. The total investment was 7 worker-months of labor spread over 2.6 calendar months.

TABLE 5 Time Investment for Financial Adviser Expert System

Phase of project	Two- or three-person system team, hr	1 expert in applic. field, hr
Establish goals and timetable	6	2
Preliminary work on key factors	20	6
Analysis of basic aspects using shell	18	2
Prototyping and experimentation	70	20
Technical design reviews	12	5
System evaluation	15	4
Manuals and final report	10	1
	50*	40

*About 7 worker-months but 2.6 calendar months.

The choice of development tools is also a critical matter. We have examined the better known shells in the preceding chapter, where it was emphasized that shells should mainly be used for prototyping. Furthermore, it has been said on repeated occasions that, whichever tool is developed to solve a particular problem, an Esystem should be created only within a framework of well-defined problem perspectives. A problem cannot be too general, since that would require a very large amount of knowledge and there is currently no way to build and maintain gigantic knowledgebanks.

Successful projects are limited to specific application areas; R1, Dendral, Mycin, VM are examples. Proper budgeting is another highlight. Typically with projects, particularly complex software projects, there is a consistent overstatement of benefits and an understatement of costs. Data processing is full of horror stories in this domain. On pure economic grounds about half the projects should never have been built. The specter of cost overruns has loomed throughout the history of software effort.

Careful audits have often suggested that, for some data processing departments (and software firms), the strategy is to underestimate costs to get a project started and then justify continuing the project by the money that has already been spent. This should not happen with Esystems. The field is too young to survive the shock. Therefore, the first section in this chapter is devoted to project management: from planning to control. A systems project must start right, or it would be better not started at all.

Directing and Controlling Esystems Projects

A project is a well-defined activity set up to produce predetermined results. It involves resources: *knowhow*, hence personnel; *money*, therefore budgets; *time*, projected in timetables; other resources, such as *computers and communications*.

As an organizational unit, the project is dedicated to the attainment of a precise, short- to medium-term goal. Projects:

- Must never be permanently structured
- Should be organized by task (diagonal structure) rather than by staff or line
- Must be dismantled upon completion

In a diagonal structure the control of performance rests on management capabilities. This is important because a project manager supervises a higher proportion of professionals than any other manager in the organization.

Project management is based on three basic concepts:

1. The project manager, hence a single point of authority and responsibility, is designated.
2. Planning and control are exerted by the project manager.
3. Organizing, staffing, and directing are under the control of the project manager.

Organizational perspectives must be observed. Staffing requirements involve the best of the available personnel. Day-to-day activities must be controlled. Midterm results should interest management—not just the end result.

A *successful project manager* must possess many qualifications: a working knowledge of several fields, a career molded in the system technology environment, a good understanding of general management problems, familiarity with the concept of profitability, the ability to control timetables, the will to establish metrics and use them, and a strong, continuous, active interest in teaching, training, and developing subordinates.

The profile of the project manager can be described by a capacity to foretell, plan, and estimate trends, an analytic and penetrating mind, knowledge to appraise alternative approaches, ability to quantify and qualify user needs, willingness to put all project documentation in writing, and appreciation of qualities, yields, costs, and human reaction.

The project manager should have an iron hand in implementing an orderly discipline and the ability to make up his or her mind when faced with difficult decisions as to the course to follow.

Not only the project manager but also the members of the team—particularly the professional expert in the domain of implementation—should be well above average. The superior person is a lover of learning, attentive to duties, careful in speech, firm in dealing with others, possessed of deep knowledge in the field, free of preconceived ideas or courses of action, dignified and at ease but not proud, and easy to serve but difficult to please.

Project organization is important. Organizational decisions will impact the cost of the project: its size, duration, extent of personnel employment, and equipment needed. Most companies have been unpleasantly surprised when they failed to control:

1. Budgets
2. Timetables
3. Personnel
4. Equipment to be acquired

All four items call for exercising better cost control. Winners apply more management to the project: tasks and budgets are better defined, changes are more rigidly controlled, performance is more closely watched through steady design reviews, and prompt action is taken to prevent or correct problems. A valid way to apply corrective action is to institute design reviews. The reviews should be held at regular intervals (biweekly, monthly) and should cover both the managerial aspects and the technical details.

An integral part of good project organization is *setting goals* and subgoals within the mission being assigned. Goals must be explicit and precise and must be put in writing. They should not be changed midterm in a project. A project should be closed down if it:

1. Fails to reach its milestones
2. Overruns its estimated costs
3. Misuses its human resources by periodically diverting them to secondary issues
4. Goes out of control

Many projects drift aimlessly because no one knows what the goals are and/or management does not know the subject well enough to exercise effective control. A related problem is continually adding new goals to the same project. This leads us to the key issue of project control. The heart of project control should be designed to highlight:

1. Cost
2. Schedule
3. Technical status

Project control should enable management to make an assessment of progress. And it should provide a sound basis for determining where special attention is required. A graphical presentation of results by milestones reached helps in the appraisal of performance, the execution of plans in accordance with established standards, and the initiation of corrective action if required. When management does not master a certain technical field, or has no time to look at detail, it should be using able consultants.

There is a critical difference between the roles of an expert as a problem solver and as an adviser. In the former role the expert focuses on the process of obtaining a concrete, accurate, and comprehensive solution to a problem. In the latter role the expert is primarily concerned with the enrichment of management's understanding of a problem area and the development of skills in handling that area.

As a consultant, the expert is expected to provide the methodology for problem solving and also to audit the project, evaluate the rules, and suggest corrective action. An advisory capacity covers a wide area, and it should therefore be properly defined at the start of the project.

Problem solving is not just writing algorithms or inference rules. It is also—if not mainly—deciding what questions should be asked by the Esystem and how to look for answers. Management would like a methodology involving concrete steps. Project management offers an example of such a methodology: from project initiation to the killing of unsuccessful projects.

Organizations must have the brains and the tools to coordinate projects, check the impact of the new or proposed systems on the existing structure, understand the implications, and plan in advance the life cycle before committing vital resources to a project. Companies which lack such pillars of good management experience the largest number of failures.

Starting the Expert Systems Project

We have seen that an intelligent knowledge-based system is one which uses inference to apply knowhow in performing a task. Such a system can be projected for knowledge handling in many areas of human thought and activity provided well-defined steps are taken.

Emphasis has also been placed on the fact that knowledge of an object is usually represented by means of relations, or assertions, that may be fuzzy. Knowledge can also be represented procedurally through a network of steps, concepts, and actions. A general method of representing knowledge of an object or a concept is by means of information frames applicable to the subject at hand. The frames may contain assertions, procedural knowledge, or links to other relevant concepts or objects.

The job of the knowledge engineer is to master the methodology and interface languages. But the engineer is (usually) not an expert in the implementation field for which the expert system is being built. That is why the close collaboration of an expert in that profession is such a necessity. From the start of an expert systems project, the project manager and knowledge engineers should pay particular attention to the major phases in systems development.

- The first and foremost phase is defining functional requirements—establishing what the Esystem is expected to do.
- The next phase is developing a data design to support the Esystem, always based on functional requirements.

A technical architecture helps describe the Esystem's major processes and how they interrelate. This is followed by system design and assurance of what the finer programmatic interfaces should contain. A parallel process is the selection of the shell and/or programming language. Experience with data processing may be helpful in some cases and inhibiting in others. It depends on how open-eyed this experience has been.

The mapping of Esystems implies some fundamental changes in the software development process. It offers new opportunities but also underlines the need for imaginative approaches and control procedures. It is just as important to take note that the way we solve a problem is influenced by the available tools. The programming language and computer architecture create a problem-solving framework. Our minds work that way. Let's use that fact to our advantage rather than have it work against us.

We need solutions able to control all the activities in software life cycle:

- Master planning
- Project management
- Interactive systems analysis
- Program design
- Development of code
- Intensive testing
- Thorough documentation
- Software maintenance

Critical for a valid expert systems development job is the interaction between the knowledge engineer(s) and the end user. This impacts on how knowledge is acquired and represented, how representations are implemented in a particular language, and how knowledge is applied to a particular situation, modified in the light of experience, and generally maintained.

Just as critical is the spirit of expert systems research. The research requires good knowledge of software engineering, but also VLSI, microprocessors, large communicating databases, and gateways for data communications. Research emphasis should also be placed on methodologies oriented to human reasoning, knowledge-intensive inference rules, and man-machine interfaces (Figure 41).

Expert systems developers are well advised not to choose a tool with more generality than is needed, to test the tool early by building a small prototype, to assure there are good explanation facilities when

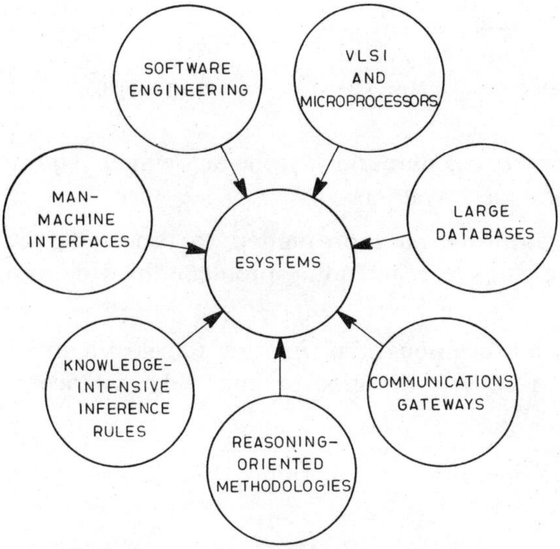

Figure 41 Expert systems research requirements and contributions from other fields.

development speed is critical, and to always focus on interactive tools and procedures. The knowledge engineer should use personal experience and problem characteristics to determine tool features. He or she must consider issues of sufficiency, completeness, and language features and focus on control methods.

Effective solutions will provide built-in explanation and interaction facilities, easy but controlled accessibility, and DBM-controlled data representation schemes. There should also be a constrained control mechanism if learning, self-modification, or advanced explanation features are needed.

Expert Systems Building

If expert systems building is a new experience for the organization, then the following advice is in order when starting the Esystems project.

1. *Carefully define in writing the field you are going to work in, and establish the goals.*

Not only should this be a very finite field but, as a general rule, it would be inadvisable to apply expert systems to:

- Problems which are too simple (say, under ten rules), since the human expert can ordinarily handle them adequately.

- Problems which are too complex (say, over 200 rules with current knowhow). Construction and search times become too long, and present hardware (micro, supermicro) has difficulty coping with them.
- Problems, such as well-structured numerical problems, which require none of the advantages of expert systems.
- Problems which rely on information more suited to processing by the human brain than by computer, including problems in wide and shallow domains.
- Areas in which there may not be enough information to select a single course of action—as when experts disagree or knowledge is incomplete.

After having clearly established the goals, and only then, proceed with the second basic step:

2. *Do research among organizations having Esystems expertise.*

It's good practice to first study all available literature in decision support systems within the chosen field and interpret what you read in terms of *your* goals. Even better, examine what has been done in DSSs within your organization and draw conclusions.

Since the expert systems field is very new, homework will provide the knowhow to ask intelligent questions. Then comes the time to get in contact with organizations that have Esystems experience. Such visits and discussions may be a tourist-type attraction or a very worthwhile enterprise. The difference rests on two factors:

- The degree of preparation
- The careful taking of notes during the meetings, followed by distillation and crystallization of the results in an appropriate report

This advice is just as valid for technological interviews as it is for the following of seminars on technology transfer. Participants in these events are delegates of their companies. They have duties to perform; they cannot just sit there daydreaming.

3. *Based on what you learn, develop YOUR methodology.*

What you learn through literature, technology seminars, and interviews with experienced users is general principles. These may be specifically applied to a chosen field of Esystems implementation—but not necessarily to *your* problem. What's more, this is somebody else's methodology, not your own.

That's why it is so important to write down in detail the experience you get in technology transfer visits and seminars. You need to do so in order to understand it better. And you need to understand it very well to build up *your own* methodology.

4. *Create a layered model, not a monolithic one.*

Speaking of layering, I have emphasized the DSS infrastructure, the location of Esystem implementation as the middle layer, and the expansion capabilities toward higher intelligence. These must always be left open. Among the determinants of a layered approach are:

- The *knowhow* which exists in the organization—and most specifically in the Esystems project team—from DSS to data communications (which is the first field to use layering).
- The *relative complexity* of the Esystems project. Here considerations include the degree of formalization of knowledge, the size of the projected Esystem, availability of external advice, and possible software and hardware constraints.
- The *degree of integration* within the company's information system, including cross-departmental transfer of expertise, integration into existing data communications networks and databases, and number of users.

Such factors affect both the nature of the Esystems application and the path of development. Generally, the greater the knowhow, the more layered the structure. The same thing is true in regard to a polyvalent implementation.

5. *Use the best expert advice for organization of facts, definition of rules, and elaboration of reasoning methods.*

This is one of the fields in which high-grade skill really pays dividends. But don't let the work with the expert become rap sessions. Structure the work, including questions and answers.

Always remember that, contrary to traditional DP, a knowledge system can communicate intelligently with the user. To do so, the knowledge system:

- Is based on a totally *different architecture* than DP
- *Proposes* an aggregate of specific issues (queries) relative to the subject addressed
- *Adapts* itself to its environment and modifies its rules
- Gives an *opinion* and *justifies* it

The expert in the professional field (the one the Esystems effort is directed to) will appreciate these features, the more so if he or she has been disgusted in the past with classical programming approaches which are incapable of profiting from human experience.

Do explain to the expert that, whereas the old-hat DP systems cannot benefit from incomplete and/or imprecise information, the expert systems can. But then also do explain to yourself that in this exciting field of artificial intelligence you must provide the ability to transit to new goals.

Let me close this section with the following thought. Esystems cannot be learned through books and conferences. The only way to get experience is to work on the development of an expert system yourself, and the time to start is now.

Learning What to Do and Applying What We Learn

There are stages in the process of expert systems realization, and it is well to take notice of them. Particularly for beginning projects, the proper division into stages helps in getting the job done well. The first is the *learning stage*. It is a period of familiarization, education, and appreciation. Companies want to become aware of what it is all about, what other companies have done, the technology that others have used, and the results that others have achieved. This helps management determine which of its operations could be helped by Esystems. At the learning stage, an expert system should have 10 to 20 rules.

The second is the *early development stage*. During this period management is sufficiently interested to do some implementation, particularly of simple applications. This is a confidence-building time during which the value of Esystems becomes apparent because of hands-on experience through prototypes; say, a 20- to 100-rules model.

Provided this experience goes well and gives some concrete results, the third period will be one of *more-advanced development*. Here research themes will be located and one or two projects attempted in the range of 100 to 500 rules, with 200 to 300 rules being a likely bet.

Such advanced development is not the true operational stage, though the Esystem being built, if successful, will be used in applications. The true *operational stage* really begins when the organization starts believing in expert systems and actively uses a system in one or more of its real-life operations *in a way leading to the industrialization* of knowhow.

A different approach in terms of effective division of the learning and implementation processes in expert systems has been taken by government bodies for project-financing purposes. Large financial and industrial organizations may be interested in adopting this approach, which is exemplified by the Alvey Directorate in the UK.

In this case, styles of activity have been distinguished starting with *show-me* projects. Their aim is that of providing immediate industrial demonstrations of existing Esystems technology. The second style is characterized by *short-term* development projects. These are aimed at producing marketable products within 2 to 3 years. One of their characteristics is low-risk development from current technology.

Remember, however, that this reference comes from government-sponsored research. In an industrial organization such a time range would be disastrous. It would kill all interest in Esystems or, worse yet, contaminate them with the very bad practices from the plain old data processing mess.

In an industrial organization, a *reasonable timetable for Esystems development is in the 4-to 6-calendar months range after the learning experience is finished.* This corresponds to a good enough *100 plus* rules level and accounts for some learning effect, but not for the training (or hiring) of knowledge engineers. The example given in the introduction, in fact, stood at the 2.6-calendar months level.

To go back to the Alvey reference, the third style of activity is *demonstrator projects.* They involve industry-led collaborative research and development aimed at building complete prototypes of possible future Esystems requiring substantial R&D work.

This is followed by the fourth style: *research themes.* They center on *medium- to long-term* directed research by collaborating teams on a limited number of carefully chosen topics. Such topics are selected among those likely to be crucial to success in building an advanced expert system or other artificial intelligence project.

Finally, the fifth style of work is *general research,* which is characterized by accelerated progress in the directed part of the research and development program. Alvey aptly suggests this will be possible only against the background of a well-balanced portfolio of high-quality, speculative research.

In a government-sponsored program, such research should involve all important aspects of artificial intelligence and related topics. Examples of the latter are software technology and man-machine interaction.

Whether expert systems research and development is an industrial or government-sponsored project, there is a direct relation between the level of management commitment and the resulting degree of technological progress. Although a modest commitment could provide support for the learning stage, it is impossible to move to real development and operations without a strong commitment from management on the implementation of expert systems.

Such a commitment should not be vague or general; it should be systems-specific. Top management should state in a policy directive that there is a main goal, that of acquiring, processing, and representing knowledge. It is wise to also qualify the areas of implementation, and I have given advice on which areas can be most fruitful—areas in which there is prior organizational experience in DSS being a specific example.

There is good news and bad news that management should consider. Some of the good news is that a recent market forecast on Esystems, made in the United States, was of huge growth over the next 10 years by areas of importance:

- Research and development
- Office
- Factory

Wherever there is a concentration of well-founded brainpower, we can expect significant results. At the same time, this and other studies have suggested that companies which fall behind in expert systems will suffer competitive disadvantages. So more good news is that Esystems are matters of competitive advantage and, therefore, of survival. They are also matters of profitability in company operations, as the body of knowledge in decision support systems helps document.

Although the lack of management commitment (or blinking lights) would strangle a project, the fact of having goals and committing resources is no guarantee of success, unless we have a properly established plan. Such a plan should address the constraints which currently exist in Esystems development and implementation.

Here comes the bad news. First of all, there is an acknowledged *scarcity of knowledge engineers*. Not only is their number small (guesstimated to be a few hundred), but most of them are in academia and hence oriented toward research on artificial intelligence rather than the development of practical Esystems which can meet decision support needs.

The problem just outlined is aggravated by the fact that management is often reluctant to trust knowledge engineers from outside the firm, whose field they do not fully understand. In many companies there are also matters of secrecy which preclude effective collaboration with human resources from outside.

A company can train its own people: *the best* currently working in computers and communications and the *willing* experts among the end users. But here comes a second constraint: the *formalization of knowledge* needed for the Esystem. I am not concerned the Esystem will formalize only static knowledge. That is an absurd argument one hears. What concerns me is the way the knowledge engineer will collaborate with the expert, formalize the knowledge, and test the system. The procedure to follow on the first two issues has been discussed. Testing is treated in the following section.

The formalization of knowledge is evidently related to the *definition of the problem*—which precedes it. This can be viewed as a related issue or by itself. Either way it reflects the lack of knowledge about Esystems among management levels and fear of the systems jargon.

It is, indeed, unfortunate that, after more than 30 years, computer people cannot communicate their knowledge to end users in a nontechnical way. This mistake should not be repeated again with expert systems.

Testing the Expert System

As Welbank suggested in the British Telecom study,* most of the expert systems that have been built so far have not been rigorously tested. Maybe they have been formally compared with a human expert and found to perform well, but there is no evidence of component tests and subsequently of system testing. That testing is one of software's weak points we know by experience with other projects. It is an issue that has, unfortunately, plagued software development at large for over 30 years.

Although it is true that the Esystems field is new and most AI projects are experimental, it is no less reasonable to suggest that there should be better ways of testing for completeness, consistency, and acceptability to the end users. Once again, as demonstrated by other software projects, the type of evaluation that is acceptable in research environments will not be good enough for actual operation. There is a significant difference between:

- The one-shot experimental project
- A computer program designed to run for production purposes
- A programming product

The one-shot experimental project concerns the designer, a laboratory, or the company the designer is working for. But there is no marketable product.

A computer program designed to run for production purposes must be very thoroughly tested. It also requires first-class documentation. Don't ever buy commodity software for which either the documentation is defective and incomplete or there is no evidence of thorough testing at both the component part and system level.

Still, the testing of a program designed for production runs is a trifle compared to what is necessary for a programming product. If we are

---

*Margaret Welbank, "A Review of Knowledge Acquisition Techniques for Expert Systems," British Telecom Laboratories, Ipswich, 1983.

talking of expert systems as the industrialization of knowledge, *the programming product quality level should be the goal.*

Feedback theory may be of assistance if we know how to apply it. The first half of Figure 42 shows a simple feedback diagram. In the second part, this has been altered to introduce expert system components in an effort to use modular sets which then can be tested module by module.

Serious testing should start with the level of the selected inference method. There are different lines along which such testing can be carried out. One is a logical comparison of the conclusions among themselves on a repetitive inference basis, other variables being kept equal. In this way the internal consistency of the adopted methodology can be checked, albeit in a way which is not separated from the rules.

Say, then, that the Esystem is running:

- It is asking valid questions.
- It is able to update its hypotheses according to the answers it gets.
- It carries on until it has no more questions to ask.
- It then stops and comes to a conclusion.

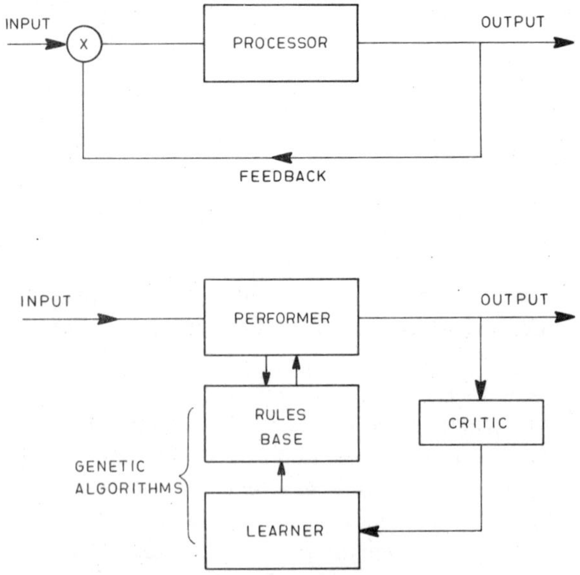

Figure 42 Top half shows a simple feedback diagram. In the bottom half, the feedback is redesigned to introduce expert system components.

How do we test this system? One way is to consider the most likely result, for instance, the outcome with the highest probability. This may be a right approach if we remember the role played by minimum and maximum probabilities for each hypothesis depending on the information currently in the knowledgebank. It will be wrong otherwise.

Another way to look at this issue is that the above approach to testing might give results if we are careful to establish a probability for each hypothesis a priori. This can be done by studying the knowledgebank and establishing a variable likelihood for each hypothesis.

We should also analyze the rules themselves and project a value for each item of evidence. Again this means scanning the knowledgebank to extract an evidence number. Subsequently we should interrogate the contributing expert on these items of evidence, preferably through the human window, by using the questions in the knowledgebank. The Esystem itself should be doing the processing work; it should present families of results which can be studied for reasonableness and dependability.

There can be a variation, and possibly improvement, of the empirical testing method. It rests on an audit procedure known as the *contention system*. It is applied by IBM to new projects with rather complex implication. Development projects at IBM are subject to active critique by key departments such as marketing and maintenance, which will be asked to handle the product and be responsible for it after the final tests have been successfully completed. The contention system has one objective: *prove what is wrong with the new product* when the audit is made, well before the completion of all development work.

In regard to expert systems, both approaches to testing rest on empirical judgment of conclusions derived from using the Esystem. If the results show the advice given by the intelligent machine to be applicable and verifiable, we can say that it has, for the time being, passed its first test.

A Test for Dependability

Pinpointing disagreements is not the only task to be done. The user still has to choose between conflicting rules, which may make even experts disagree over which one is right. In this case, as Waterman suggests, rules should be tagged with their author's name, and those from an expert who participated in the design project should take precedence.

The dependability test can be extended over a range of conceptual validation:

1. What kind of inference capabilities are implied when somebody is an expert?

2. What kind of understanding has an expert (in a specified domain) that others lack?
3. Does the Esystem demonstrate this sort of understanding?

The questions should then become more specific:

4. What are the specific processes in the Esystem that comprise expert reasoning?
5. Are we sure all processes that should be there have been incorporated?
6. Have we put in more rules than are really necessary?
7. What part of the Esystem assures relations between bodies of experience?

Then comes the toughest question of all:

8. Are we sure the incorporated rules (all of them) are complete among themselves and noncontradictory?

This is the second level of expert system testing, and it is much more detailed. It should not be done prior to investigation of reasonableness and dependability because the system being built might have to be rejected altogether. But there are also issues we cannot test in this first phase.

Even if an Esystem and the human expert had the same semantic knowledge, that is, knew the same facts, the expert's experience could have allowed him or her to build up better definitions of how to use it. Some deviation may exist at this early stage.

Human experts are generally expected to show better reasoning as they learn more. Their reasoning becomes somewhat more automatic and faster as they learn how to use the knowledge they once acquired as facts.

In its state of infancy, that is, the tests following design, the expert system will not have comparable responses. Reference to applied experimental psychology may be useful to supply some learning curves—and therefore allowance to permit the Esystem to pass the *first-level test* even if the human expert is not fully happy with it.

The *second-level test* on the completeness of the system of rules with which the knowledgebank is endowed is completely different. Here the critical question should be Would Einstein, Newton, Descartes, Galileo, or Euclid have been satisfied with the system of rules?

Experience allows the facts we once learned to be related to each other in ways that improve our decisions. Factual knowledge becomes integrated with experience, but giving a right answer is no evidence of correct functioning. Even a broken watch is right twice per day. From mathematics and physics to artificial intelligence, a man-made system must pass the test of self-consistency in the system of signs and rules that compose it. Hence, the second big test is the investigation of the logical form of the selected methodology.

The goal should be to determine the character of the selected methodology and the nature of the rules. But the mathematical proof is independent of that. It is a test of completeness in a system sense. I have been told on a couple of occasions that this requirement of self-sufficient and noncontradictory rules is not self-evident because of the novel approaches that have been chosen. New solutions should always be welcome, but with mathematically proven consistency.

The rules embedded in the expert system must represent a noncontradictory aggregate, beyond the fact that methodology itself should reflect a world of possible experience or, more precisely, our world of experience. Apart from the requirement of explanatory reference and mathematical completeness, there are software characteristics to be tested. Based on his experience with planning and controlling the work associated with Operating System 360, Fred Brooks suggests that there is an order of magnitude of difference between a common DP applications program and a programming product which is systems-oriented.

This is the third fundamental test, and let's recall that software reliability is built in at the drafting board. Careful attention should be paid to that fact. Don't wait till the end to test software reliability. It will be too late. With the advent of fourth-generation languages we have gained a great facility in *prototyping*. Let's use it. As we have seen in the preceding chapter, it can be employed to advantage with expert systems.

Fourth, another issue most important to all software projects should be watched carefully. Complete documentation not only of the design but also of the tests and of subsequent maintenance is very important. A different group of knowledge engineers may need to alter a system that was built by a previous team. Documentation on the structure of the system and on the rules must be very explicit if the engineers are to do the maintenance work effectively.

For any intervention, a record should be kept of the reason for adding or deleting any rule to or from a knowledgebank. A record should also be kept of how the Esystem has been released to its users and the problems that might have shown up with the original version. It is most important that the documentation not be manual but kept by computer. Manual documentation is an obsolete process done by the unwilling who has been asked by the unable to do the unnecessary. Manual documentation is messy and difficult to upkeep. With software projects, documentation soon becomes obsolete. Worse than being useless, it is misleading. Not only should the computer be the expert system's documentation partner but also a data dictionary and DBMS facilities should be constantly used.

These points help emphasize that, in each and every Esystems project, extensive testing is an indispensable phase and should precede implementation. Only after all tests have been properly done can we say that we have transformed system design into machine intelligence to be applied to the job to which the expert system is addressed.

Chapter

12

Applications of Expert Systems

"The only way not to succeed is not to try."
EDWARD TELLER

A Bird's-Eye View of Current Applications

In the chapter on expert systems shells we talked of affordable commodity software which may produce useful applications. Such applications might be goal-directed or data-driven depending on whether causes or consequences of known facts are to be inferred. Examples of analysis include interpretation, prediction, and monitoring.

Esystems are also used in tasks characterized by expertise which is usually goal-directed. The expertise involves putting together actions, events, or objects to build up a plan or solve more complex problems. Planning and designing, but also assembling and repairing, are examples.

Computer-aided instruction and process control are areas of applications which require both analysis and synthesis. Esystems can also be used as front-ending and interfacing tools. In such applications they function as dialog means assuring that all proper questions are asked and a two-way communication is effectively established.

With this background in mind, we can appreciate the very significant range of applications to which Esystems have been put. Here are a few examples in alphabetic order:

1. ACE: cable maintenance, analysis of performance of cable aggregates
2. Art of Negotiating: simulates a negotiating session, guides in framing a strategy
3. Bacon: analysis and synthesis for room planning
4. Blah: analysis for income tax advice

5. Communication Edge: analysis and synthesis to prepare business meetings
6. Emes: management of power allocation of electrical components in spacecraft
7. Fies: analysis for fault isolation and detection
8. Finex: expert system for financial analysis beyond the intelligent spreadsheet level
9. HAM-RPM: analysis and synthesis for hotel reservations
10. IDT: DEC's intelligent diagnostic tool
11. Induce: a structural learning program with good noise immunity
12. Inet: an Esystem with knowledge about factories and warehouses
13. Intellect: interface for access to dBase II and VisiCalc
14. ITA: automates robotics inspection task
15. Kipus: analysis of unemployment situation
16. Lunar: analysis of Apollo II lunar rock samples
17. Nand: natural-language interface to another expert system
18. NTC: network troubleshooting consultant able to give interpretative analyses of Ethernet/Decnet problems
19. Plidis: control over emission of pollutants
20. Pol: analysis and synthesis for loading of ships
21. SCCES: calculation of risks of factors involved in stress-corrosion-cracking
22. Straight Talk: intelligent database access
23. Sysan: preparation of documentation concerning program library
24. VMS Expert (TVX): assisting users of a VMS operating system
25. XCON: DEC's extensively used commercial Esystem
26. XSEL: an interactive salesperson's assistant to configure VAX and PDP II

This list has purposely excluded the medical field, which is a well-known area in Esystems implementation. The examples given disprove the popular thought that Esystems are practically indivisible from medical or more generally diagnostic issues. A variety of topics are fertile ground for Esystems applications.

Although planning and diagnosis are often thought to be the best grounds for the implementation of intelligent machines, other fields may present opportunities for getting really exciting results. An expert system developed at Stanford University by Lenat discovered the idea of prime numbers from about 100 basic concepts in the mathematical theory of sets and rules to manipulate them with.

Expert systems form one of the key areas in microelectronics which can provide management with a leading edge. As Figure 43 documents, a leading edge offers competitive advantages but is also subject to constraints. Expert systems are on the side of the advantages, and that for two key reasons:

1. They represent contained financial risk, but the benefit can be high.
2. They are a novel approach which can be implemented in short timetables and show results.

The large variety of cases of useful applications of expert systems brings into perspective the key role to be played by the knowledge engineer: to interpret the expert's answers to questions about the method of knowledge representation and then integrate those answers into the growing knowledgebank.

As emphasized in the section on knowledge acquisition, the systems specialist must be able to draw analogies to help the professional expert structure important aspects of his or her knowledge in the application area. The specialist must challenge by (1) posing counterexamples which seem to violate the expert's hypotheses and (2) raising conceptual difficulties and then helping the expert resolve them. That is the stuff of which successful Esystems applications are built.

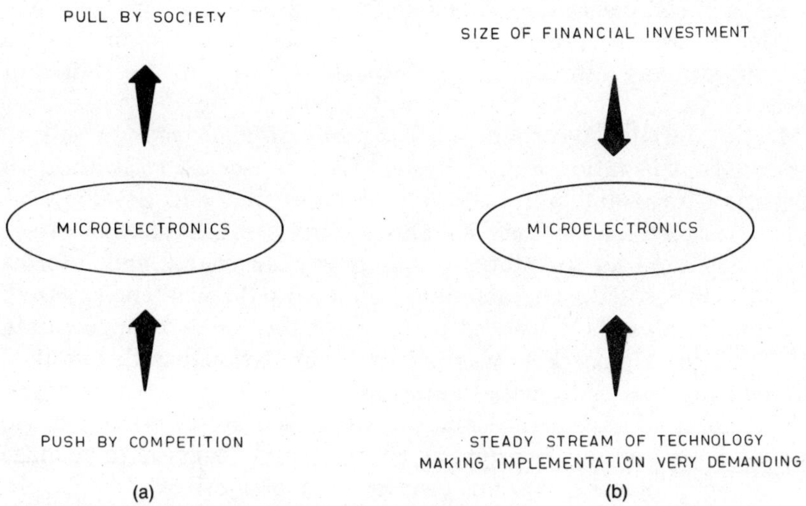

Figure 43 Choosing a policy: (*a*) leading edge; (*b*) constraints on leading edge. Policies are necessary to overcome such constraints.

Proprietary Applications

Developed by AT&T, Automated Cable Expertise (ACE) is an expert system that contains distilled knowledge in the form of if-then rules. This knowledge comes from the people who know cables best: the telephone company cable maintenance experts.

ACE differs from other more commonly found Esystems in two ways:

1. It manipulates massive amounts of data
2. It obtains this information automatically from distributed databases

This expert system has been working since 1982 to help the cable maintenance force of the Southwestern Bell Telephone Company. It monitors and analyzes the performance of cable aggregates and serves over half a million customers in several metropolitan areas. It also makes recommendations.

An important reason for its success is that it is not programmed with all logical answers to all possible questions. It has a set of about 500 rules to follow. As for methodology, it runs through the cable records of a city and can handle a conglomeration the size of Fort Worth overnight. Such a job would take a human expert up to a week.

By collecting its information from other computer programs, detecting recurring patterns, requesting additional data, and testing this data against its expert-derived rules, ACE isolates problems much earlier than a human counterpart could. It provides information on both specific trouble types and locations. The human window is well designed. When ACE has a recommendation to make, it communicates via a video. The dialog is user-friendly. That is critical because its main goal is to work on systems and free human experts to work on the causes of problems.

At Martin Marietta Aerospace, three expert systems have been built to date. Fies (Fault Isolation Expert System) is a rule-based fault isolation and detection program built with internal research and development funds and designed for space station power subsystems. A microprocessor continuously monitors the status of the power subsystem and informs the Esystem when data characterizing fault situations is encountered. The system isolates the fault and performs or recommends appropriate correction. The original Fies was software simulation-based, but it is now being integrated into actual hardware.

Emes (Energy Management Expert System) is a prototype rule-based system developed under government contract and designed to manage the allocation of power to various electrical components of a spacecraft. It is also designed to permit graceful degradation of critical system components under abnormal conditions. Emes is intended for use in future space station applications. Martin Marietta has also designed a fault-handling expert system for satellite propulsion. Telemetry data is passed to the Esystem, which then identifies potential faults and develops work-arounds.

The third implementation reference is the Intelligent Task Automation (ITA) project. Its goal is to fully automate robotic inspection tasks and also to integrate robotics, computer vision, path planning, and task scheduling. Future artificial intelligence efforts on this project will include the addition of exception-handling capabilities to the already functioning planning system.

In another development, there is an interesting Esystems front end to the stress-corrosion-cracking (SCC) problem. The SCC Expert System (SCCES) was written to calculate the risk of various factors involved in SCC, such as crack initiation, when evidence is supplied by the user.

The evidence concerns such things as temperature of the fluid and the condition in the metal surface. SCCES consists of a knowledgebank of rules and facts specific to the SCC domain but linked to commercially available packages. The knowledgebank was constructed by two corrosion specialists and a knowledge engineer.

A leading industrial firm is now in the process of developing a decision support–expert system superstructure over its large inventory of classical DP programs. Depending on the specific application area, the approach ranges from the provision of dialog through a human window to thorough restructuring with objective management analysis and synthesis (Figure 44).

At IBM's command center in Kawasaki, Japan, the *AOS* (Automated Operations System on 3031) expert system runs thirteen mainframes (3031 to 3081), all with MVS. Only one operator is required instead of thirteen operators, plus support personnel, per shift.

AOS responds to all commands (from initiation on) typically done by an operator. In a parallel but more limited sense, a Yorktown Heights development YES-MVS (Yorktown Expert System) replaces operator interaction with the scheduler. It will be a common feature on Sierra Series. Both Esystems take care of jobs that run for days and are resident in the computer, never leaving it. That's the way to go. You can't let operators run large-scale aggregations of computers and communications.

At BBN, work progresses on several expert systems including an automated data network design tool, a radar intercept operator-training aid, and a steam propulsion system teaching tool. There is also a pharmaceutical plant configuration system. BBN scientists developed software used to control robots in a National Bureau of Standards (NBS) automated factory demonstration laboratory. They are also active on a

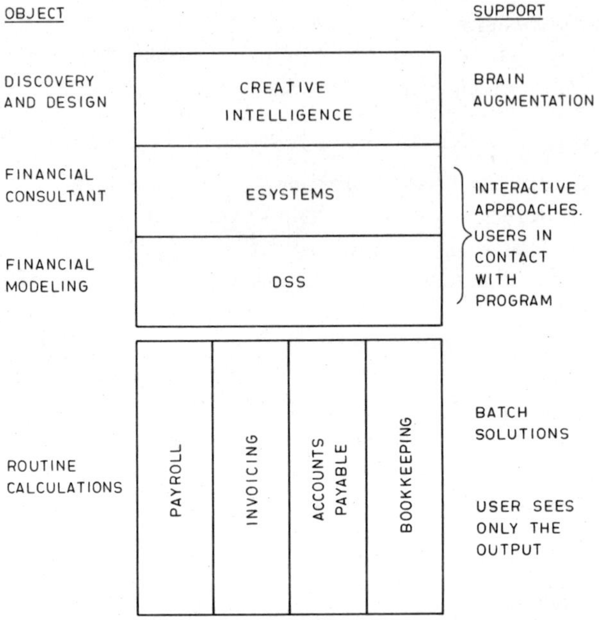

Figure 44 An approach to Esystems: from classical DP understructure to creative intelligence.

sophisticated natural-language interface capable of translating English queries into computer commands.

Work is in progress on connected-word speech recognition technology applied to computer-based training and simulation, high-quality, 16-kBPS (kilobits per second) speech systems, and speech compression. One additional product is at an early stage of development: RS/Expert, a statistical advisory Esystem.

One of the richest libraries of expert systems is provided by Digital Equipment Corporation. Here is an impressive list:

1. *The Expert Configurer* (XCON) is an extensively used commercial expert system.

Formerly referred to as R1, XCON was initially developed at Carnegie-Mellon University as a 500-rule prototype. Written in OPS5, this Esystem is used on a daily basis in Digital's worldwide manufacturing operations to configure most VAX and PDP-11 computers that are on order—prior to manufacturing them. XCON currently utilizes over 2400 rules to accomplish this task. It takes less than 2 minutes to configure most VAX systems.

2. The *Expert Selling Tool* (XSEL) is an adjunct to XCON that helps salespeople to interactively configure computer systems to prepare correct quotes.

This work can be done right in the customer's office. XSEL can submit orders to XCON in batch mode. It is also used to train salespeople.

3. *Expert Site Preparation Tools* (XSITE) acts as site planning assistant.

XSITE helps in the layout and design of a computer room. It runs after the components are selected, by using XSEL.

4. *Intelligent Network* (INET) is a frame-based simulation system with knowledge about factories, warehouses, and distribution centers and how to move material from one unit to another.
5. *Intelligent Scheduling Assistant* (ISA) schedules shop floor activity and manufacturing activity.
6. *Intelligent Business System* (IBUS) and its subset *Intelligent Logistics Assistant* (ILOG) help with the execution of orders and order flow.

Their expertise centers on problems in manufacturing. IBUS also teaches people how to manage change and how to focus on persons, rather than software, in a changing environment.

7. *Intelligent Diagnostic Tool* (IDT) assists technicians in diagnosing systems that do not pass manufacturing verification tests.

IDT uses search techniques to locate fail modules within a system.

8. *AI Spear* is a computer system failure analysis tool for TU78 tape drives.

AI Spear detects intermittent failures by analyzing the system error log. Such failures are often impossible to find with conventional diagnostic programs.

9. *Knowledge Based Test Assistant* (KBTA) is an Esystem to aid hardware test engineers.

It implements a complete test programming environment from the acquisition of device information to the synthesis of test programs.

DEC has also developed an Esystem to enhance software functionality:

10. *VMS Expert* (TVX) assists users of the VMS operating system.

TVX tutors users about utilities, commands, and functions provided by the OS, diagnoses error conditions the user may encounter, and helps to tailor sets of commands converting the user's stated goals into VMS primitives.

11. *Network Troubleshooting Consultant* (NTC) gives interpretative analysis and consultative advice on Ethernet- and Decnet-related problems.

Another interesting Esystem reference is Baroid's Mudman. Baroid invented drilling mud in the 1920s and is now the largest mud company in the world (about $400 million per year). Mud is a lubricant needed in drilling oil wells. Baroid has a knowledgebase of 65 years of mud experience embedded in the knowledge of mud experts.

When Baroid sells drilling mud to an oil firm, it also assigns a mud engineer to stay at the site and solve problems. It takes about three years to train a mud engineer. No conventional algorithms are universally applicable.

As stated on numerous occasions, this is an ideal ground for the development of expert systems. Baroid's Esystem Mudman uses pattern matching and heuristics. It provides able assistance as an expert consultant, serves the company's client base, and extends the knowhow available from the human experts.

Commodity Applications

Dr. Fischer (University of Pennsylvania, Wharton School) and Dr. Jaikumar (Harvard), both of Dart, Inc., made a model to handle truck deliveries. It:

1. Computes distance
2. Estimates loading capacities
3. Adds time constraints
4. Includes quality of roads
5. Reflects maximum allowable speed
6. Incorporates other factors affecting delivery

The model supports color graphics, with on-screen shapes, tracking routes, and stops by truck. Among the users are Air Products and Chemicals (which handles liquid oxygen distributed to 3500 customers over 22 million miles), Exxon, and Hershey Foods. Another customer, Edward Don, employs it for restaurant supply purposes affecting 1100 customers. The user says efficiency has been increased 10 percent.

Dupont/Clinical Systems Division typically handles 1500 customers in 1000 cities in the United States and Canada. With the model's assistance it has been able to serve 3000 customers.

One of the goals at the City of Scottsdale is an expert system as a forecasting tool for growth, types of industries to be located in the city area, income to be generated, investment for infrastructure, and running expenses.

By using Voras, a semantic network language, an Esystem coordinates information throughout the Mediterranean for the French Navy. *It was developed in 3 months.* As Feigenbaum suggested, Esystems can be developed in from 3 days to 10 weeks if we have clear goals and proper brainpower.

The British Post Office (BPO) uses Esystems for staff allocation. Written in micro-Prolog by a nonprogrammer, construction of the prototype took only 2 weeks. As its designer commented, "The problem was not the language, but the interface."

Let's take a couple of examples from commodity software. *Communication Edge* (by Human Edge) helps its user prepare a strategy for business meetings that require communication between two people.

1. The program *asks* its user scores of questions about the personalities of the participants.
2. The program then presents the user with a response on how to maximize the encounter and deal with possible personality clashes.

The better the user knows the other person, the better the program works. For instance, it might urge the user to study certain details, or it might suggest perseverance. Another product of the same firm, the "MindProber" delivers a personality analysis on an individual, including speculation about attitudes toward work and ability to cope with stress.

Different sourcing provides the *Art of Negotiating*, which simulates a negotiating session in a given area such as contracting. This software (provided by Experience in Software, Berkeley, Calif.) forces its user to define the issue under negotiation including the way the opponent would define it. It also prompts the user to:

- Rank his or her own goals and needs
- Do the same for goals and needs of the opponent
- Identify disputed items
- Try out different negotiating strategies
- Eventually find common ground

Should it not be possible to find common ground, the program helps the user select whether he or she wants to pursue an adversarial strategy or a conciliatory course.

Tutorials and strategic aids are a value-added feature. The user who is not certain of an opponent's firmness on a particular position can access a list of methods to test the opponent. The methods range from leaking information to the press to changing one's own position and watching the opponent's reaction.

Using Expert Systems within the DP Organization

Wertz describes an expert system written in Lisp which allows the development of Lisp programs. Modules are indexed and archived according to ancestor-descendent relations with other modules, dates, version numbers, and so on. This supports a software developer, because at any instant the current program consists of modules best fitted for a given job. Program update is fully done by the Esystem, which also guides the hand of the developer.

Software development can be one of the most rewarding areas of Esystems implementation. Defense contractors, for example, are mounting a major joint research effort to develop ways to drastically cut the costs of writing computer programs. Each member company, including TRW, Boeing, Lockheed, McDonnell Douglas, and Ford Aerospace, contributes $1 million per year to help support about 140 full-time researchers. The researchers will develop:

1. Artificial intelligence and expert programs to assist in writing software
2. A database of standard software modules to simplify the writing of new programs

One of the fields which has begun to attract proper attention is the use of artificial intelligence in *declarative* language constructs. The programmer declares what he or she thinks is true about the solution to a problem, and the computer:

- Searches for the solution(s)
- Checks each candidate solution against what is known to be true of correct solutions
- Discards candidates that fail at least one of the tests
- Preserves what survives the testing

List-processing languages are declarative languages. Each fact or rule is a statement about the world, but it is also a piece of the program because the program is an invisible set of procedures which treat each new calculation as a single uniform kind of search. The search takes place automatically in the space of all possible solutions that are governed by the constraints imposed by the given *facts plus rules*.

This view of programming is new. It permits the user to program without programming, because the user states what he or she knows to be true about real life and the system finds the answers to questions consistent with that information through a process of automatic search. Even users who have no previous exposure to computers or conventional programming languages can employ this AI approach to build their own well-defined worlds in which they can explore consequences of design choices and learn about both deductive and inductive reasoning.

This development makes *incremental evaluation* of code feasible. Under system control, a routine can execute itself to examine its operating characteristics. It can also test cases. Although languages like Lisp and Prolog easily permit incremental evaluation because of their structure, there is no reason why the approach should not be used through agile front ending with other languages. Old software in Cobol or Fortran may also be executed under the control of an intelligent development system, provided that the system fits around the old software automatically through a *support environment* in which the piece of old software still plays its normal part.

Such problems are being studied in current work on software tools and development environments in connection with American defense projects, as well as by Alvey in the UK and Esprit in the Common Market. Significant is the fact that, in the past few years, a new type of commercial software has begun to appear. It ranges from an English language *front end for databases* to expert systems building tools.

A relational database management system makes it feasible to modify storage structures quickly without regard to record management. At the same time, there is no danger of losing stored data. An expert system improves upon the situation through the provision of intelligent interfaces and interactive controls.

Expert Database Systems represent the convergence of research in artificial intelligence and database management. As such, they play an ever-increasing role in database administration by providing intelligent, knowledge-intensive access to large shared databases. Typically, they:

1. Support efficient user interfaces and natural-language question and answer facilities
2. Endow database systems with reasoning, planning, and justification capabilities

3. Provide sophisticated tools to support indexing, manipulation, and evolution of large databases
4. Integrate AI and DBMS functionality into new software and hardware environments

The goal, achieved by cross-fertilization of ideas, is effective specification, prototyping, testing, and debugging of complex database applications.

Addressing Software Issues

Today, reasonably simple Esystems addressed to software issues are practical. They are being implemented by self-taught teams to produce the first significant results at relatively low cost. Expert systems for software development are not inherently complex, risky, or demanding. This statement is valid at the current state of the art as long as we choose a small rule-based application and build a relatively simple support environment.

In my judgment, the preferred approach should be a combination of rapid prototyping and top-down design. That makes sense in software engineering, though it is not easy to manage during a project if the programming language cannot be expressed in a natural fashion. Esystems provide an able solution by creating the support environment.

The support environment, as well as the final product, does not have to be influenced by the characteristics of the list-processing language in which it is written (Prolog, Lisp, or Shell). It is enough that the language to be chosen is adequate to express all of the ideas and tools needed to develop an agile solution extending the life of available software.

The subject can have a most significant impact on the data processing profession. A British research team aiming at a comprehensive classification of Esystems distinguished among three aspects in the context of DP/MIS operations:

1. Applications which might have a DP/MIS dimension, such as fault finding
2. Expert system extensions to the functionality of existing DP/MIS systems
3. Ability to incorporate AI approaches into DP/MIS and methodologies

The latter should aim at attaining shorter development times, more flexible and maintainable systems, and greater cost benefit. Early results from ongoing experience show it can be done.

The team referred to concentrated on the third of the above approaches. It concluded that, although expert systems could not be a panacea for DP, they could contribute usefully. For instance, data validation appeared to be a promising area.

A parallel research project suggested that relational database systems might represent a bridge between the two extremes of traditional von Neumann architecture and the use of artificial intelligence. Among the suggested tools were:

- Esystems shells
- Approaches to normalization
- Off-the-shelf AI languages
- A route to more sophisticated relational database systems

A third project concentrated on the relation between expert systems and software engineering. Its conclusion was that Esystems can help determine an appropriate environment, map logical data models into a physical database, and support the work of the analyst.

For instance, intelligent interfaces can be built to examine the actual use of a database and suggest database restructuring. They can also tutor users in concepts such as normalization, planning testing strategies, and assisting in sizing a given job—in short, guiding the user in how to employ the object system.

Esystems can analyze faults, train specialists, offer operations advice, feature decision support, provide project management, and improve project estimation. A good field was felt to be the rapidly growing area of end user computing.

In conclusion, although the DP/MIS and expert systems cultures are very different, current research on cross-fertilization serves to dispel misconceptions. It also suggests important DP areas in which knowledge-based techniques might be valuable.

We can forecast that, within a few years, the computing environment will feature both conventional DP/MIS and Esystems. Classical DP activity will be surrounded by a new and fast-growing area of intelligent computing. End user applications and DP/MIS methodologies are amenable to knowledge engineering.

Expert Systems in Manufacturing

One of the success stories of expert systems is the use of Esystems in production environments. This ranges from production planning and scheduling to coordinating production shops, assuring in-process banks, and managing inventories. AI in robotics is one of the better known and most challenging applications areas.

Expert systems implementation in manufacturing should be focused along either or both of two main lines of reference (Figure 45):

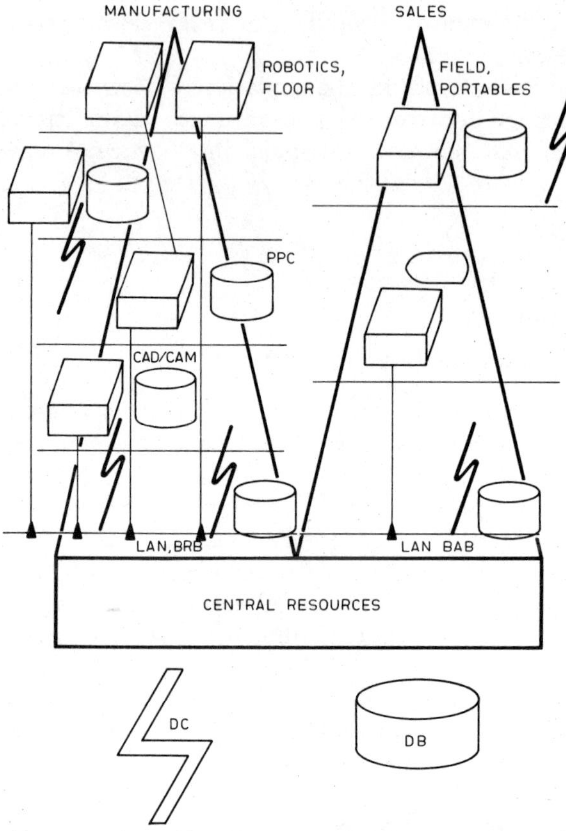

Figure 45 Expert systems in manufacturing should be developed along engineering-production and marketing-sales lines.

1. The technical organization, from CAD/CAM to robotics
2. The marketing and sales organization with its associated activities

Both areas are challenging, and the first section of this chapter has given real-life examples. Where to begin is often a matter of company culture.

Just as they find a fertile field in extending the life cycle of classical DP applications, so Esystems can play a similar role in manufacturing. Examples of possible implementations are job allocation, projecting and handling physical failures, facing catastrophes, assuring recovery and restart of automated production processes, administering robots, bettering the rules, and projecting long-term requirements, as well as facing day-by-day requirements as they develop.

In many of these implementations the time span for the development of an expert system can be quite contained. For instance, in a factory-planning case it took a couple of days of steady work to create a simple system containing a dozen rules. There were at least two conditions to each rule.

To create the expert system, the designer started by listing all of the possible equipment this type of factory might need. The list was entered into the program as a protocol of alternatives, and two or three types were listed for each required piece of equipment.

The options available for each alternative were at the center of the logic trails on the computer. To apply the Esystem, the user answers a series of questions with choices based on the types of products to be made. Each response moves the system into a logic chain leading to the selection of a machine tool. At any point in the process, the user can ask to see the rule upon which the program is basing its questions (or answers). If need be, the user can also ask to see all of the evaluated conclusions to make a personal determination.

In a factory quality-control application, coordinate-measuring machines were used to obtain data from component parts. An Esystem was designed to digitize that data. Now a manufactured component can be compared with the design in the computer. The system suggests the needed corrective action.

Expert systems are a vital component of computer-integrated manufacturing (CIM), a strategy built on the automation of information flow throughout a production firm. CIM is implemented by gradually connecting individually computerized tasks, and it requires intelligent communications links among previously isolated computer systems throughout the organization.

Successful expert systems implementation should, however, start at the design stage. Knowledge-based systems have already been implemented with most commendable results in VLSI design, placement techniques for printed-circuit boards, prototyping, computer-aided design, optoelectronics, solid-state microwave devices, component and system testing, robot studies, robot assembly, and quality assurance.

Intelligent programs are being used for signal discrimination, knowledge about the sender, understanding English words, complex code handling, and broader context knowledge. Successful AI projects are ranging from detection of desirable messages through overlapping coded information to promising prospects for intelligent communications.

Robotic vision is an often-talked-about subject of AI implementation. We spoke about it in the chapter on artificial intelligence. Rather than be repetitive, let's now stress issues connected with man-machine communication and smart assistance to the end user in a product-oriented sense. The first example is not precisely an expert system, but it is microprocess-based, emphasizes the human window, and has Esystems potential.

Map display as a navigation aid for autos is one of the applications for extending the life or usefulness of an existing product. By using an augmented dead reckoning scheme that compares a vehicle's movements with stored map data, the system operates without external signals. Comparisons continuously correct the system's calculation of the vehicle's location to within 16 meters (50 feet). The map display is updated every second.

The display shows the vehicle at its center. When the driver turns, the map rotates so that the road ahead is always at the top. The system has a zoom feature that permits the driver to look at smaller or larger regions, and it can automatically display destinations specified by the driver.

Potential models can use compact laser disks to provide enough storage for pictures of tourist attractions. They can also incorporate a question-and-answer interface. Commercials aimed at visitors also serve as electronic travel guides.

The integration of expert systems and graphics is a promising area in engineering design and manufacturing. An advanced design tool developed at General Motors Research Laboratories uses computers to generate visual images from mathematical data with such accuracy that in-depth aesthetic evaluations of new concepts may be made prior to creating a physical model.

The system is completely interactive. By choosing from a menu on the screen, the designer can redefine display parameters, select a viewing orientation, and mix a color. Each part of an object can be assigned a surface type with associated color and reflectance properties.

Built-in lighting controls generate realistic highlights on simulated surfaces composed of different materials. An unlimited number of light sources can be independently aimed at an object and the light concentration adjusted to simulate spotlight and floodlight effects. The lighting model determines the intensity of the reflected light that reaches the eye from a given point on the object. It takes into account the reflectance properties of the surface as well as the physics of light reflection.

Another feature is the ability to portray a variety of different materials and lighting conditions realistically. The color seen from a surface is really a combination of two colors:

- Diffuse reflection, the color of the surface or material itself
- Specular reflection, the color of the reflected highlights

The ability to simulate reality through graphics is one of the computer's strong points. But the more we approach real-life situations, the

more we need intelligent machines. Since the easier parts
aided design have now become integral features of the en
ture, the profession is moving to more complex approaches
systems are necessary.

Designing objects which require complex patterns, molds, and dies calls for a system that enables the designer to carry out work beyond what has traditionally been performed by the pattern maker. Three-dimensional visualization on color screens makes it feasible to work with fewer physical models. All that requires machine intelligence.

While technology is forging ahead, problems are encountered in achieving successful introduction of expert systems into a manufacturing organization. They include accurate identification of requirements, system evaluation and selection, training, overcoming resistance to change, and integration with other internal computer-based developments. In large firms these problems can be compounded by scale, geographic distribution, and diverse product ranges.

This is written as a warning that although knowledge engineering permits the development of Esystems in manufacturing, the corporate culture may reject it. Management will therefore be well-advised to take all steps which can assure acceptance. As cannot be too often repeated, education is a focal point.

Expert Systems in Banking

The banking industry is facing a time of increasing competition and lower profits in its classical role of financial intermediary. This is fostered partly by deregulation and partly by the competitive market forces.

New strategies are necessary, and one of the ways to support profit goals and survive is to use high technology as a competitive tool. Expert systems are part of this picture, and Battelle is doing a worldwide study to establish the impact of expert systems on financial institutions.

Although the current expert system implementation in the banking industry varies widely from one institution to another, there are some recurrent issues which suggest a trend. Among the fields of higher potential are risk analysis, foreign operations, portfolio management, balance sheet evaluation, tax advising, treasury operations, credit approval, and data processing applications.

Some banks have a tendency to develop their own Esystem in house, while others seek assistance from outside sources. Another way is to buy a shell, involve specialist Esystem houses for training, but then proceed with in-house development. Just one software house specializing in expert systems did six projects for the financial industry over 12 months:

1. *Credit risk adviser.* This was done on a PC from the prototype level to the applications model. The bank intends to use it throughout its operations.
2. *Bank service adviser.* It has the purposes of informing the client on service needs, advancing solutions offered by the bank, and keeping the management of the bank informed on branch office services.
3. *Currency exchange.* It assists in an interactive dialog at two levels: with the bank employee and with the client.
4. *Investment adviser.* The bank has set very clear rules; the Esystem executes them. The knowledge engineer did not need to find the rules from the expert; the rules were embedded in bank policies.
5. *Telephone selection procedures.* Front-ending the services offered by the PBX.
6. *Accounting procedures.* This was originally developed for one of the big US accounting firms and then enriched with auditing capabilities.

A leading financial institution developed, with internal resources, an expert system to act as portfolio investment adviser. In this capacity, the Esystem typically follows rules used by an expert investor:

- Interest rate developments (lower rates)
- Revenues (steady or rising)
- Balance sheets (well balanced)
- Price/earnings (no high ratio)

An expert investor will look first at numbers and then at intangibles: type of industry, current products, rate of new product introduction, and quality of management. The Esystem qualifies judgment by interlinking those factors.

The rules embedded in the expert system avoid stocks of companies whose earnings are expected to be disappointing or whose estimated earnings are likely to fall. It gives precedence to *performing stocks*, that is, stocks of companies that report earnings in excess of the consensus estimates or the consensus estimates of which improve over time.

Part of the role given to the expert system is to establish an investment strategy directed at finding such stocks. This can be done by human experts, but much ability is required to consistently estimate earnings more accurately than the consensus. The Esystem is able to estimate earnings better than the consensus, and to do so consistently.

The reason why this estimating is quite difficult for a human expert is that the consensus is based on the efforts of similarly educated people with similar access to information. This is the essence of the stock market mechanism.

When analysts go out on a limb to recommend securities for purchase, they are saying that the stocks are undervalued relative to their expectations and that they are reasonably confident about those expectations. Furthermore, the recommendation in itself implies expectations different from consensus expectations, which presumably are already reflected in the stock price.

For this reason, leading brokers limit their universe to the recommended list and depend on backtesting to gain foresight as to future earnings. The expert system also does backtesting. Two ranking measures are used in the backtests:

1. Standardized unexpected earnings. This is defined as the unexpected earnings less the consensus estimate for quarterly earnings that existed just prior to the earnings announcement. The difference is divided by the standard deviation of earnings estimates.
2. Standardized estimate momentum. This reflects the change in estimate over a given period: the consensus estimate at the end of the period less the consensus estimate at the beginning of the period. Again the difference is divided by the standard deviation of estimates at the beginning of the period.

As a portfolio investment adviser, an Esystem capitalizes on the two ratios and also makes use of the wealth of information available in public databases. Using the standard deviation of estimates in the denominator of the measures gives a higher ranking to a stock whose originally tight consensus is a positive surprise or is revised.

Shearson Lehman suggests that an investment strategy based on purchasing stocks with the highest values by either of the two statistics would have outperformed a passive portfolio by a significant margin over the backtest period. To document this thesis, a test was performed quarterly from 1976 to 1984.

It is also proper to note that the theory concerned implies some market inefficiency insofar as it suggests that prices do not respond immediately to changing expectations, that such expectations respond gradually to new information, and that there is serial correlation in estimate errors. Overestimates for one quarter are usually followed by overestimates for the next quarter.

On another occasion, a system projected for risk analysis contains the following modules (Figure 46):

1. Bank strategist
2. Environmental assessor

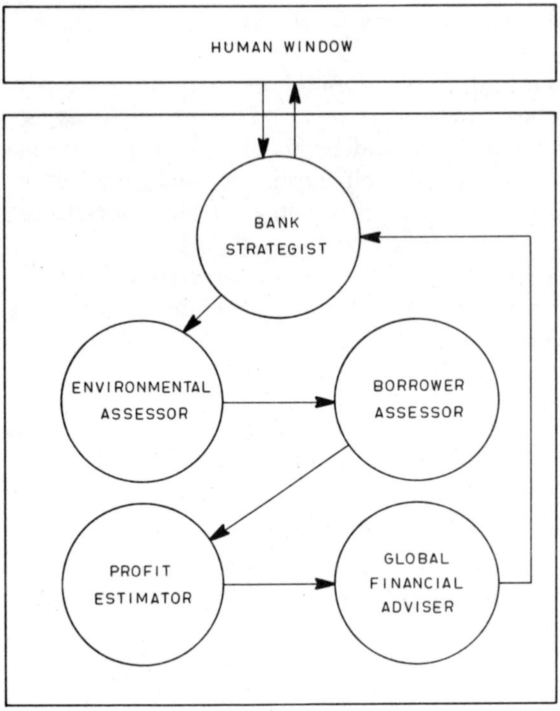

Figure 46 Modules contained in a system designed for risk analysis.

3. Borrower assessor
4. Profit estimator adjusted for risk
5. Global financial analyst and adviser

The *bank strategist* examines how the potential transaction fits within the strategic objectives of the bank. Its reference is company-confidential information, but it need not be visible to the average user. Only the results are presented.

The *environmental assessor* looks at the external business and financial climate. It takes into account industry trends and market forecasts—both global and specific to the product line(s) featured by the prospective borrower. Access to public databases is a must.

The *borrower assessor* studies both the financial and nonfinancial pluses and minuses of the firm. The analysis of financial statements is formalized and is therefore generally applicable to all borrowers.

A methodology also is developed for the assessment of management quality and other human resources. The same thing is true of the breadth of the product line, the orientation and extent of investments in research and development, the markets to which the prospective borrower appeals, and the quality of the marketing organization.

Based on that information, the *profit estimator* determines the risk and profit embedded in the projected transaction. This cannot be done as a monolith. Therefore, it must take the form of confidence intervals. The volume of references necessary for this job is quite complex, but knowledge can be formalized. Furthermore, stages 2 and 3 have already produced valuable references on which the Esystem can capitalize.

The *global financial adviser* thus obtains all information necessary to ascertain the financial strengths and weaknesses of a proposed deal. Once the evaluation of the prospect is done in absolute terms, it is compared to a global database of ongoing risk-adjusted loans. Thus it is positioned in terms of potential risk and profit within a real-life environment. Such an approach can find implementation in other fields. If the global database is properly updated in regard to results, the financial adviser will be able to provide valuable references for management decision. This same process can also assist the expert system in documenting the advice it is giving.

Finally, to assure consistency of purpose, the results of the global financial adviser are fed back to the bank strategy module and communicated to the banking executive through the human window. This is one of the best examples of what has so often been described as the implementation domain of expert systems.

As emphasized in the Preface, the use of expert systems in business improves the *dependability of the decision-making process*. Humans forget relevant factors, especially if they are under stress or time is critical. Intelligent machines don't forget, and they are immune to pressures.

Expert systems offer increased consistency in the relative importance given to different decision factors. They also present greater accessibility and better explanatory capabilities. Human experts can be on holiday, on call, or otherwise be unavailable. *The industrialization of knowhow sees to it that the intelligent machine is always at your service.*

Acronyms and Abbreviations

AI	artificial intelligence
AOS	Automated Operating System
ASCII	American Standard Code for Information Interchange
BPW	bits per word
CAD	computer-aided design
CAM	computer-assisted manufacturing
CIM	computer-integrated manufacturing
DARPA	Defense Advanced Projects Agency
DB	database
DBA	database administrator
DBMS	database management system
DML	data manipulation language
DOD	Department of Defense
DP	data processing
DSS	decision support systems
EBCDIC	Expanded Binary Coded Decimal
EDP	electronic data processing
Email	electronic mail
Emes	Energy Management Expert Systems
EMycin	Empty Mycin
ESS	expert support systems
Esystems	expert systems
ETL	Electrical Laboratory (Japan)
4GL	fourth-generation language
GESCO	General Electric Supply Company
GPS	General Problem Solver
Icenter	information center
ID	identification
IPL	information-processing language

Isoft	integrated software
IST	Innovative Science and Technology Office
IVD	Interactive Videodisk
KAS	Knowledge Acquisition System
kBPS	kilobits per second
Kbytes	1024 bytes
LAN	local area network
LIPS	logical inferences per second
Mbytes	megabytes (1 million bytes)
MCC	Microelectronics and Computer Development Center
MIPS	million instructions per second
MIS	management information system
MITI	Ministry of International Trade and Industry (Japan)
MMI	man-machine interface
NBS	National Bureau of Standards
NCC	network control center
OA	office automation
OS	operating system
PDS	Personal Decision Series
PSI	Personal Sequential Inference
R&D	research and development
ROI	return on investment
SBA	vulnerability analysis method (Sweden)
SCC	stress-corrosion-cracking
SCCES	SCC expert system
SDI	Strategic Defense Initiative
2-D	two-dimensional
3-D	three-dimensional
UCSD	University of California at San Diego
VLSI	very large scale integration
WS	workstation

Index

Accounting model, 35
Accounting procedures, 220
AI Spear, 209
Alpha-beta procedure, 143
Alvey Directorate, 118, 194, 195, 213
American Hospital Study, 15
Ariel of AT&T, 130
Arrow Electronics, 15
Arthur Andersen, 12
Artificial intelligence (AI), 20, 38, 75, 79, 138
Artificial intelligence (AI) developments, 76
Artificial intelligence (AI) implementation, 83
Associative database, 113
AT&T (American Telephone and Telegraph), 206
Authors, 85
Automated office system, 23
(*See also* Office automation)
Automated Operations System (AOS), 207
Automated reasoning, 149
Avis, 15

Back-end functions, 120
Backward-chaining methodology, 93, 142
Backward reasoning, 139
Bangor Punta Corporation, 10
Bank of America, 5
Bank Services Advisor, 116, 220
Bank strategist, 222
Bankers Trust, 9, 37, 159
Baroid, 210
BBN, 207
Bergen-Brunswig, 14
Betriebswirtschaftliches Institut der Kreditgenossenschaften, 14, 129
Boeing, 212
Borrower assessor, 222
British Telecom, 115
Brook Bond Oxo, 13
Budgeting, 186
Business strategy, 9

Callable objects, 85
Carnegie Mellon, 94
Chevron, 15
Chief executive officer (CEO), 69
Commodity shells, 170
Communicating databases, 82, 114
Communications, 37
  and computers, 8, 9, 82, 83
  man-machine, 139
  PC-to-mainframe, 25, 26, 38
Communications networks:
  and computers, 83
  private and public, 6
Communications protocols, 16
Compiler, 101
Computer(s), 16
  and communications, 8, 9, 82
  and communications networks, 83
Computer-aided design (CAD), 130
Computer-aided instruction, 203
Computer-integrated manufacturing (CIM), 217
Computer literacy, 30
Computer programs (*see* Software)
Computer simulation, 34
Conceptual dependence, 153
Constraint propagation, 146

Credit risk adviser, 220
Currency exchange, 220

Data communications disciplines, 100
Data dictionary, 157
Data manipulation language (DML), 100
Data processing (DP), 5, 63, 135
  electronic (EDP), 40
Data processing/word processing (DP/WP), 38
Data transparency, 39
Database(s), 31
  associative, 113
  communicating, 82, 114
  global, 98, 111, 112
  management-oriented, 24
  public, 6
Database management orientation, 119
Database management system (DBMS), 16, 100, 202
  relational, 120, 167, 213, 215
Dataland, 127
Decision-oriented systems, 125
Decision support, 64
Decision support system (DSS), 26, 32, 34, 68, 71, 74, 82, 126, 140, 177, 196
Deduction, 148
Deductive approaches, 150
Defense Advanced Research Projects Agency (DARPA), 76
Dendral, 95, 111, 112
Department of Defense (DOD), 76, 166
Dependability, 199
Descriptive model, 34
Design classification, 90
Development tools, 186
Dialog management, 79
Digital Equipment Corp., 206
Dipmeter Advisor, 115
Distriphar, 14
Document handling, 85
Documentation, 201
Dynamic model, 35

Einstein, Albert, 2, 74, 134, 150
Eisenhower, Dwight, 32
Electronic data processing (EDP), 40
Electronic teller, 129
Email, 64
Empirical contents, 135
Empirical testing method, 199
EMycin, 81, 142
Energy Management Expert System (Emes), 206
Engineering workstation, 16
Environmental assessor, 222
Error rates, 119
Esprit, 213
Eurisko, 104
Expert Configurer (XCON), 206
Expert Database Systems, 213
Expert investor, 220
Expert Selling Tool (XSEL), 209
Expert Site Preparation Tools (XSITE), 209
Expert support systems (ESS), 71, 72, 141
Expert systems (Esystems), 16, 20, 62–70, 73, 74, 79–84, 92, 94, 98–102, 105, 106, 108–111, 114, 115, 124, 126, 130, 139–141, 143, 157, 160–162, 164, 165, 168, 169, 176, 177, 184–186, 189, 190, 193, 194, 196–198, 200–206, 212, 214–217, 219–221, 223
  functionality and purpose of, 95
Expert systems developers, 190
Expert systems methodology, 74, 83
Expert systems software, 149
Explanation generator, 81
Explanatory interface, 114

Facts, 98
Factual knowledge, 181
Fault Isolation Expert System (Fies), 206
Feedback theory, 198
Fifth-generation languages (5GL), 64, 119
Financial model, 34
Ford Aerospace, 212
Forecasting, 67
Formalization of knowledge, 197
Forsyth, Richard, 141
Forward and backward pruning, 143
Forward chaining, 142
Forward pruning, 143

Fourth-generation languages (4GL), 7, 63, 105, 106, 119–121
Front-end tools, 120
Functional model, 136
Functions, 85
Further definiens, 91
Fuzziness, 155
Fuzzy environment, 154
Fuzzy logic, 155–158
Fuzzy set, 144, 154, 155, 157, 158

Galilei, Galileo, 135
General Electric Information Systems, 10
General Electric Supply Company (GESCO), 11, 15
General Motors (GM), 7, 8
General Motors Research Laboratories, 218
General Research, 182
Global database, 98, 111, 112
Global financial adviser, 223
Gould Industries, 10
Graphical systems support, 126
Graphics, 125
Graphics languages, 126
Graphics presentation, 7
Graphics solutions, 127
Guidon, 95

Hardware, 16
Heuristics, 111
Hitachi, 158
Hopper, Max, 5
Human Edge Software, 182
Human window, 94, 114–116, 118, 175

IBM (International Business Machines), 199
Incremental learning, 160
Induction, 148
Inductive approaches, 150, 151
Inference, 133, 135, 143
Inference engine, 80, 81, 114, 140, 176
  logical, 136
  meta-, 93
Information center, 21–25, 28
Information center implementation, 25
Information elements, 100, 101, 123, 137
Information engineering solutions, 63
Information sciences, 74
Information system, 4, 5, 26, 86
Information technology, 8
InfoTym, 176
Integrated software (Isoft), 16, 37
Integration, 19, 97
Intelligent Business System (IBUS), 209
Intelligent Diagnostic Tool (IDT), 209
Intelligent knowledge-based system, 189
Intelligent Logistics Assistant (ILOG), 209
Intelligent Network (INET), 209
Intelligent programs, 217
Intelligent Scheduling Assistant (ISA), 209
Intelligent system, 135
Intelligent Task Automation (ITA), 207
Intelligent workstations, 7, 16–20, 38, 39, 41
Interacting subproblems, 145
Interactive dialog procedure, 67
Interactive videodisk (IVD), 128, 130
Interconnected frames, 91
Interfaces, 114, 115
  explanatory, 114
  linguistic, 121
  man-machine, 117–118
  user-friendly, 125
Investment adviser, 220

Jastrow, Robert, 78
Judgmental knowledge, 181

Kas, 95, 96, 112
Knowhow, 102, 193
Knowledge, 90, 100, 109, 135
  factual, 181
  formalization of, 197
  judgmental, 181
  meta, 89
  procedural, 181

Knowledge acquisition, 98, 102, 104, 105, 114, 149
Knowledge-acquisition system, 103
Knowledge-based systems, 217
  intelligent, 189
Knowledge Based Test Assistant (KBTA), 209
Knowledge engineer, 91, 100, 103, 105, 107, 111, 144
Knowledge engineering, 78–80, 84, 87, 103, 135
Knowledge engineering systems, 110
Knowledge information network, 85
Knowledge management, 81, 97, 98
Knowledge network, 87, 88
Knowledge representation, 78, 110
  basic criteria of, 89
Knowledge representation language, 90, 165
Knowledge revolution, 7
Knowledge utilization, 78
Knowledgebank, 65, 79–81, 93, 97–99, 101, 105, 110, 111, 114, 140, 199, 205
Knowledgebank management, 99, 119

Large search space, 145
Layered structures, 100
Lex, 162
Linguistic interface, 121
Lisp, 81, 142
Litton Industries, 2
Local area networks (LANs), 7, 10
Lockheed, 212
Logical constructs, 133
Logical inference engine, 136
Logical operators, 110
Lone Star Cement, 10

McCarthy, John, 165
McDonnell Douglas, 176, 212
Machine, 132
Machine learning, 160
McKesson Pharmaceuticals, 15
Man-machine communications, 139
Man-Machine Interface (MMI) by Alvey, 118
Man-machine interface language, 116
Man-machine interfaces, 117

Management, 1
  middle, 13, 23
    responsibilities of, 5, 6
  top, 13, 23
    responsibilities of, 12
  (*See also* Knowledge management; Project management)
Management information systems activities, 24
Management productivity, 4
Manager, 1
  (*See also* Project manager)
Martin Marietta Aerospace, 206, 207
Matrix presentation, 89
Memory, 101
  episodic, 101
  semantic, 101
Menu(s), 123
Menu management, 123
Menu selection, 175
Menu window, 124
Metadendral, 95, 103, 104, 111, 162
Meta-inference engine, 93
Meta knowledge, 89
Metropolitan Insurance Company, 12
Michie, Donald, 182
Middle management, 13, 23
  responsibilities of, 5, 6
MIT (Massachusetts Institute of Technology), 94, 127
Modeling, 34, 67
Models, 108, 137, 138, 140
  accounting, 35
  descriptive, 34
  dynamic, 35
  financial, 34
  functional, 136
  reference, 136, 137
Molgen, 95, 96
Mothercare, 13
Mycin, 95, 96, 103, 112, 144

National Bureau of Standards (NBS), 207
Natural-language access, 81
Natural-language programming, 116
Network Troubleshooting Consultant (NTC), 210
Nixdorf, 65, 128
Noah, 95, 96, 147
Numeric procedures, 144

Office automation (OA), 6, 23, 33, 74
One-dimensional programming, 121
Online query system, 125
Operating system (OS), 16
Owens Corning Fiberglass, 10

Packet assembly and disassembly, 39
Parsing, 92
Pattern recognition, 158
PC-to-mainframe communications, 25, 26, 38
PC-to-mainframe connections, 7, 121
Pecos, 107
Perot, H. Ross, 7
Person-to-person interaction, 119
Personal computer (PC), 10
Phrase parameter, 110
Physical concepts, 133
Piper Aircraft, 10
Planning, 25
  strategic, 2–4, 87
Plausible reasoning, 146
Private and public networks, 6
Problem solving, 189
Problem-solving framework, 190
Procedural knowledge, 181
Process control, 203
Professional, 5, 8, 13, 23
Profit estimator, 223
Programming language, 164
Programming language shells, 163
Programs, computer (*see* Software)
Project(s), 186, 188
Project control, 188
Project management, 184, 187–189
Project manager, 187
  responsibilities of, 27
Project organization, 187, 188
Prolog, 81, 142
Prospector, 112
Protocols, 39, 40, 100
  communications, 16
  higher-level, 18
  low-level, 18
Prototype, 164
Prototyping, 105, 106, 163, 172–176, 214

Quel of Ingres, 121
Query systems, 121
  online, 125

Reference model, 136, 137
Refinement strategies, 147
Relational DBMS, 120, 167, 213, 215
Retrieval, 121
Risk Adjusted Return on Capital (RAROC), 156, 159
Risk assessment, 159
Robotic vision, 217
R1, 113
Rosie, 81
Routing capabilities, 175
Rules, 98, 114, 201

Search strategies, 144
Semantic analysis, 92
Semiexpert system, 67
Sensory reasoning, 159
Service quality control, 159
Shearson Lehman, 221
Shell, 81, 105, 168, 174, 176
Sideways chaining, 143
Simplicity, 97
Simulation, 173
  computer, 34
Small search space, 144
Smith, Roger, 7
Software, 16, 17, 19, 135
  expert systems, 149
  integrated, 16, 37
  intelligent programs, 217
Software development, 212
Software engineering, 82
Software modules, 100
South East Electricity, 12
Spatial reasoning, 158
Speech processing, 127
Spreadsheet, 35–37
SQL of IBM, 121
Stanford University, 94
Strategic information system, 5
Strategic plan, 4
Strategic planning, 2, 3, 87
Strategy, 2
Strategy formulation, functions of, 3
Stress-Corrosion-Cracking Expert System (SCCES), 207
Sylvania Commercial Lighting Division of GTE, 10
Symbol manipulation, 79
SYN, 95, 96, 111, 112, 146
Systems approach, 24
Systems architecture, 86

Task planning systems, 159
Taxonomical constructs, 90
Taxonomy, 91
Technical architecture, 190
Teknowledge Inc., 181
Telephone selection procedure, 220
Temporal reasoning, 159
Top management, 13, 23
  responsibilities of, 12
Transaction processing, 125
Translator, 92
Two-dimensional programming, 121

Uncertain data, 154
Unification algorithm, 147
USAA Insurance, 12
U.S. Department of Defense (DOD), 76, 166
United Technologies, 10
User-friendly interface, 125
User interface design, 118

Very large scale integration (VLSI), 112, 190
Videodisks, 129, 130
VMS Expert, 209

WestTrak, 11
Westvaco, 11
What-if, 35
Whitbread, 11
Workstations, 12
  engineering, 16
  intelligent, 7, 16–20, 38, 39, 41

YES-MVS by IBM, 103, 207

ABOUT THE AUTHOR

DIMITRIS N. CHORAFAS has been involved in the computer field since 1953, making him an "old-timer" in a very young industry. He has worked as a programmer, analyst, designer, project manager, and, for the past 25 years, advisor to presidents of leading firms. He has worked with many corporations in Europe and America, including IBM, DEC, Honeywell Information Systems, Olivetti, AEG-Telefunken, UNIVAC, Nestlé, Omega, The Diebold Group, Worthington, Commerzbank, Dresdner Bank, Credito Commerciale, Instituto Bancano Italiano, Banca Provinciale Lombarda, Credit Agricole, Von Tobel Bank, and the Union Bank of Switzerland. In his dual status as international management consultant and university professor (at UCLA, George Washington University, Georgia Institute of Technology, the University of Washington, and others), he has traveled to 60 different countries. A Fulbright Scholar, Dr. Chorafas has written 55 books and many technical papers. He conducts seminars around the world.